Poverty in America

Poverty in America

A Handbook

Third Edition

John Iceland

UNIVERSITY OF CALIFORNIA PRESS

Berkeley · Los Angeles · London

University of California Press, one of the most
distinguished university presses in the United States,
enriches lives around the world by advancing scholarship
in the humanities, social sciences, and natural sciences. Its
activities are supported by the UC Press Foundation and
by philanthropic contributions from individuals and
institutions. For more information, visit www.ucpress.edu.

University of California Press
Berkeley and Los Angeles, California

University of California Press, Ltd.
London, England

© 2013 by The Regents of the University of California

Library of Congress Cataloging-in-Publication Data

Iceland, John.
    Poverty in America : a handbook /
John Iceland. — 3rd ed.
        p.   cm.
    Includes bibliographical references and index.
    ISBN 978-0-520-27636-9 (pbk., alk. paper)
    1. Poor—United States—History.   2. Poverty—United
States—History.   3. Economic assistance, Domestic—
United States—History.   I. Title.
HC110.P6I25   2013
339.4'60973—dc23   2012042288

Manufactured in the United States of America

22   21   20   19   18   17
10   9   8   7   6   5

To Mia, Jakob, and Jeannie

Contents

List of Illustrations   *ix*
Preface   *xi*
Acknowledgments   *xiii*

    Introduction   *1*
1. Early Views of Poverty in America   *11*
2. Methods of Measuring Poverty   *22*
3. Characteristics of the Poverty Population   *39*
4. Global Poverty   *61*
5. Causes of Poverty   *79*
6. The Great Recession   *114*
7. Poverty and Policy   *130*
    Conclusion   *157*

Notes   *165*
References   *179*
Index   *205*

Illustrations

FIGURES

1. Poverty Thresholds for Four-Person Families, 1947–2011 / 35
2. Poverty Rates, by Measure / 36
3. Official Poverty Rates by Age, 1959 to 2011 / 41
4. Ratio of Family Income to the Poverty Threshold, 2011 / 44
5. Percentage of Households with Various Consumer Goods, 2009 / 46
6. Share of Total Population and Poor Population in High-Poverty Neighborhoods, 1990 to 2005–2009 / 56
7. Percentage of People Living on Less Than $1.25 a Day, by Region, 1981–2005 / 63
8. Infant Mortality by Region, 2010 / 65
9. Relative Poverty Rates for Selected Countries, Mid-2000s / 70
10. Absolute Poverty Rates for Selected Countries, Mid-2000s / 72
11. Death Rates among Children 1–19 Years of Age, by OECD Country, Mid-2000s / 73
12. Father-Son Earnings Elasticities, by Country / 75
13. Poverty Rates and the Gross Domestic Product, 1929–2011 / 82
14. Cumulative Growth in Average After-Tax Income, by Income Group, 1979–2007 / 84

15. Shares of Income after Transfers and Federal Taxes, 1979 and 2007 / 85

16. Percentage Change in Median Usual Weekly Earnings, by Educational Attainment and Gender, 1979–2010 / 86

17. Official Poverty Rates by Race and Hispanic Origin, 1959–2011 / 91

18. Women's Median Annual Earnings as a Percentage of Men's Earnings for Full-Time, Year-Round Workers, 1960–2011 / 101

19. Percentage of Births to Unmarried Women by Race and Hispanic Origin, 1940–2009 / 103

20. Poverty Rates of Families by Family Structure and Race and Hispanic Origin, 2011 / 104

21. Poverty Rates, Using the National Academy of Sciences Poverty Measure, with and without Government Assistance, 2007 and 2010 / 124

22. Spending on Government Programs, 1970 to 2009 / 140

23. Spending on Programs as a Percentage of the Federal Budget, Fiscal Year 2010 / 141

24. Percentage of Households That Report Receiving Income from Selected Programs, by Poverty Status, 2009 / 142

25. Percentage Point Decline in Pretransfer Poverty Produced by Government Transfers (Social Insurance and Means-Tested), 2004 / 143

TABLES

1. Poverty Rates for Individuals by Demographic Characteristics / 42

2. Percentage of People Reporting Various Hardships / 45

3. Poverty Rates by Region, Metropolitan Status, and State, 1999 and 2011 / 52

4. Intergenerational Mobility across the Earnings Distribution / 76

5. Poverty Rates by Nativity and Race and Hispanic Origin, 2011 / 96

6. Poverty Rates by Group, before and after the Great Recession, 2006–2011 / 123

Preface

Much has changed since I wrote the second edition of *Poverty in America*. The Great Recession and its aftermath have brought new attention to the problems of poverty and inequality. My goal here is to provide a fresh look at patterns and trends in poverty and help contextualize them. This is necessary for providing a basis for an honest political discussion of what ails us and what we can do about it. That is not to say that information alone leads to specific policy solutions. Policy is always guided in part by people's values. But having a better understanding of a problem is necessary for more wisely choosing a course of action that will ultimately help further one's goals.

This edition contains numerous changes from the previous one. First, this edition contains two new chapters. Chapter 4 discusses global poverty, and chapter 6 tackles the Great Recession. There was a limited discussion of poverty in the international context in the previous edition, but I opted for a fuller treatment here. There is much we can learn about poverty in the United States by comparing our experience with those of other nations. The new chapter on the Great Recession discusses both its causes and effects on American society. Although the recession officially ended in 2009, its impact on both the U.S. economy and its politics has been far reaching. One empirical chapter was eliminated from this edition, chapter 6 in the previous edition, "Why Poverty Remains High, Revisited"; the information in this chapter, although originally useful, became increasingly dated.

Second, in addition to adding and subtracting these chapters, I updated other ones so that they engage in extended discussions of recent poverty debates. I discuss, for example, how the recession helped spawn the Tea Party and Occupy Wall Street movements. The chapter on the causes of poverty delves into the debate about whether culture or changing economic conditions are more responsible for increases in female headship and nonmarital fertility, especially among the white population, in recent years. The chapter on policy discusses the contrasting visions of government's role in society that permeate current policy debates, including the debate on President Obama's Patient Protection and Affordable Care Act, or "Obamacare."

I sought to make this edition more accessible for students of poverty by adding vignettes throughout the book to illustrate theoretical arguments and statistical findings. For example, I discuss newspaper accounts of Apple's Foxconn factories in China to illustrate why many U.S. manufacturing jobs have gone overseas as well as the difficult working conditions faced by many people in developing countries. I provide short accounts of the psychological toll of losing a job during the recession and stories of the hardships experienced by people who are desperately poor. This helps humanize poverty for people with relatively little firsthand knowledge of what it means to be poor.

Finally, I updated all of the tables and figures in this edition so that they contain the latest information available. This involved eliminating some tables and figures and adding new ones. Naturally, the text accompanying these tables and figures was likewise updated.

In short, the second edition of *Poverty in America* was beginning to show its age. This edition provides basic updates to facts and figures, but, more importantly, it engages in the most recent research and current political debates on poverty. In the wake of the deepest recession since the Great Depression, the time is ripe for a renewed discussion of poverty in America.

Acknowledgments

I would like to thank a number of people who helped in the development of this book, including its earlier editions: Gordon Fisher, Patricia Ruggles, Daniel T. Lichter, Andrew Beveridge, Josh Kim, Susan Ferber, Leif Jensen, and Charles Ferrer. A special thanks to Naomi Schneider at the University of California Press, who has provided invaluable advice, direction, and support for this project over the years. My thanks as well to Mari Coates and Stacy Eisenstark at the University of California Press for their dedicated work.

I have the deepest gratitude for my friends and family for their support and encouragement, including my wife, Jean, who inspired me to write this book and is always there for me. I would like to thank my children, Jakob and Mia, for the light they bring into our lives; and my parents, Harry and Joan, for all they have done and continue to do. Finally, I would like to thank all of my other family members, including Charles, Debbie, Matthew, Josh, Matt, John, and Edna.

Introduction

Poverty will always be with us. This is not a new idea. From the Gospel of John to today many have despaired that poverty is an enduring feature of society, even as they search for ways to alleviate it. But is this true? Will poverty really always be with us?

The last fifty years, much like the fifty years before it, have been an economic roller coaster. In 1964 President Lyndon Johnson boldly proclaimed the War on Poverty, making it the centerpiece of his domestic agenda. Then, after nearly a decade of true progress against poverty in the United States—the poverty rate declined from 19 percent in 1964 to 11 percent in 1973—progress stalled. The 1970s and early 1980s saw two recessions and a simultaneous bout of high inflation and unemployment. This led Ronald Reagan to quip, in 1988, "My friends, some years ago the federal government declared war on poverty—and poverty won." Nevertheless, the good economic times were hardly over for good. The 1990s were generally a decade of very healthy economic growth during which both high- and low-income Americans experienced increases in their standards of living. In 2000, President Clinton's Council of Economic Advisors predicted the dawn of a new era in which the business cycle of boom and busts would soon be but a memory. Unfortunately, a mere decade later—after another two recessions, including the near economic catastrophe of the Great Recession of 2007–9—the economic and political mood of the country seemed to reach a new low. There was a feeling that America's best days were in the past, and it was only a matter of time before other countries—especially China—would take the mantle as the new global superpower.

This mood was accompanied by bitter competing visions of what ailed the United States and what it could do to regain its footing. Conservatives felt the problem was too much government stifling economic growth and infringing on people's freedoms. Their remedy was tax cuts and smaller government. Progressives thought the problem was underinvestment and runaway inequality that thwarted opportunity. Their answer was targeted spending and investment in basic physical infrastructure and human capital. For a variety of reasons, political moderates lost their voice and polarization and gridlock set in.

The question remains: did we really lose the War on Poverty? We certainly did not win; the official poverty rate is higher today than it was a generation ago. However, it is not fair to say it was lost either. The "war effort" was relatively short in duration, more or less ending by the early 1970s. Moreover, official poverty statistics also mask some improvements in poverty, as programs today are less likely to deliver cash benefits that are counted in official poverty statistics and more likely to include noncash or near-cash benefits that are not, such as in the form of Medicaid, housing subsidies, and the Earned Income Tax Credit. The 2000s notwithstanding, median incomes and standards of living rose through most of the post-1960 period. People today have access to a greater array of useful (and entertaining) consumer products (including smartphones and tablets) that were almost unimaginable in President Johnson's day.

Nevertheless, many Americans continue to struggle to gain a foothold in the middle class. Growing inequality since the 1970s has made matters worse. College costs have soared, as have health care and child care costs in many parts of the country. Families have become more fragile, and marriage is in retreat. High-paying blue-collar jobs appear to have gone overseas for good. The United States *has* lost ground to other rapidly growing countries. Many of our political leaders seem consumed by petty bickering and are unable or unwilling to rise to these challenges.

At this juncture we need to refocus our attention on simmering—some might say festering—problems in America. Poverty is one of these. This book draws new attention to this issue. My basic goal is to answer the following questions: Why does poverty remain so pervasive? What does it mean to be poor? Are particular groups of people (e.g., ethnic minorities, single-parent families) inevitably more likely to be poor?

What can we expect over the next few years? What are the limits of policy?

I advance several arguments throughout this book. First, views of poverty vary over time and place. What it means to be poor today is not the same as what it meant in the early twentieth century. Nor is the standard of what constitutes poverty in the United States the same as that in the developing world. Second, the persistence of poverty in the United States reflects more than just an aggregation of individual failings. Structural factors, such as the way we understand and define poverty, the inherent features of our economic system that produce income inequality, other social inequities, and our policy responses to these problems shape current trends. Third, antipoverty policies constitute a relatively small part of the federal budget and have only a moderate impact on poverty. The effect of policy on poverty is limited by the role of government in society that the public supports. Public sentiment is in turn affected by trust in government and the tension between individualistic and communitarian values. Social and ideological conflicts, confusion about the causes of poverty, and parochial concerns all stand in the way of efforts to reduce poverty and inequality.

These analyses are based on a synthesis of a wide range of quantitative and qualitative studies and a firsthand examination of information collected in a variety of social surveys, such as the decennial census and the Current Population Survey. The strength of these data is that they provide us with a comprehensive overview of poverty across the United States. My goal here is to provide a comprehensive understanding of the general nature and causes of poverty in America by combining this information with the historical record and social scientific theory.

WHY LOOK AT POVERTY?

There are several reasons why poverty continues to be a critical issue in the United States. First, the hardship that often accompanies poverty plainly has adverse effects on individuals' physical and psychological well-being. A number of studies have shown that children raised in poor families are less healthy and worse off in terms of their cognitive development, school achievement, and emotional well-being.[1] Poor adolescents, for example, are more likely to have low self-esteem, act out antisocial behaviors, and become delinquent. Poor individuals are also more likely to have health problems and die at younger ages. Some of the harmful effects of poverty are due to low income, while others result from conditions that often accompany poverty, such as family instability and low levels of education. Poverty often begets more poverty, as those who grow up in poor families are more likely to be poor themselves as adults. Many people also argue that the continued suffering of some Americans in the midst of plenty is morally troubling.

Second, poverty has broad economic consequences. Economies thrive in societies with a vibrant middle class. Much of the strong economic growth in the United States in the twentieth century was fueled by the expansion of consumer markets. As the demand for new products soared, so did technological innovation, productivity, and wages and benefits. Declining levels of poverty contribute to a healthy economy by increasing the number of people who can purchase goods and services; that increase in turn stimulates economic growth and raises average standards of living. One study suggests that the costs associated with childhood poverty total about $500 billion per year in the United States, or the equivalent of nearly 4 percent of GDP. This is based on a rough estimate of what is lost through forgone earnings (due to, for example, low education), crime, and the health costs of growing up poor.[2]

Third, high levels of poverty have serious social and political consequences. Poor people often feel alienated from mainstream society. Poverty also provokes social disorder and crime, and it reduces public confidence in democratic institutions if people do not feel their needs are being addressed by the prevailing system. The ghetto riots of the 1960s, as well as the Los Angeles riots in 1992, for example, reflected the economic, social, and political marginalization of African Americans in U.S. cities. The unequal distribution of resources has contributed to the fragmentation of society we experience today, both nationally and globally.

MYTHS ABOUT POVERTY

There are many common myths about poverty. A frequent misperception, for example, is that a majority of the poor are African Americans, often residing in inner cities. Even though blacks are overrepresented among the poor, they make up less than one-quarter of the population living in poverty. Another common misperception is that the poor do not work; in fact, over 60 percent of poor families have at least one worker.[3] Many believe that poor families are trapped in a cycle of poverty that few escape. However, there is considerable cycling into and out of poverty, and a significant proportion of Americans are poor at some point in their adult lives. Some suppose that welfare programs are a major part of the federal budget. Aside from Medicaid, however, welfare programs constitute a modest share of such spending.

Another common assumption is that poverty represents a fixed measure of economic deprivation. Yet the historical record reveals that people's views of what it means to be poor have varied considerably both over time and across location. Not only are poverty standards lower in developing countries than in the United States, but American standards of poverty were much lower in the early part of the twentieth century than they were just decades later.

A final misperception I will mention here is that current disagreements about public spending reflect distinctly modern social issues. Quite the contrary, debates about the effect of government transfers on markets, individual conduct, and poverty go back to the nation's earliest days. From the beginning, Americans have argued about the relative importance of alleviating hardship, on the one hand, and discouraging and limiting socially undesirable behaviors, on the other. The problem with these debates is that they often have been based on only a partial understanding of the causes of poverty, and people also have different goals and priorities when seeking to address them. /

ORGANIZATION OF THE BOOKS

In chapter 1, I discuss views of poverty in America from the colonial era to the present. Familiarity with the historical context helps inform current poverty and inequality issues. For example, one way in which current debates on public spending echo past debates lies in how we decide who is worthy of support. There has long been a distinction between the "deserving" poor (those deserving of public support), such as the elderly, and the "undeserving" poor, such as able-bodied men and unmarried mothers.

Even as some of the central policy issues on how to address poverty have remained the same, views of what it means to be poor have changed over time. As standards of living have risen, so have assessments of how much money it takes to support a family. Dollar estimates early in the twentieth century were about 50 percent of the estimates made a little over half a century later. Many believe that the current official poverty line, devised in the 1960s and updated annually to account for inflation, is now too low. In 2011 the average poverty line for a family of four was $23,021.

In chapter 2, I review alternative methods of measuring poverty. As the number of antipoverty initiatives grew in the wake of Lyndon Johnson's War on Poverty, it became clear that a standard poverty measure was needed to assess the effectiveness of these programs. The official poverty measure defines poverty lines for families of different sizes and composition and compares a family's reported income to that line to determine if the family is poor. These poverty lines are updated annually for inflation. This official poverty measure remains in use to this day, though not everyone agrees that it represents the best way to estimate economic deprivation.

The two basic types of poverty measures are absolute measures and relative measures, each of which has several variants. Absolute measures, such as the current U.S. official measure, typically attempt to define a truly basic needs standard and have thresholds that remain constant over time. Relative measures, on the other hand, define poverty in terms of comparative disadvantage, and thus what constitutes poverty changes as living standards change. Each of these measures has its own strengths and weaknesses, and both are informative about the changing nature of economic well-being in society.

In my view, the best general measure of poverty has both absolute and relative components. The central notion underlying poverty is that poor individuals are unable to meet basic needs, regardless of general living standards. Yet poverty is relative in that the amount of money people believe they need to live within society rises as overall standards of living rise. One way to keep an absolute poverty measure meaningful is simply to update it by adjusting poverty thresholds every generation or so (or as needed). An alternative is a quasi-relative measure recommended by the National Academy of Sciences (NAS) Panel on Poverty and Family Assistance.[4] Its basic strength is a poverty line that rises as spending on basic goods increases. Because of this and other advantages, this measure is a strong challenger to the current official U.S. poverty measure.

Chapter 3 describes the poverty population in detail. In 2011, for example, 15 percent of the U.S. population, or 46.2 million people, were poor according to the official measure. Poverty rates are a little higher when using the NAS measure and significantly higher if using a common relative measure. Poverty is more pervasive among some demographic subgroups—such as blacks and Hispanics, children, people with less education, and female-headed families—regardless of the poverty measure used. A significant proportion of people report experiencing various material hardships, such as sometimes not having enough food to eat or missing utility payments. However, both rich and poor Americans alike report having basic consumer items such as TVs and refrigerators.

Evidence from studies looking at the dynamics of poverty indicates that a majority of people who fall into poverty remain in poverty for only a short time. Nevertheless, many families frequently move into and out of poverty, and a significant proportion of the poor also suffer long-term poverty spells. Studies show that the large majority of children who grow up poor do not remain so as adults. Nevertheless, as adults they are considerably more likely to be poor than those who did not grow up poor.

Poverty varies widely across states and regions. Although poverty became more concentrated in central cities in the 1970s and 1980s, it became less so thereafter. In recent years suburban poverty has become more widespread. Several pockets of rural poverty have persisted over decades. Some argue that people living in high-poverty neighborhoods (and in remote rural areas) are not only spatially isolated from mainstream society but often socially isolated as well. Many social problems, such as crime, welfare dependency, drug use, and substandard educational outcomes, are more common in high-poverty areas. Concentrated poverty has a variety of sources, including the lack of economic opportunities in many areas of the country and high levels of racial, ethnic, and class segregation.

Chapter 4 discusses U.S. poverty in the global context. When comparing poverty in the United States with poverty in countries around the world, two findings stand out. First, poverty in developing countries qualitatively differs from that in the United States and other developed countries. In impoverished countries, particularly in South Asia and Africa, a high proportion of the population fails to earn even $1.25 a day. Infant mortality levels are high and life expectancies are relatively low in these countries. Absolute global poverty, however, has declined in recent decades, and especially in rapidly industrializing countries such as China and India. While debates on the effects of globalization continue, these countries, at least, represent cases where globalization has served to increase general standards of living.

A second theme of this chapter is that although the United States has virtually the highest gross national product (GNP) per capita in the world, it has higher levels of both absolute and relative poverty than other rich countries in Northern and Western Europe. It also has higher levels of relative poverty than just about all European countries, as well as lower levels of economic mobility than many of them. Differences in spending on programs that assist the low-income population help explain these poverty differentials. /

In discussing the causes of poverty in chapter 5, I consider not only conventional theories about the effect of individual characteristics, such as educational attainment, but also theories that focus on the impact of structural factors. Understanding the workings of economic systems and social inequality is essential for explaining why poverty exists and why members of some groups are more likely to be poor than others. For example, factors that account for the historical racial-ethnic gap in poverty include not only differences in educational attainment and the prevalence of female-headed families but also residential segregation, economic inequality, and discrimination.

Some of the rapid decline in poverty among minorities over the last half century reflects the fall of legal barriers and the decline of discrimination. Today, past poverty, economic dislocation, wealth differentials, and family instability are barriers at least as important as racism and discrimination in explaining poverty levels among blacks and Hispanics. Nevertheless, despite this progress, racial and ethnic disparities remain a critical problem in America.

While men continue to earn more than women in the labor market, gender differences in pay have been gradually declining. The pay gap between male and female full-time workers is smallest among younger cohorts. Women today are more likely to receive college diplomas and many kinds of professional degrees than men. This suggests that gender inequality will continue to decline in the coming years and perhaps even leave men at a socioeconomic disadvantage at some point in the future.

Single-parent families are considerably more likely to be poor than other families. Single parents face the challenges of supporting a family on one income and often paying for child care while they work. Lower levels of education among individuals who head such families also contribute to their lower earnings. Although there has been a significant decline in the poverty rate among single-parent families (and especially female-headed ones) over the decades as the employment and earnings of single parents has grown, such families nevertheless remain particularly vulnerable to poverty and material hardship.

Chapter 6 examines the causes and effects of the Great Recession of 2007–9. This recession resulted from the bursting of the housing bubble and the subsequent crisis in the banking industry. By October of 2009, the national unemployment rate had doubled to 10 percent. High unemployment declined only very slowly in the subsequent months and years. The root causes of the Great Recession were rising inequality (which made it more difficult for many families to attain a middle-class lifestyle), the loosening of bank lending rules and the corresponding rise in consumer debt, and the rise of the mortgage securitization industry with relatively little regulatory oversight. Government bailouts of many companies deemed "too large to fail" and a subsequent economic stimulus package, though viewed with suspicion and resentment by many, likely served to prevent an even larger economic calamity.

Consequences of the recession included higher poverty, greatly reduced wealth, greater food hardship, and more young adults living with their parents. Political responses to the crisis varied widely, ranging from, on the conservative side of the political spectrum, the rise of the Tea Party movement in 2009 and 2010 to, on the liberal side, the Occupy Wall Street movement in 2011. Although these specific movements may have ebbed, their underlying philosophies live on and continue to inform political debates on poverty.

Chapter 7 examines policy issues. Historically, American welfare policy has been characterized by a perennial tension between the goal of giving aid in a humane manner to those in need and the attempt to ensure that such efforts do not promote dependence or provide work disincentives. Colonial programs tended to provide sufficient benefits to needy community members, though they were unkind to outsiders and able-bodied men. The poorhouses of the nineteenth century attempted to supply very basic care while discouraging residents from becoming dependent on handouts. These institutions ended up doing little to address the roots of poverty. Scientific charities at the turn of the twentieth century sought to professionalize welfare assistance; their efforts to reform the poor morally often failed miserably.

In the 1930s, the Great Depression showed that local efforts alone were insufficient to combat poverty in times of a national economic crisis. It became clear that poverty, even among able-bodied individuals, can result from broader structural forces. In the post–World War II period, even as living standards grew, so did concern that not everyone was benefiting. The War on Poverty and the civil rights movement in the 1960s sought to bring prosperity to those who had previously been ignored by policy or had only marginally benefited from it, such as racial and ethnic minorities. These movements brought considerable change, though many believed that welfare policies were too expansive and did not do enough to prevent dependency. Welfare reform in the 1990s changed that by ending cash aid as an entitlement all poor people could receive. In recent years, debates about the nature and scope of our health care system have come to the fore. As of the time of this writing, these issues are far from resolved.

Some of the frustration with government policies that aim to help low-income Americans in recent years has stemmed from misperceptions about the size of various government programs. Controversial programs such as cash welfare assistance consume only a relatively small part of the federal budget, and, indeed, government transfers are often not large enough to lift the recipients' income over the poverty line. The relatively popular social insurance programs, such as Medicare and Social Security, make up the largest proportion of income-assistance spending. The cost of medical benefits has risen by more than the cost of other programs since the 1970s. These social insurance programs lift the greatest number of people out of poverty, especially among the elderly. The Earned Income Tax Credit is more effective for helping working families with low wages. Medicaid is an important medical benefit targeted to the low-income population.

Today's welfare system once again attempts to strike a delicate balance: providing at least some sort of safety net while also not discouraging work and industriousness. We continue to see substantial poverty and inequality in America today, particular in the wake of two recessions in the 2000s and sluggish job growth even during economic recoveries. The country is deeply divided on how to address these issues and is engaged in an ongoing ideological battle about the proper role of government in society. This suggests that any efforts to reduce poverty in the near future will be, at best, incremental.

CHAPTER I

Early Views of Poverty in America

What is poverty? When I ask this question of my students, a common response is something like, "Being poor means not having a lot of money." This makes sense, but it is still rather vague. Although we commonly fumble about for a more precise answer, many of us nevertheless feel we can certainly recognize poverty when we see it. The historian James T. Patterson, for example, relates the following report from a social worker during the Great Depression: "Chicago, 1936: One woman wrote to a relief station as follows: 'I am without food for myself and child. I only got $6.26 to last me from the tenth to the twenty-fifth. That order is out and I haven't anything to eat. We go to bed hungry. Please give us something to eat. I cannot stand to see my child hungry.'"[1] I venture that even the hardest-hearted would grudgingly agree that this is poverty. As one moves away from this kind of obvious example, however, it becomes more difficult to distinguish just what people mean when they refer to "the poor," as opposed to lower-income people more generally.

In 1993 the General Social Survey fielded the following question about poverty (they haven't asked it since): "People who have income below a certain level can be considered poor. That level is called the 'poverty line.' What amount of weekly income would you use as a poverty line for a family of four (husband, wife, and two children) in this community?" Answers ranged from as low as $38 to as high as $2,305 per week (all of these figures are in 2011 inflation-adjusted dollars). The average response was $524.[2] Most families would find it difficult to live on $38 a week. At the other extreme, $2,305 per week seems excessive as a minimum standard. At what point does luxury become a necessity? More to the point, why did this question elicit such a wide variety of responses?

Although poverty is a concrete phenomenon for those who live it, what people judge to constitute poverty varies across both time and place. A working-class laborer in a developing country would likely be considered poor in Western Europe. In fact, the World Bank uses a poverty standard of $1.25 or $2 per person per day, or $1,369 to $2,190 per year, for a family of three in developing countries.[3] In contrast, the average official poverty threshold for a family of three in the United States was $17,916 in 2011. It should be noted that this comparison is not altogether easy to make, as there are some poor regions around the world where people get by on subsistence farming and where relatively little money is exchanged.

As far back as 1776, Adam Smith noted the importance of social perceptions in determining what constitutes economic hardship. In the *Wealth of Nations* he defined the lack of "necessaries" as the experience of being unable to consume "not only the commodities which are indispensably necessary for the support of life, but whatever the custom of the country renders it indecent for creditable people, even of the lowest order, to be without."[4] More recently, Peter Townsend observed that people are social beings who assume many roles in a community—worker, citizen, parent, friend, and so on. He maintained that poverty should be defined as the lack of sufficient income for people to "play the roles, participate in the relationships, and follow the customary behavior which is expected of them by virtue of their membership of society."[5]

In order to understand who we, as a society, consider poor, therefore, we must begin by examining how our own views have evolved. This chapter begins by tracing views of poverty in America before 1900. I place these views in their economic, social, and political context, noting how these forces subsequently affected twentieth-century efforts to measure and understand poverty. I end by describing the emergence of the current official poverty measure in the 1960s.

VIEWS OF POVERTY BEFORE 1900

Views of poverty reflect social conditions. A common assumption during the U.S. colonial period was that the roots of poverty lay primarily not in structural economic causes but in individual misbehavior.[6] The poor were often categorized as either "deserving" or "undeserving" of public support. Voluntary idleness was regarded as a vice, and in early colonial times unemployed men were often either bound out as indentured servants, whipped and forced out of town, or put in jail. In 1619, the Virginia assembly ordered that idle able-bodied persons should be bound over to compulsory labor. Likewise, in 1633 the General Court of Massachusetts decreed harsh punishment for those who spent their time "idly or unprofitably."[7] Yet hardship among the elderly and children was usually viewed more sympathetically, as many colonists recognized that poverty was widespread and sometimes unavoidable. Communities therefore often accepted responsibility for the well-being of the elderly in need.[8]

By the early nineteenth century, many craftsmen and farmers displaced by the mechanization of agriculture and the mass production of goods struggled to earn a living, as did unskilled laborers.[9] These groups constituted an economically insecure "floating proletariat," some of whom traveled extensively to find jobs. Some became "tramps," jobless men and, to a lesser extent, women who moved continuously from place to place in search of employment.[10]

The distinction between the deserving and undeserving poor persisted through the nineteenth century. In 1834, for example, the Reverend Charles Burroughs spoke about the differences between poverty and pauperism: "The former is an unavoidable evil, to which many are brought from necessity, and in the wise and gracious Providence of God. It is the result, not of our faults, but of our misfortunes. . . . Pauperism is the consequence of willful error, of shameful indolence, of vicious habit."[11]

The word *pauper* generally refers to someone receiving relief or assistance, usually from local or county governments. As illustrated in the quote above, the public has tended to have a dim view of people who seek assistance, and paupers have generally been considered as members of the "undeserving" poor. The poor were also sometimes stigmatized with other labels such as "dependent, defective, and delinquent."[12]

The nineteenth century saw the growth of poorhouses, also known as "indoor relief," as a method for dealing with the poor. Starting in the 1830s, state governments began to write laws mandating that counties have a poor farm or poorhouse. Many of those who needed short-term aid nevertheless still received from local agencies or private charities "outdoor relief," which did not require those seeking help to enter institutions.[13] The poorhouses were harsh; their purpose was to deter all but the most desperate from applying for help. Poorhouse inmates were expected to work as a form of punishment, moral training, education, and reform.[14] It was not until the beginning of the twentieth century that poorhouses fell out of favor, as public officials and social professionals realized that such institutions did little to reduce poverty and sometimes even exacerbated family instability when family members were interned in these institutions.[15]

Contemporary concerns about the geographical concentration of poverty echo fears voiced by many nineteenth- and early twentieth-century commentators. Indeed, in the middle decades of the nineteenth century, some middle-class and wealthy city residents began to build new homes in areas just outside cities such as New York and Boston in order to avoid the poor who lived in the cities themselves.[16] Michael Katz recounts how, in an 1854 annual report, Charles Loring Brace, the head of New York City's Children's Aid Society, argued that the "greatest danger" to America's future was the "existence of an ignorant, debased, and permanently poor class in the great cities. . . . The members of it come at length to form a separate population. They embody the lowest passions and the most thriftless habits of the community. They corrupt the lowest class of working-poor who are around them. The expenses of police, prisons, of charities and means of relief, arise mainly from them."[17]

S. Humphreys Gurteen, a writer and preacher, also decried the problems of both poverty and pauperism in his 1882 description of poor city districts: "large families huddled together in tenements and shanties which barely afford protection from wind and storm; dwellings where the laws of health are defied, where the most ordinary sanitary arrangements are unknown, and where 'boards of health' fail to penetrate; . . . human forms, even those of children, shivering in rags; hunger written upon care-worn faces; and despair everywhere triumphant." He blamed these problems on the abandonment of the poor by the well-to-do, on immorality, and on the ineffectiveness of charity, which he believed fostered dependence.[18]

Nevertheless, apart from these small, highly visible "slum" districts, cities were not nearly as segregated by class as they have been in recent decades. Urban working-class neighborhoods were in constant flux, with steadily employed workers sharing the same buildings, streets, and residential districts with those who were less steadily employed.[19] This is a natural consequence of the fact that poverty was endemic in cities and rural areas across the country.

Katz ventures that perhaps half the population of typical nineteenth-century cities was poor, though this judgment is based more on contemporary notions of poverty than on the standards of the time.[20] He does note, however, that the "working-class experience was a continuum; no clear line separated the respectable poor from paupers."[21] According to another estimate, roughly 10 to 20 percent of late nineteenth-century Americans lived in a family with a member who had "tramped" at some point, that is, moved from place to place in search of work.[22] The receipt of government aid was far less common. According to an analysis of 1860 census data, 7.9 people in 1,000 received public relief.[23] Robert Hunter, in his 1904 book *Poverty,* estimated that at least 10 million people were poor, which represented about 12 percent of the American population in that year. He noted that this was largely a guess and that the actual number was likely much higher.[24] John Ryan, an advocate of a "living wage," used a less severe poverty standard and estimated that closer to 40 percent of wage earners were living in poverty at the time.[25] As bad as some of the city slums were, the incidence of poverty was actually much higher in rural areas in general and in the South in particular. Sharecroppers and tenant farmers suffered from hard times after 1860, with some leaving for mill villages where working conditions were terrible and wages low.[26]

Poverty among African Americans was likewise endemic. Largely concentrated in southern and rural areas, black sharecroppers struggled to earn a living. Blacks were barred by law or custom from a large range of full-time jobs, especially outside black communities, leaving agricultural wage labor as the most common occupation.[27] As the new system of Jim Crow laws, disfranchisement, and racial violence escalated during the late nineteenth century, southern blacks began to migrate to northern cities in growing numbers. This migration north would swell in the following century. Most blacks who lived in cities were employed as common laborers or as domestic and personal servants. Opportunities for promotion and advancement were very uncommon for blacks in these and other occupations.[28]

Because of their precarious economic position, African Americans were more likely to receive public assistance in some cities.[29] W. E. B. DuBois, in his well-known study *The Philadelphia Negro,* estimated that about 9 percent of black families were very poor and another 10 percent were simply poor, earning less than $5 per week.[30] As there was no official poverty measure at the time, DuBois's estimates of poverty are based on his own assessment, and his standard of poverty was meager compared with most other appraisals. Although African Americans made up about 4 percent of Philadelphia's population in the 1890s, they constituted about

8 percent of those either residing in the city's almshouses or receiving assistance from the county poor board or aid for orphans.[31] DuBois believed that high levels of poverty among African Americans had a number of causes, including the legacy of slavery, white racial beliefs and discriminatory practices, low levels of skill and education, and, in industrial cities, competition from immigrants.[32]

The United States continued its rapid industrialization and urbanization in the early twentieth century. Between 1860 and 1920 the nation's urban population increased from about 20 percent of the total U.S. population to over 50 percent. Immigrants from Europe poured into eastern and midwestern cities in growing numbers. And beginning in about 1915 and continuing for the next thirty years or so, the migration of blacks in search of better economic opportunities in northern cities accelerated. Corporations with large factories in industries such as steel and automobiles found a large pool of cheap and willing labor in the immigrant and black communities.[33]

Industrialization was accompanied by economic growth, as real per capita income in 1929 was one and half times greater than it was in 1900. Standards of living rose by several other measures as well, including size and quality of housing, the number of home appliances, and health. For example, in 1930 life expectancy at birth was sixty years, up from only forty-seven years in 1900.[34] Nevertheless, a large part of the workforce, especially those in peripheral industries, remained vulnerable to periodic and often severe downturns in the economy. Sugrue describes the plight of these workers: "Trapped in insecure jobs with small companies increasingly marginal to a market dominated by large corporations, they shared with their nineteenth-century predecessors susceptibility to bouts of poverty."[35]

The collapse of the stock market in October 1929 and the ensuing Great Depression, which stretched throughout the 1930s, brought economic hardship to nearly all corners of the country, though rural areas were often hit the hardest. In 1933 a full quarter of the labor force was unemployed.[36] As one report from a social worker documented, "Massachusetts, 1934: About the unemployed themselves: this picture is so grim that whatever words I use will seem hysterical and exaggerated. And I find them all in the same shape—fear, fear driving them into a state of semi-collapse; cracking nerves; and an overpowering terror of the future. . . . They can't pay rent and are evicted. They . . . are watching their children grow thinner and thinner; fearing the cold for children who have neither coats nor shoes; wondering about coal."[37]

Much of the economic progress of the previous decades had been dashed and the natural optimism of the American people was shaken. Years passed with high unemployment and growth that was uneven at best. Just as the country seemed to be emerging from the depression, the economy again sputtered and sank in 1937. Despite Franklin D. Roosevelt's efforts to expand the safety net—bitterly opposed by free-market conservatives at every turn—only massive expenditures on the war effort in the early 1940s and the resurrection of associated industries brought back prosperity. Meanwhile, hardship flourished, and poverty could no longer be blamed solely on individual morality and misbehavior, for the role of larger economic forces was plain to see.

It was in this social and economic context—poverty, progress, and collapse—that an interest in studying and documenting poverty and other economic indicators blossomed. There was a growing recognition that in order to address economic problems, one had to have solid information about the economy with which to make informed decisions.

THE BEGINNING OF POVERTY MEASUREMENT

It was not until the late nineteenth and early twentieth centuries that techniques to measure and study poverty began to be developed, in part because many social science disciplines and statistical methods themselves were only in youthful bloom. Sociology itself arose in the nineteenth century through the writings of such people as Auguste Comte, Herbert Spencer, and Karl Marx.[38] Although economics has a longer history, the discipline's sophisticated quantitative methods are more recent in origin. In short, although there has long been an interest in issues related to poverty, the "science" of examining poverty began only in the last couple of centuries.

Concerned about working-class unrest that fed the revolutions of 1848, European statisticians began to study the incomes and expenses of working-class families in about 1850. This lead to the development of "standard budgets," which basically refer to the cost of goods and services that families need to achieve a certain standard of living. Influenced by these studies, early efforts in the United States to develop standard budgets began between 1870 and 1895. Sometimes different budgets were constructed for people of different social classes or occupational groups. Although most were constructed to represent a minimum subsistence level, others were meant to represent minimum comfort levels.[39]

Charles Booth came up with the term *line of poverty* in his well-known multivolume study of poverty and society in London.[40] He defined poverty in the following way: "The 'poor' are those whose means . . . are barely sufficient for decent independent life; the 'very poor' those whose means are insufficient for this according to the usual standard of life in this country."[41]

In fact, it was around the end of the nineteenth century when the word *poverty* became associated less with receiving public relief or private charity (i.e., "pauperism") and more with having insufficient income to live appropriately. This concept of poverty became widely accepted among the social workers, social scientists, and others who studied these issues more systematically in the first two decades of the twentieth century. It was also around this time that people began to accept the view that poverty was also due to economic and other social factors rather than just individual weakness.[42]

In a careful review of early poverty measurement efforts, Gordon Fisher suggests that these attempts to define poverty (or income inadequacy) inform us not only about economic deprivation but also about the social structure of the time and the social processes by which poverty lines are drawn. Illustrating the tendency of successive poverty lines to rise in real terms as the real income of the general population rises, early budgets and other measures of income inadequacy were quite low by recent standards (all comparisons below adjust for inflation). For example, Fisher notes that the 1890–91 report of the Iowa Bureau of Labor Statistics included a standard budget showing the "minimum cost" of "the necessary living expenses of laboring men with families" that was roughly equal to 52 percent of today's official poverty threshold for a family of five.[43]

DuBois's 1896–97 poverty line (which was meant to be a standard budget rather than a bare-necessities demarcation line) of $5 a week, or $260 a year, represents only about 26 percent of the official poverty line for a family of five. This poverty line was markedly lower than every other contemporary American standard budget. In his classic 1904 volume *Poverty*, Robert Hunter used a poverty line of $460 a year for an averaged-size family in northern industrial areas, and $300 for such a family in the rural South. To live at the poverty line, he stated, was to use the "same standard that a man would demand for his horses or slaves."[44] Other minimum subsistence budgets and poverty lines developed before World War I tended to represent from 43 to 54 percent of the current official poverty line.[45]

Some Progressive Era advocates of the poor recognized that the standard budget methodology could be misused in ways that were unfair to working-class families. In 1918 William Ogburn, a University of Washington professor who had gone to work for the National War Labor Board, noted in a discussion of standard budgets, "We can not go on the assumption that the housewife can purchase food value with the skill of a domestic-science expert, or that she has the will power of a Puritan, or that no allowance would be made to the man for drinks and tobacco."[46] Indeed, Fisher notes:

> Lower-income homemakers were consistently being expected to show a skill in food buying that would have actually been greater than that of most middle-class homemakers—and were being stigmatized as "ignorant" and having "poor buying habits" when they failed to exhibit such impossible talents. Scott Nearing's trenchant analysis was correct: any "superwoman" who could live up to the expectations of such budgets would not have to be subjected to them in the first place, as she would already be earning almost twice the poverty level in private industry.[47]

Into the 1940s there was still no consensus in the literature regarding "poverty" or "poverty lines." Federal government employees, labor union personnel, advocates for income redistribution and greater economic growth, and a handful of academics tried to develop or revise poverty lines during the 1946–65 period, but many were unaware of the work being done by others in different organizations.[48]

Between 1949 and 1958 a common low-income line that was often cited, originally proposed by the congressional Subcommittee on Low-Income Families (SLIF), was equal in constant dollars to 81 percent of today's official poverty threshold for a family of four. The poverty lines offered after 1958 and before the official poverty line was introduced in 1965 tended to be even higher, again reflecting growing standards of living of the time.[49]

THE DEVELOPMENT OF THE OFFICIAL POVERTY MEASURE

The late 1950s and early 1960s saw the publication of several books and reports that drew people's attention to poverty. One was John Kenneth Galbraith's *The Affluent Society*. Galbraith argued that, while rising standards of living reduced hardship, the materialism of American consumer culture contributed to inequality and that poverty remained entrenched in many parts of the country. He also discussed

the relative nature of poverty: "In part [poverty] is a physical matter. . . . But . . . it is wrong to rest everything on absolutes. People are
poverty-stricken when their income, even if adequate for survival, falls
markedly behind that of the community. Then they cannot have what
the larger community regards as the minimum necessary for decency;
and they cannot wholly escape, therefore, the judgment of the larger
community that they are indecent."[50]

In 1962 Michael Harrington's *The Other America: Poverty in the
United States* was published; reviews of this book and other contemporary reports caught the eye of the Kennedy administration and influenced its views and policies on poverty issues. Harrington's basic aim in
the book was to draw attention to the poverty that persisted despite the
plenty that many Americans enjoyed. He argued that the poor, black
and white alike, were subjected to a chronic suppression of their living
standards. This led to a culture of poverty that was perpetuated by an
endless cycle of neglect and injustice.[51]

Within the Kennedy administration, the economist Walter Heller,
chairman of the Council of Economic Advisors (CEA), wanted to
"launch a Kennedy offensive against poverty."[52] The CEA favored
doing so within the framework of the broader economic agenda they
had been pursuing since 1961, which aimed at faster economic growth
and full employment by means of tax cuts. Robert Lampman, a CEA
economist at the time, also sought to devise a politically acceptable definition of poverty that would focus less on income inequality and more
on the amount needed to achieve a minimum living standard. A nar-
rower income definition would lend itself to the growth-centered economic policy (as opposed to income redistribution policies) the CEA
was advocating.[53]

After Kennedy's assassination in 1963, President Lyndon Johnson
decided to adopt Kennedy's emerging plan as his own, and in fact to
make it a centerpiece of his domestic agenda. Johnson announced his
ambitious War on Poverty in his January 1964 State of the Union
address. In 1965 Mollie Orshansky independently published an article
in the *Social Security Bulletin* in which she presented two sets of poverty
thresholds, "economy level" and "low-cost level." These were a refined
and extended version of thresholds that she had described in a July
1963 *Social Security Bulletin* article.[54]

At that time, poverty measurement had been a major item on the
research agenda of the Office of Economic Opportunity (OEO). Influenced by views on the political feasibility and desirability of defining

poverty as a lack of income, the OEO adopted the lower of Mollie Orshansky's two sets of poverty thresholds—the set based on the economy food plan—as a working definition of poverty for statistical, planning, and budget purposes. In 1969 the U.S. Bureau of the Budget (now the Office of Management and Budget) designated the thresholds as the federal government's official statistical definition of poverty. The weighted-average nonfarm poverty threshold for a family of four was $3,128 for the base year, 1963. In the following chapter I discuss this measure, as well as other types of poverty measures, in more detail.

CHAPTER 2

Methods of Measuring Poverty

The current official poverty measure, devised in 1965 and adopted by the federal government in 1969, has lived to a ripe old age. Some would assert *too* ripe an age, especially given changing living standards over the last half century. Unlike in the 1960s, most women today work, and many of these families need child care. Health care costs have surged, and housing takes up a larger share of a family's budget than it used to. People of all political stripes say the poverty measure is hopelessly outdated, and, as a consequence, new efforts have cropped up to provide a more accurate portrait of poverty in the United States.[1]

So if there is bipartisan support for changing the official measure, why hasn't a new one been adopted yet? The short answer is that although there are elements of the official poverty measure that all agree need to be changed (such as the measure of people's income, which is clearly flawed), there are some fundamental differences in opinion on what a "poverty" measure should, well, measure.

Consider the following stark assertion about the meaning of poverty, written in 1904: "Whether it be directly through starvation, or indirectly through sickness brought on by insufficient nourishment, poverty must necessarily lead to the extinction of the physical life."[2] Most would agree that equating poverty with starvation and death is too severe an approach. There are many people who are struggling to make ends meet, some even homeless, but who are not at death's door. But should poverty refer to a severe state of material deprivation? Or are notions of poverty inextricably linked to social standards of living, as alluded to in the previous chapter?

The debate continues today. A 2011 report by a conservative think tank in Washington, D.C., argued, "Most of the persons whom the government defines as 'in poverty' are not poor in the ordinary sense of the term," as the majority of the poor have amenities like air-conditioning, cable TV, a refrigerator, an oven and stove, a microwave, and a clothes washer and dryer. The report further asserts that "the major dietary problem facing poor Americans is eating too much" and that "most poor families stated that they had had sufficient funds during the past year to meet all essential needs."[3]

Stephen Colbert, a comedian and faux conservative political commentator on his show, *The Colbert Report,* provided a retort to this report. "A refrigerator and a microwave?" asked Colbert. "They can preserve and heat food? Oolala! I guess the poor are too good for mold and trichinosis." Colbert's subsequent discussion with Peter Edelman, a former aid to Robert Kennedy who was a guest on his show that day, focused on how government programs have been instrumental in alleviating much of the severest of poverty that once plagued a significant proportion of the U.S. population.[4] The underlying theme was that poverty is perhaps not as severe as it once was, but that does not mean that many people are not struggling to meet what are widely considered basic needs.

This chapter focuses on these issues by reviewing the basic types of poverty measures, discussing their advantages and disadvantages, and describing a poverty measure recommended by a National Academy of Sciences panel that is a strong contender to replace the current official one.

WHAT IS POVERTY?

Poverty, as defined and applied in this book, essentially refers to economic, or income, deprivation. Two basic types of poverty measures are *absolute* measures and *relative* measures. Absolute measures, such as the current U.S. official measure, typically attempt to define a truly basic—absolute—needs standard and therefore remain constant over time. Relative measures, which are more commonly used by researchers and policy makers in Europe though used less in the United States, define poverty as a condition of comparative disadvantage, to be assessed against some relative, shifting, or evolving standard of living. The key distinction between the measures is not necessarily in the specific monetary value of the respective poverty thresholds (though absolute thresholds are usually lower), but rather in how these thresholds are updated over time. Absolute poverty lines remain constant, while relative ones rise as standards of living rise.[5]

In the 1990s, a U.S. National Academy of Sciences research panel devised a *quasi-relative* measure, which combines elements of absolute and relative measures.[6] Since that time, additional research has resulted in additional adjustments and refinements to the panel's recommended measure. This quasi-relative measure has certain qualities that, in my view, make it conceptually and practically the most viable and useful type of general poverty measure in the United States, even though different types of measure can be informative when trying to understand different social and economic conditions.

Absolute Measures

Absolute poverty measures have thresholds, or poverty lines, that remain constant over time. These measures are descended from the work on standard budgets and poverty lines described in the previous chapter. The assumption underlying most absolute measures is that there is a subsistence level of income or consumption below which people should be deemed economically disadvantaged or deprived. Early advocates of the poor who developed standard budgets typically attempted to come up with a dollar figure representing the amount of income below which a family or person risked being without adequate shelter, clothes, or food. Although absolute thresholds do not necessarily represent a severe measure of deprivation, it is nevertheless implicit that they are developed by "experts" with reference to basic physiological needs.[7]

The official U.S. poverty measure is an excellent example of an absolute measure that achieved a wide degree of support and consensus. The current official poverty measure has two components: poverty thresholds and the definition of family income that is compared to these thresholds. Mollie Orshansky of the Social Security Administration constructed poverty thresholds by using the "Economy Food Plan" (the lowest-cost food plan) prepared and priced by the U.S. Department of Agriculture. She described her poverty thresholds as a "relatively absolute" measure of poverty, inasmuch as they were developed from calculations that made use of the consumption patterns (at a particular point in time) of the U.S. population as a whole. Nevertheless, the measure is considered an absolute one because it does not change as standards of living change. The plan was designed for "temporary or emergency use when funds are low." It allowed for no eating at restaurants, called for careful management of food storage and preparation, and was designed to provide a nutritious but monotonous diet.[8]

To get from the food plan cost to an overall poverty threshold figure, Orshansky used information from the 1955 Household Food Consumption Survey, which indicated that families of three or more people spent about one-third of their after-tax income on food in that year. She therefore multiplied the costs of the food plan for different family sizes by three to come up with thresholds for those families.[9] Thresholds have been updated yearly for inflation using the Consumer Price Index (CPI). The definition of family resources used to compare to the thresholds is the Census Bureau's definition of income, which consists of gross annual cash income from all sources, such as earnings, pensions, interest income, rental income, and cash welfare. A family and its members are considered poor if their income falls below the poverty threshold for a family of that size and composition.[10]

The main advantage of absolute poverty measures is that they are conceptually easy to understand and intuitively appealing. There is, after all, an "absolutist core" in the idea of poverty.[11] For example, if there is starvation and hunger, then there is clearly poverty—regardless of how high or low the overall standard of living. Furthermore, the history of research on standard budgets exemplifies the widely held belief that there is some amount of money we need to survive, and that people making less than that amount face substantial economic hardship.

The main disadvantage of absolute poverty measures is that as standards of living change, generally so do people's perceptions of what poverty means. Fisher describes how poverty lines and minimum subsistence budgets before World War I were, in constant dollars, generally between 43 and 54 percent of Mollie Orshansky's poverty threshold for 1963. A U.S. Works Progress Administration "emergency" budget for 1935 was equal to 65 percent of Orshansky's poverty threshold, and Robert Lampman's low-income line for 1957 was 88 percent of that threshold.[12]

Economists describe this phenomenon as the income elasticity of the poverty line—the tendency of successive poverty lines to rise in real terms as the real income of the general population rises. Reviewing a number of studies on the issue, Fisher estimates that the amount of money people think it takes to "get along" rises between 0.6 and

1.0 percent for every 1.0 percent increase in the income of the general population.[13] He finds similar general patterns in Britain, Canada, and Australia. Thus, it could be argued that poverty measures are useful only to the extent that they tell us something meaningful about the conditions in a particular society. Poverty is by its nature at least somewhat relative; people are poor when others think of them as poor.[14]

The official U.S. poverty measure has some advantages and disadvantages unrelated to the fact that it is an absolute poverty measure. On the positive side, it has achieved a level of consensus that no other poverty measure in the United States can claim. As an analytic tool, it has provided much useful information about trends in economic well-being. First among its many problems is that the definition of money income used is flawed: gross cash income inadequately captures the amount of money people have at their disposal to meet economic needs. Second, the thresholds are not very refined and have become outdated. There are also other, less central, technical criticisms, such as the unit of analysis (the family) and the source of data used for official poverty statistics. These shortcomings are now discussed in turn.

Regarding the definition of income, a family is considered poor if its gross cash income falls below the family's designated poverty threshold. Cash income includes earnings and other items mentioned earlier.[15] Yet many argue that in-kind or near-money government benefits that can be used to meet basic needs—such as food assistance cards, housing subsidies, and the Earned Income Tax Credit (EITC)—should also be counted as resources. The omission of these items from the official definition of resources has become increasingly serious in recent years because government policies designed to aid low-income families have progressively been concentrated in these noncash programs.[16]

Furthermore, some argue that the current income definition does not take into account variation in expenses that are necessary to hold a job and to earn income—expenses that reduce disposable income. These expenses include taxes paid, transportation costs for getting to work, and the cost of child care for working parents with children. Child care expenses in particular have risen significantly since the time when the poverty measure was originally devised. At that time, women were much more likely to stay home and care for their children than they are today, when a majority of mothers work to help their families make ends meets. All of these expenses are taken into account in the resources definition of an experimental poverty measure described in more detail below, but they are not in the current official income definition.

Official poverty thresholds are also seriously flawed. First, they are constructed rather crudely, and thus they have become outdated. Although the thresholds were originally constructed based on the cost of a food budget, which was then multiplied by three, more recent data indicate that food comprises closer to one-eighth—not one-third—of families' expenses.[17] A more refined threshold could price out the cost not only of food but also of other necessities, like shelter and clothing. Some argue that thresholds should also be adjusted for geographic differences in the cost of living, since families in, say, New York City have greater income needs than families in rural Mississippi.[18] The official measure does not take these differences into account.

Among other issues, the official poverty measure uses the family as the basic unit. That is, a person is considered poor if his or her family income falls below the poverty threshold for a family of that size and composition.[19] A problem with this definition is that cohabiting couples are treated as separate units, as if they did not pool resources at all. The rapid growth in the number of cohabiting couples and people living in nontraditional housing arrangements has magnified the effect of this issue in recent years.[20] A more detailed discussion of the official measure, its problems, and potential alternatives is contained in the volume authored by the National Academy of Sciences Panel on Poverty and Family Assistance, *Measuring Poverty: A New Approach,* and in more recent research on how to best implement the panel's recommendations.[21]

Relative Measures

Relative poverty can be defined as comparative economic deprivation. It is based on the notion that poverty is relative to a society's existing level of economic, social, and cultural development. Implicit is the assumption that people are social beings who operate within relationships. Those whose resources are significantly below the resources of others, even if they are physically able to survive, may not be able to participate adequately in social organizations and relationships, and are thus incapable of fully participating in society.[22] Adam Smith argued that to be poor was to lack what was needed to be a "creditable" member of society. In the *Wealth of Nations* (1776), he noted, "A linen shirt, for example, is, strictly speaking, not a necessity of life. The Greeks and the Romans lived, I suppose, very comfortably though they had no linen. But in the present times, through the greater part of Europe, a creditable day-labourer would be ashamed to appear in public without a linen shirt."[23]

Relative measures can take different forms. The most common method is setting a threshold at a percentage of the median household income. The European Union currently uses 60 percent of median income as its standard calculation, which they refer to as an "at risk of poverty rate."[24] Analysts comparing poverty across countries in the developed world have often specified a poverty threshold at half the median income, and of course other relative methods are also possible, such as 70 percent or 40 percent of median income.[25]

Relative measures have advantages and disadvantages. Proponents of the measure argue that the relative notion underlying these measures fits with both the historical record and changing views of poverty as described above. Furthermore, sometimes real needs do indeed rise in richer countries. For example, although a car may be a luxury in some countries, in a society in which most families own cars and where public transportation is scant, a car is often needed to find a job and commute to work. Furthermore, once someone owns a car, he or she is required to purchase car insurance. In her book *Nickel and Dimed: On (Not) Getting By in America,* Barbara Ehrenreich describes how the lack of affordable housing drives up housing prices for the poor. For example, she reports that a trailer park in Key West convenient to hotel jobs was charging $862 a month for a half-size trailer (in 2011 dollars), forcing lower-wage workers to search for housing further away in less fashionable areas. She argues, "Insofar as the poor have to work near the dwellings of the rich—as in the case of so many service and retail jobs—they are stuck with lengthy commutes or dauntingly expensive housing."[26]

It is no surprise, then, that relative measures tend to be popular in wealthy industrialized countries. The Organization for Economic Cooperation and Development (OECD) notes that, since very extreme hardship such as starvation is very uncommon in advanced industrialized societies, absolute subsistence poverty lines have little meaning.[27] Some researchers argue that poverty should be thought about in terms of exclusion from standards of living generally available to others in the same society. Social exclusion has therefore become a common theme in discussions about poverty in Europe. At a 2000 meeting of European Union countries, for example, the leaders declared, "The number of people living below the poverty line and in social exclusion in the Union is unacceptable."[28]

The notion that poverty has an important social component cannot be overstated, as it applies to poverty in the developing world as well. For example, in 2010 it was reported that India's mobile phone subscribers totaled around 564 million (or close to half of the country's population of 1.2 billion). At the same time, only 366 million people had access to proper sanitation.[29] However, just because an individual has a popular consumer good (a cell phone) that was not widely available, say, twenty years ago, does that mean he or she is not poor. Given both current standards of living and the social context, it can be argued that a cell phone, although usually not needed to avoid starvation, is a very useful social and economic tool. In many countries with lousy landline infrastructure, cell phones have become a substitute. In addition to meeting entertainment needs, they are often used in the developing world as a tool to find jobs, sell goods, transfer remittances, and conduct other kinds of monetary exchanges.[30] In short, a cell phone is now seen as a necessity by many people even in developing countries.

Detractors point out a few disadvantages of relative poverty measures. Some find these measures conceptually unappealing, believing that poverty should reflect a very low, subsistence level of well-being. That is, they believe that only people who are deeply deprived of very basic goods—like food and shelter—should be considered poor.[31] Value judgments about what are necessities (beyond the most basic of goods) should play no role in determining who is poor.[32] Second, relative measures can behave in deceptive ways over time, such as during periods of rapid economic growth and recession. In particular, relative thresholds often decline in bad times as median incomes fall. This could result in a decline in measured poverty rates, even though low-income people are faring worse.[33] Some empirical work in the United States, however, suggests that this is often not the case; relative poverty rates *do* tend to rise during recessions.[34]

Yet there are notable examples of relative poverty reacting counter to the business cycle. For example, in the late 1990s, when the Irish economy grew at an annual rate of 7 or 8 percent, unemployment fell, and wages rose, the relative poverty rate, as measured by the numbers living below 50 or 60 percent of average income, rose. This produced skepticism among politicians and the public about the meaningfulness of reported relative poverty rates there. Similarly, the Czech Republic, Hungary, and Poland all went through serious recessions in the 1990s, but relative child poverty rates, which used a poverty line based on a fixed percentage of average income, did not.[35] The UNICEF Innocenti Research Centre has noted that relative poverty is really about inequality, with a focus on the bottom end of the income distribution; its premise is that what constitutes an acceptable quality of life changes over time and that falling behind the average by more than a certain amount means effective exclusion from the normal life of society.[36]

Another set of arguments occasionally levied against relative poverty lines is that they are often too much of a moving target to be addressed by policy because they change over time or that relative poverty cannot be eliminated.[37] However, relative poverty, using the measures described above, can theoretically be eliminated if there is very little economic inequality. It is therefore more accurate to say that absolute and relative poverty measures provide different yardsticks for measuring the success of social programs. Absolute poverty tends to be more responsive to economic growth, which raises average living standards. Meanwhile, relative poverty is more responsive to income inequality, which reflects the distribution of resources in society. Which measure one deems of greater importance from a policy standpoint could influence one's choice.

An additional challenge, though not necessarily a drawback, of relative measures is that consideration has to be given to the reference group. That is, should relative poverty be measured in relation to the average standards of living for the country, subnational, or perhaps community level? Most relative measures use the nation as the reference point, but standards of living often vary across states, provinces, and communities in most nations.[38]

Other Poverty Measures

Researchers have devised numerous other measures, some of which are variations of either absolute or relative measures, depending on how they are implemented. The goal here is not to provide an exhaustive list but merely to mention that many other measures of poverty are possible and can be informative.

Consumption measures compare not a family's income but rather its consumption of goods to a poverty threshold. If the family spends little, this is an indication of actual material deprivation—of insufficient consumption of basic items such as food and shelter. Conceptually, this represents a powerful and appealing measure. Consumption measures can be either absolute or relative, depending on how the threshold is designed and implemented. That is, one can use an unchanging (absolute) threshold or one that changes with standards of living. Proponents of consumption measures argue that such measures are preferable to income poverty because people may be more likely to underreport their income than their consumption.[39] The main problem with consumption measures is that few large-scale surveys ask the relevant questions on family consumption patterns needed to construct a consumption poverty measure. In addition, it could be argued that some people consume little by choice. It is thus possible to classify relatively wealthy or high-income individuals as poor if they simply choose to spend little. Conversely, people sometimes meet their consumption needs by going into debt. It is not clear, for example, if someone who has lost their job and is temporarily making ends meet by borrowing money should be considered "poor" or not.

Hardship measures are based on respondents reporting a lack of food, heat, access to health care, or adequate housing, to name a few possible dimensions.[40] Hardship measures tend to be close to absolute measures in spirit, though they can also be defined in terms of hardships relative to a particular society's norms. One issue with hardship measures is that there is no consensus yet on what exactly they should measure. Some define them in terms of inadequate consumption of basic goods, while others define them in terms of poor physical living conditions. A wide variety of indicators are possible, including those relating to housing, nutrition, medical well-being, and neighborhood quality. Within all these categories there are several possible measures. To combine them into an index is challenging. Hardship measures may also reflect preferences and tastes (for example, some people do not mind not having basic consumer items) rather than involuntary deprivation.[41] Nevertheless, there is still growing interest in hardship measures because they are generally easy to understand and intuitively meaningful.

Social exclusion has traditionally referred to marginalization. Studies of exclusion typically consider the degree to which the economically deprived suffer from multiple forms of social deprivation, including, for example, consumption of goods, employment, political engagement, and social interaction.[42] The government of the United Kingdom has defined social exclusion as "a short-hand term for what can happen when people or areas suffer from a combination of linked problems such as unemployment, poor skills, low income, poor housing, high crime environment, bad health and family breakdown."[43] Such people are alienated from, and living on the fringes of, mainstream society. In the United States, the term *underclass* was once popularly used (and is still sometimes used) to describe a segment of the population, mainly African Americans in highly segregated inner cities, that suffered social exclusion.

A. B. Atkinson has identified three elements of social exclusion: 1) relativity—individuals are excluded from a particular reference community or society; 2) agency—people are excluded by an act of people or institutions, such as employers, schools, or government service agencies; and 3) dynamics—exclusion is a function not just of current circumstances but also of future prospects.[44] A challenge with measuring social exclusion is that there is as yet little widespread agreement on its precise conceptual definition and how best to operationalize it.

Some have advocated even broader measures of poverty, viewing it as a multidimensional experience. The United Nations, for example, uses a poverty measure defined as a "lack of income and productive resources to ensure sustainable livelihoods; hunger and malnutrition; ill health; limited or lack of access to education and other basic services; increased morbidity and mortality from illness; homelessness and inadequate housing; unsafe environments and social discrimination and exclusion."[45]

These views of poverty have been influenced by the work of Amartya Sen (a Nobel Prize winner in Economics), who has argued that conventional income poverty measures overlook the core problem associated with poverty—that of *capability deprivation*.[46] Capabilities are what allow people to obtain what is intrinsically important to them, such as good health, adequate food and shelter, education, and so on. Sen sees low income as one of the major causes of poverty, since it can be a principal reason for a person's capability deprivation. But there are other factors that can affect people's capabilities, such as age, gender, and race in societies that offer unequal opportunities to people based on these kinds of characteristics. To support the use of these measures, the United Nations publishes a large number of social indicators for countries where such data are available.[47]

These indicators provide very valuable tools for understanding patterns and trends in well-being in both developed and developing countries. Nevertheless, this book tends to focus on income poverty rather than on the other, often harder to define and operationalize, measures described above. Income poverty measures offer a straightforward, easy-to-understand approach to gauging the extent to which people may lack the income to meet basic needs.

A Quasi-Relative Poverty Measure

In response to the increasingly apparent weaknesses of the official poverty measure described earlier, the U.S. Congress appropriated funds for an independent scientific study of poverty measures in the early 1990s. The job fell to the National Research Council of the National Academy of Sciences (NAS) (now called the National Academies), which established the Panel on Poverty and Family Assistance. This panel reviewed several alternative approaches to measuring poverty, noting that the decision to accept or reject any particular one must involve subjective judgment as well as scientific evidence. It did, however, recommend specific changes, some within a range, to the official poverty measure in its 1995 report, *Measuring Poverty: A New Approach*. In subsequent research undertaken by the Census Bureau, a few experimental poverty measures based on variations of the panel's recommendations were implemented and published.[48]

Specifically, the NAS-inspired measure, now called the Supplementary Poverty Measure (SPM) by the U.S. Census Bureau, is devised in the following way. First, the SPM poverty thresholds are calculated based on how much people report spending on food, clothing, shelter, and utilities, plus a small additional amount to allow for other needs (such as household supplies, personal care, and non-work-related transportation). Unlike the official U.S. poverty measure, these thresholds are further adjusted for variations in housing costs by state and metropolitan area. Thresholds are updated annually to reflect real growth expenditures on this basic bundle of goods.[49]

The SPM measure is essentially relative in nature because the thresholds are updated based on changes in real expenditures, which typically rise as the general standard of living rises. The recommended measure is quasi-relative rather than wholly relative because the proposed update would be based on consumption expenditures for only basic categories of goods—food, clothing, housing, utilities—which would be expected to rise less rapidly than total consumption expenditures or median income.

In the SPM measure family resources are defined as the value of cash income from all sources, plus the value of near-money benefits that are available to buy goods covered by the new thresholds, minus "nondiscretionary" expenses. Cash income sources include wages and salaries, interest income, and cash welfare assistance. This element of the SPM resource definition is the same as the current official Census Bureau definition of income. However, the SPM resource definition then also includes near-money benefits such as food assistance cards, housing subsidies, school breakfast and lunch subsidies, and the Earned Income Tax Credit. Nondiscretionary expenses subtracted include taxes, child care and other work-related expenses, out-of-pocket medical costs, and child support payments to another household. Taxes represent a nondiscretionary expense. Child care and other work-related expenses (such as commuting expenses) are also subtracted because, the NAS panel argued, these costs are often incurred if parents are to work and earn labor market income to meet their basic needs.[50]

The SPM measure addresses some of the weaknesses of both purely absolute and purely relative measures, though certainly not all of them. One remaining weakness is that it is computationally more complex than the current official measure. Some people will also object to its incorporation of a relative element if they simply dislike relative approaches to measuring poverty.[51] Nevertheless, the SPM measure is clearly a more refined measure than the current official poverty measure in both the construction of the thresholds and the definition of income used. It also has the advantage of increasing, in real terms, as spending on basic items increase, so that it reflects changes in real standards of living. Yet it is not responsive to changes in consumption patterns of other, more discretionary items—such as luxury goods—that may occur. It is also designed to gauge the impact of government programs on poverty, as both cash and noncash government benefits are taken into account in the measure of family income.

COMPARISONS OF THRESHOLDS AND MEASURES

Figure 1 compares four-person (two adults, two children) poverty thresholds of four common measures for the years 1947–2011: the threshold of the official U.S. poverty measure, the threshold used in the SPM,[52] a relative threshold based on half the median after-tax family income, and a threshold based on popular opinion of what poverty means (termed here a "subjective" threshold). Specifically, the subjective threshold was calculated by using answers from the question, "People who have income below a certain level can be considered poor. That level is called the 'poverty line.' What amount of weekly income would you use as a poverty line for a family of four (husband, wife, and two children) in this community?"[53] This question was last asked in the General Social Survey in the 1993, so there is no more recent information on it in the figure.

Since the official threshold is updated solely on the basis of inflation, the threshold dollar amount has remained unchanged (all amounts are given in 2011 dollars). In contrast, subjective and relative thresholds

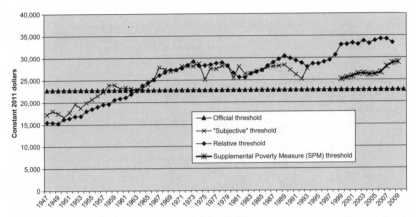

FIGURE 1. Poverty Thresholds for Four-Person Families, 1947–2011. SOURCES: Official and SPM thresholds are from U.S. Census Bureau 2010c. Relative thresholds 1947–92 are from National Research Council 1995, 132–33. Relative thresholds 1993–2010 are from author's tabulations of 1994–2011 Current Population Survey data. Subjective thresholds are from National Research Council 1995, 138–39. Many of the National Research Council 1995 thresholds are from Vaughan 1993. NOTES: The thresholds are for two-adult, two-children families. Relative thresholds represent one-half the median after-tax income of this type of family. The "subjective" poverty thresholds for 1947–89 are from Vaughan 1993, table 1, derived by assuming a constant relationship of the poverty amount to an amount to the response to the "get-along" question. See Vaughan 1993 and National Research Council 1995 for more details. The SPM thresholds are based on expenditures on food, clothing, shelter, and medical expenses (termed "FCSUM-CE").

track each other fairly closely over the period. They are below the official threshold until the late 1950s and early 1960s, after which they surpass the official threshold. By 1993, with the official threshold at $22,811, the subjective threshold was $27,621, and the relative threshold was $27,973. The relative poverty threshold rose rapidly in the strong economy of the late 1990s, reaching $33,026 in 2000. Since then it has hovered at about that amount (in 2008, for example, the relative threshold was $33,418), as family incomes remained stagnant over the 2000s and then declined after the beginning of the Great Recession in late 2007.

Note that the subjective and relative thresholds cross the official threshold in the period just before the official threshold was originally devised. At that time, then, there would have been little difference between poverty rates estimated using any of these three methods. However, since that time there has been an increasing disjuncture between these poverty rates. The Census Bureau's SPM measure begins

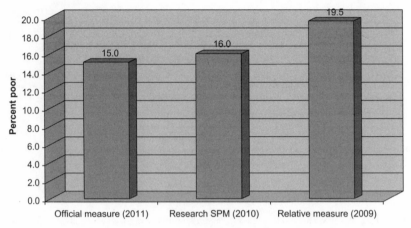

FIGURE 2. Poverty Rates, by Measure. SOURCES: The official poverty rate is from ·
DeNavas-Walt, Proctor, and Smith 2012. The SPM measure is from Short 2011a. The
relative poverty measure is from Short 2011b.

only in 1999. According to the figure, SPM thresholds are higher than
the official one (for example, the SPM threshold was $29,052 in 2009,
compared to the official threshold of $22,811 in 2011 dollars).

Figure 2 depicts poverty rates estimated using the official measure,
the SPM measure, and a typical relative measure in 2009–11. Note that
there are actually many ways a relative poverty measure can be constructed, even after deciding on the particular threshold. The relative
measure used here employs a threshold equal to one-half the after-tax
family-sized adjusted median family income. The income definition
used in this relative measure refers to total disposable household
income.[54] Unsurprisingly, results show that poverty rates are lowest
when using the official poverty measure (15.0 percent) and highest
when using the relative measure (19.5 percent). The SPM measure (16.0
percent) falls between them, though it is considerably closer to the official measure.

THEORETICAL ISSUES REVISITED

Poverty measurement research efforts in the United States are in flux.
There is some movement away from absolute methods of measuring
poverty toward more relative measures, though there are a few staunch
defenders of the former. In the end, the method adopted will likely
depend in part on theoretical considerations. Does *poverty* refer to a

subsistence standard (that is, the amount of money required to survive) or to *economic marginalization* (deprivation relative to social norms and standards)? Can there be such a thing as a legitimate absolute poverty measure that remains constant over time? As I indicated above, many commentators would contend that defining an absolute standard has serious drawbacks, for the meaning of poverty is grounded in time and place.

The quasi-relative measure provides a compromise between the extreme absolute and relative ways of measuring poverty. Most of all, it addresses the unrealistic assumption behind purely absolute measures—that there can be a single, unchanging absolute standard. Even the current official measure, although nominally absolute, is still partially relative in that it reflects the standards of the time it was constructed. The quasi-relative measure also addresses the conceptually unappealing nature of purely relative measures—the implicit denial that there is such a thing as purely basic needs. For example, if most people in a society have two luxury cars, should we really consider someone with only one to be poor? The quasi-relative measure explicitly accepts the fact that some relativity is inherent in measuring poverty, but it strives to measure deprivation in relation to the acquisition of an absolutely basic set of goods and not luxury goods.

SUMMARY

Poverty refers to economic deprivation, but views about what, precisely, constitutes poverty and who the poor are still vary across both time and place. Poverty measurement efforts over the years have shown that as overall standards of living rise, so do the thresholds deemed necessary to sustain a minimum level of living.

The two basic types of poverty measures are *absolute* measures and *relative* measures. Absolute measures, such as the current U.S. official measure, typically attempt to define a truly basic needs standard, and they therefore remain constant over time. Relative measures, on the other hand, define poverty in terms of comparative disadvantage, which is assessed against changing standards of living. Each of these measures has different strengths and weaknesses. Yet, if used appropriately, they can also complement each other, as there are a variety of legitimate ways to think about economic deprivation.

In my view, the best general measure of poverty has both absolute and relative components. If people cannot meet basic needs, they are poor, regardless of overall standards of living. However, poverty is relative in that people's beliefs about the money needed to get along rises as overall standards of living rise. One way to keep an absolute poverty measure meaningful is simply to revise it by adjusting poverty thresholds every generation or so, or as needed. An alternative is the quasi-relative measure recommended by the National Academy of Sciences Panel on Poverty and Family Assistance, currently termed the Supplemental Poverty Measure by the U.S. Census Bureau. Because of its strengths, this measure is a viable candidate to supplant the current official U.S. poverty measure.

CHAPTER 3

Characteristics of the Poverty Population

During a time of persisting unemployment and high poverty after the Great Recession, it was not difficult to find stories about people struggling to get by.

At a food pantry in a Chicago suburb, a 38-year-old mother of two breaks into tears. She and her husband have been out of work for nearly two years. Their house and car are gone. So is their foothold in the middle class and, at times, their self-esteem. "It's like there is no way out," says Kris Fallon. She is trapped like so many others, destitute in the midst of America's abundance.

There's Bill Ricker, a 74-year-old former repairman and pastor whose home is a dilapidated trailer in rural Maine. He scrapes by with a monthly $1,003 Social Security check. His ex-wife also is hard up; he lets her live in the other end of his trailer.

There's Brandi Wells, a single mom in West Virginia, struggling to find a job and care for her 10-month-old son. "I didn't realize that it could go so bad so fast," she says.

Ken Bargy, 58, had to stop working five years ago because of his health and is now on disability. His wife drives a school bus in a neighboring town. He sends his children, 15 and 10, to school 20 miles away. In the back of the trailer, he offers shelter to his elderly mother, who is bedridden and dying of cancer. The $18,000 the family pieces together from disability payments and paychecks must go to many things: food, lights, water, medical bills. There are choices to make. "With the cost of everything going up, I have to skip a light bill to get food or skip a phone bill to get food," he says. "My checking account is about 20 bucks in the hole."[1]

In this chapter I take a closer look at exactly *who* the poor are, focusing on information collected from social and economic surveys. My goal is to provide an accurate portrait of the poor, describing their demographic profile, what kinds of hardships they experience, how long they tend to remain poor, and where in the United States they are concentrated. This baseline information is essential to both understanding the causes of poverty (the focus of chapter 5) and formulating policy responses that make sense (chapter 7). However, because a wholly statistical portrait of poverty is necessarily incomplete, it is important to remember that behind all of these numbers are names and faces, people whose stories are as varied as their number.

POVERTY IN THE UNITED STATES OVER TIME
AND ACROSS GROUPS

Figure 3 shows poverty rates over time and for different age groups. After a steady decline in the American poverty rate between 1959 (the first year for which government statistics on poverty are available) and 1973, progress stalled, then poverty noticeably worsened in the wake of the severe economic recession of 2007–9 (discussed in detail in chapter 6). Whereas 22.4 percent of Americans were poor in 1959 and only 11.1 percent were in 1973, by 2011 the official poverty rate was 15.0 percent, indicating that 46.2 million Americans lived in poverty.[2]

The elderly experienced the most notable improvements in poverty over the period 1959 to 2011. The poverty rate among the elderly was 35.2 percent in 1959, considerably higher than the poverty rates for both children (27.3 percent) and those 18 to 64 (17.0 percent). But by the late 1990s, the elderly poverty rate was equal to that of adults 18 to 64, whose poverty rates remained stagnant after 1973, and by 2011, the elderly poverty rate, at 8.7 percent, was considerably lower than the poverty rate of adults 18 to 64 (13.7 percent). A great deal of the reduction in the elderly poverty rate is due to the impact of Social Security and other such programs. Meanwhile, child poverty rates declined from 1959 to 1973, only to rise thereafter. In 2011, 21.9 percent of children were poor—far higher than the poverty rate of others. Clearly, the social safety net does a better job of helping the elderly than children in the United States, reflecting the political muscle of older Americans today.[3]

Poverty rates vary by the measures used. Table 1 shows poverty rates across different demographic groups using the current official measure

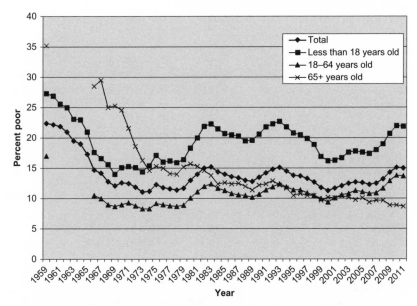

FIGURE 3. Official Poverty Rates by Age, 1959 to 2011. SOURCES: DeNavas-Walt, Proctor, and Smith 2012, table B2.

of poverty, a relative poverty measure, and the Supplemental Poverty Measure (SPM). As described in chapter 2, the current official poverty measure is an absolute one, where the thresholds are meant to represent a truly basic needs standard and remain constant over time. The relative measure has thresholds that change over time as standards of living change; the reasoning behind this measure is that individuals whose resources are significantly below the resources of others, even if they are physically able to survive, are marginalized from mainstream society. The relative threshold used here is equal to one-half the median household income in the United States adjusted for household size.

The SPM measure is a quasi-relative poverty measure combining absolute and relative elements. It is relative because the thresholds are updated based on changes in real expenditures for certain consumption categories but is less than fully relative because only basic categories of goods and services—food, clothing, housing, and utilities—are considered. The amount spent on these items tends to rise less rapidly than median family income. The SPM measure also aims to correct some of the technical deficiencies of the official measure. In particular, it aims to more accurately measure a family's disposable (net) income by including

TABLE 1 POVERTY RATES FOR INDIVIDUALS BY DEMOGRAPHIC CHARACTERISTICS

	Official Poverty Measure (2011)	Research SPM (2010)	Relative Poverty Measure[a] (2009)
All persons	15.0	16.0	19.5
Age			
Under 18	21.9	18.2	25.9
18–64 years	13.7	15.2	16.9
65 years and older	8.7	15.9	19.6
Race/ethnicity			
White	12.8	14.3	–
White, non-Hispanic	9.8	11.1	13.2
Black	27.6	25.4	34.1
Asian	12.3	16.7	–
Native American	29.5	–	–
Hispanic (any race)	25.3	28.2	33.2
Family type			
In married couple family	7.4	9.9	11.9
In female householder family	34.2	29.0	39.0
In male householder family	16.5	22.7	22.6
Homeownership			
Owner	8.0	9.7	11.3
Renter	30.5	29.4	37.4
Education (of those age 25+)			
Less than high school	25.4	–	–
High school	14.9	–	–
Some college	11.1	–	–
College graduate +	5.1	–	–
Citizenship status			
Native born	14.4	14.7	18.4
Foreign born	19.0	25.5	26.9
Naturalized citizen	12.5	16.8	17.8
Not a citizen	24.3	32.4	33.7

[a] The relative threshold equals half the median family income adjusted for family size in 2009. See text for details.

SOURCES: The SPM measure is from Short 2011a. The relative poverty measure is from Short 2011b. Most of the official measure poverty rates, with the exception of those described below, are from DeNavas-Walt, Proctor, and Smith 2012. The Native American poverty rate is available only using the official measure in U.S. Census Bureau 2012i. Poverty rates by educational attainment are from U.S. Census Bureau 2012m. Poverty rates by family type are available are from U.S. Census Bureau 2012l.

noncash benefits, such as food stamps, and by subtracting nondiscretionary expenses, such as work-related expenses and out-of-pocket medical costs. Under this measure, thresholds also vary across geographic areas with different costs of living.

While 15.0 percent of the population was poor according to the official measure, poverty rates are higher when using either the SPM (16.0 percent) or relative measure (19.5 percent). The official poverty rate among whites was relatively low, at 12.8 percent. Among minority groups, poverty rates ranged from just 12.3 percent among Asians to 29.5 percent among Native Americans. More than one-fourth of both African Americans and Hispanics were poor as well. Education is highly correlated with poverty. Although 25.4 percent of people with less than a high school degree were poor, only 5.1 percent of college graduates were poor in 2011. People living in married-couple families were considerably less likely to be poor (7.4 percent, according to the official measure) than those in male householder (16.5 percent) or female householder (34.2 percent) families. Citizenship status also matters; native-born people and naturalized citizens have relatively low poverty rates, while noncitizens have a considerably higher one.

SPM poverty rates were higher than official ones, with the exception of poverty rates among children, African Americans, and renters. SPM poverty rates tend to be higher because of their reliance on higher poverty thresholds (see chapter 2). The SPM's inclusion of noncash benefits (such as food assistance) intended to improve the economic situation of the poor affects some of the patterns observed in table 1. They serve, for example, to lower the poverty rates among children more than among adults.[4]

Relative poverty rates are higher than both the official and SPM poverty rates, mainly because their poverty thresholds are also higher, though the patterns across groups tend to be similar, with a few exceptions. For example, while adults sixty-five and over have lower poverty rates than those eighteen to sixty-four when using the official poverty measure, the elderly have higher poverty rates than other adults when using the relative measure, mainly because many of the elderly have modest fixed incomes above the official poverty line but below the relative one.

THE DEPTH OF POVERTY AND MATERIAL HARDSHIP

The official poverty measure discussed above tells us something about the extent, or breadth, of poverty across demographic groups and over time, but only at specific threshold cutoffs. Figure 4 therefore shows

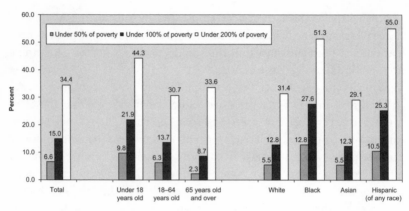

FIGURE 4. Ratio of Family Income to the Poverty Threshold, 2011. SOURCE: U.S. Census Bureau 2012k.

levels of "extreme" poverty (the proportion of people with family incomes less than half the official poverty threshold) and near poverty (the proportion with family incomes less than 200 percent of the poverty threshold). (The official poverty threshold was $22,811 for a four-person family in 2011.) While the overall official poverty rate was 15.0 percent in 2011, a smaller proportion of people—6.6 percent— were in extreme poverty, while about a third of all people were near poor and poor. As might be expected, rates of extreme poverty are higher among children and African Americans and lower among whites, Asians, and the elderly.[5]

Table 2 shows reports of selected measures of four types of hardship: food security, health care, housing and neighborhood conditions, and meeting basic needs. About 14.5 percent of the population reported some level of food insecurity in 2010. Food insecurity is defined as a household having difficulty at some time during the year providing enough food for all their members due to a lack of resources. A smaller percentage (5.4 percent) reported very low food security, defined as insufficient food intake of some household members due to a lack of resources.[6] With regard to health care, 15.7 percent of the population lacked health insurance, though a smaller proportion—6.8 percent— reported not seeing a doctor when it was necessary. Between 5 and 10 percent of households reported a problem with a leaking roof, pests such as mice or cockroaches, or a lot of trash or litter on their streets.

About 6.1 percent of households missed a rent or mortgage payment due to insufficient funds, nearly 1 in 10 missed a utility bill for

TABLE 2 PERCENTAGE OF PEOPLE REPORTING VARIOUS HARDSHIPS

	Percent
Food security[a] (2010)	
Food insecurity	14.5
Very low food security	5.4
Health care	
Did not have health insurance (2011)	15.7
Did not see a doctor when needed to (2005)	6.8
Housing and neighborhood conditions (2005)	
Leaking roof	4.9
Problem with pests in house	9.8
Trash or litter on streets	7.3
Meeting basic needs	
Unpaid rent or mortgage (2005)	6.1
Unpaid utility (2005)	9.8
Telephone disconnected (2005)	4.2
Reported not meeting essential expenses at one point during year (2005)	14.4
Children in families affected by a foreclosure (2007–9, annual average)	4.3
People using an emergency shelter during the year (2009)	0.5

[a] Food insecure households had difficulty at some time during the year providing enough food for all their members due to a lack of resources. Very low food secure households are those where the food intake of some household members was reduced and normal eating patterns were disrupted due to limited resources.

SOURCES: Food security figures are from Coleman-Jensen et al. 2011. The proportion of people without health insurance is from DeNavas-Walt, Proctor, and Smith 2012. All 2005 figures are from U.S. Census Bureau 2009. Estimates of people using an emergency shelter are from U.S. Department of Housing and Urban Development 2010. Foreclosure data are from Annie E. Casey Foundation 2011.

the same reason, and 14.4 percent reported more generally that they were not able to meet an essential expense at one point during the year. In 2007–9, during the period when the housing bubble burst, over 4 percent of children per year lived in families affected by a foreclosure. The actual incidence of homelessness is considerably lower. In 2009, an estimated 0.5 percent of the population used an emergency shelter at some point during the year—though this still translates into 1.56 million people. On a single night in 2009, there were an estimated 643,067 sheltered and unsheltered homeless people nationwide.[7]

A significant number of poor American households own common consumer items, though there was variation across items considered. Figure 5 indicates that in 2009, 41 percent of poor households owned their own home, as compared to 68 percent of all households, and

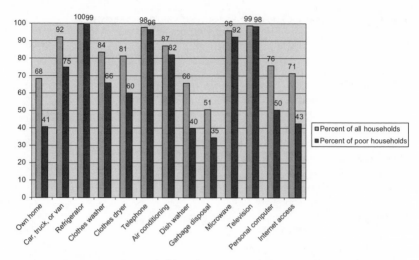

FIGURE 5. Percentage of Households with Various Consumer Goods, 2009. SOURCES: Most items are from U.S. Census Bureau 2011a. Data on possession of microwaves, televisions, personal computers, and Internet access come from U.S. Energy Information Administration 2009.

about three-quarters of poor households owned a car, truck, or van, compared to 92 percent of all households.[8] Most people (poor and non-poor alike) owned refrigerators, telephones, microwaves, and televisions. However, about half of the poor lacked a personal computer, and more than half did not have Internet access at home. The fact that many poor households owned a number of the consumer goods listed suggests that poverty in the United States differs in nature from poverty in many developing countries (see chapter 4). In the United States a wide variety of consumer items are also available at a range of prices and quality levels. It is relatively easy, for example, to find a secondhand television for a few dollars in most places around the country at discount retailers, not to mention on Craigslist or eBay. Even used cars, although not within the reach of everyone, are not prohibitively expensive for a majority of people.

However, in the United States people who do not have access to a car may have trouble holding a job, given the decentralized character of many American cities and the inadequacy of many local public transportation systems. The poor also often pay more for goods and services than the nonpoor, as supermarkets offering low prices are less often located in poor urban neighborhoods or rural places than in affluent ones.[9] It could also be argued that American families that do not own some basic consumer goods may both feel marginal and be treated as such; they may lack sufficient income to, as Peter Townsend put it, "play the roles, participate in the relationships, and follow the customary behavior" of their society.[10]

One study examined how many Americans lived below a truly subsistence poverty line used to measure absolute poverty in developing countries—less than $2 a day. It found that in 2011, 1.5 million families (less than 2 percent of all U.S. families) met this definition over the course of at least a month, but that this number had nearly doubled from 1996. When families' receipt of food assistance is included in the measure of family resources, the number of extremely poor families was substantially smaller (795,000), indicative of the importance of this benefit.[11] For these very poor families, life is desperate:

> Magdalyn March, 30, of Birmingham, Ala., can relate to those living in extreme poverty. In 2006, she lost a seasonal job at a packing warehouse, split with an abusive boyfriend and was caring for her two children. She received about $200 a month in government cash assistance and $282 in food stamps [well above the $2 a day threshold].
>
> March and her children lived in a motel when she was with her boyfriend. When he left, she couldn't afford the room, and she and her children were kicked out. March stayed with friends and relatives for a few nights at a time but ended up in a homeless shelter.
>
> She credits the shelter, First Light, with helping her find a job as a waitress at a chain restaurant and affordable day care. She says she still struggles. She needs glasses and has to go to the dentist but can't afford it. March and her children are living with her mother now.[12]

THE DYNAMICS AND INTERGENERATIONAL TRANSFER OF POVERTY

Most poverty data come from studies conducted at one point in time or from annual studies conducted on a different set of people every year. It has only been in the last forty years or so, when researchers began analyzing new information from longitudinal studies (which follow the same set of people for several years) that a dynamic view of poverty emerged. The findings from these longitudinal studies surprised many people and changed the conventional wisdom about how individuals and their families experience poverty over time.

Previously, many believed that there was a permanently dependent "underclass," mired in poverty year after year and utterly dependent upon the government or others.[13] And, while surveys indicate that poverty is a fairly constant feature of society—the poverty rate, for example, has fluctuated little, from about 11 to 15 percent, since the mid-1960s—the longitudinal data show that a majority of poor individuals remain poor for only short periods of time. Furthermore, a relatively high proportion of people experience poverty at one point during their lifetime.[14] One study estimates that about half of Americans will experience at least one year below the poverty line between the ages of twenty-five and seventy-five. The likelihood of experiencing poverty varies considerably by race and education, with a majority of blacks, and nearly all blacks without a high school degree, experiencing poverty at some point, compared with well under a third of white high school graduates.[15]

Spells of poverty, however, tend to be short. Different studies have estimated that anywhere between 45 and 59 percent of individuals who enter poverty have a spell length of only one year, and 70 to 84 percent have a spell length of less than four years.[16] Only 12 percent of poverty spells last ten years or more.[17] Likewise, spells of serious food insecurity also tend to be short. Nearly four in five of people living in households with food problems in a given year no longer reported such food problems two years later.[18] If we calculate poverty using a monthly rather than an annual time frame, we see even more turnover in the poverty population. For example, while 29 percent of all people were poor for at least two consecutive months from 2004 through 2006, only 3 percent of people were poor for every month during the same period of time.[19] Of course, many of those who are poor for just a few months are people have higher annual incomes but work seasonally.

Despite the brief duration of many poverty spells, it is quite common for people who leave poverty to fall back into it some time later. In fact, when measuring poverty on an annual basis (the most common way), about half of those who end poverty spells return to poverty within five years. Accounting for multiple spells shows that approximately 50 percent of blacks and 30 percent of whites who fall into poverty in a given year will be poor in five or more of the next ten years.[20] This suggests that although the proportion of people who are chronically poor is low, there is a larger proportion of people who are economically insecure and at high risk of poverty.

A number of factors affect the length of time people are poor. As might be expected, people are less likely to escape poverty in recession years than in other years.[21] In addition, the longer one is in poverty, the less likely it is that one will escape it. One's work skills may erode, or the growing gap in a resume may make someone less attractive to employers over time.[22] Families headed by white men tend to leave poverty more quickly than those headed by others, such as black women.[23] About 62 percent of whites who experience poverty are poor for less than four years, while only 39 percent of blacks who experience poverty are poor for less than four years.[24] The time in poverty for Hispanics falls in between.[25]

A related issue is the extent to which poverty is passed from one generation to the next. According to conventional wisdom, the debilitating effects of poverty are passed on from generation to generation. The belief that people were trapped in long-term poverty was one of the motivations for President Johnson's War on Poverty.[26] If poverty is indeed routinely "transmitted" across generations and unequally distributed across demographic groups, U.S. norms of fairness and meritocracy can justifiably be called into question.

Research has shown that there is close to a 50 percent correlation between fathers' and sons' income, indicating that one's family background is quite important.[27] On the one hand, the good news is that the current generation of adults is generally better off than their parents, as median incomes in the United States have grown over time. For example, a 2007 study indicated that the median family income for adults who are in their thirties and forties was 29 percent higher than their parents at the same age ($71,900 versus $55,600, adjusted for inflation). Two out of three Americans have higher incomes than their parents.

On the other hand, because a child's economic position relative to others in society is so heavily influenced by that of his or her parents, 42 percent of children born to parents in the bottom fifth of the income distribution remained at the bottom, while 39 percent born to parents at the top fifth remained at the top. Only 6 percent of children born to parents at the bottom made it to the top of the income distribution.[28] As is discussed in more detail in chapter 4, this kind of relative economic mobility is, contrary to conventional wisdom, actually lower in the United States than in most of Europe.[29]

Researchers argue about the factors that explain the significant correlation of income across generations. Three common theories focus on 1) family and environmental stresses, 2) resources and investments, and 3) cultural perspectives.[30] According to the family and environmental stress perspective, poor families experience high levels of stress in their everyday environments, and this may hinder children's development. The stress may be the result of difficulty encountered in paying bills and meeting other basic needs or from a general vulnerability to adverse events. This psychological distress in turn affects marital and parenting relationships, with the result that parents may become more punitive and inconsistent and less nurturing and stimulating. This hampers children's socio-emotional, physical, cognitive, and academic development, which in turn increases their likelihood of becoming poor as adults. For example, because of family stress poor children may be more likely to act out in school, receive poor grades, and ultimately drop out of school.

According to the resource and investment perspective, children's development is affected by a combination of their "endowments" and parental investments. Endowments include both their genetic abilities and the values and preferences that their parents impart to them. These values may include an emphasis on doing well in school. Also important are the time and money that parents invest in children, such as by reading to them at night, purchasing books to further their education, paying for quality day care when they are young, or buying a house in a safe neighborhood with good schools. These investments help children learn, maintain good health, obtain a good education, and avoid poverty as adults.

According to cultural perspectives, poor people who are marginalized and have no opportunity for upward mobility respond by adapting their behavior and values. The resulting culture of poverty is characterized by "little impulse control and an inability to delay gratification, as well as feelings of helplessness and inferiority."[31] This culture manifests itself in sexual promiscuity, drug use, a high incidence of single-parent households, and crime in poor communities. A common criticism of cultural perspectives is that often they do not differentiate the behavior of individuals from their values. Many of the poor actually share middle-class values, but they do not see how acting upon these values might eventually lead to success, leading them to behave in ways that are often self-defeating. For example, while many poor young women want to get married and see the benefits of marriage in an abstract sense, they may have children out of wedlock because not many people around them are getting married and there seem to be few "marriageable" men with stable employment with whom to form a lasting family (see chapter 5 for an expanded discussion of the possible role of culture in causing increases in nonmarital childbearing).[32]

Thus, the research suggests that the first two perspectives—those that focus on family and environmental stress and on resources and investments—best explain the intergenerational transmission of poverty. However, it should be said that there is still uncertainty about the contribution of each perspective, as it is often difficult to untangle the complicated connections between them.

THE GEOGRAPHY OF POVERTY

One's community is not only the site of many social interactions, but it can also greatly affect one's educational and economic opportunities. The economic, social, cultural, and political features of places vary tremendously across the United States. Many cities in the Northeast and Midwest, for example, had economies based on manufacturing for many years. Deindustrialization in the post–World War II era had a profound effect on people living in these cities. Many who had worked in manufacturing plants lost their jobs as plants closed and moved their operations to the South or outside the country. These people were forced to find other types of employment, and some became poor.

This type of local change helps produce considerable differences in the extent of poverty across states, regions, and metropolitan areas. Concentrated poverty—which refers to the high incidence of poverty in specific neighborhoods or groups of neighborhoods—also varies within specific metropolitan areas. These geographic dimensions of poverty are discussed below.

Poverty by Region, State, and Metropolitan Status

Poverty rates in the fifty states and the District of Columbia ranged from 8.8 percent in New Hampshire to 22.6 percent in Mississippi in 2011 (see table 3). Reflecting the national increase in poverty between 1999 and 2011, only one state (Wyoming) and the District of Columbia experienced declines in poverty over the period. The states experiencing the largest increases in poverty included Michigan (7.0 percentage points), Indiana (6.5 percentage points), and Georgia (6.1 percentage points), which experienced steep declines in manufacturing (including the auto industry) and/or construction over the period, especially during the severe recession in the last years of the decade.

Although poverty rates vary considerably by state, differences across broader regions are rather modest. In 2011 the poverty rate was a little lower in the Northeast (13.1 percent) and Midwest (14.0) than the South (16.0) and West (15.8). Historically, poverty rates have been lower in the Northeast and Midwest than in other parts of the country, and especially in the South. In 1969, for example, the poverty rate in the

TABLE 3   POVERTY RATES BY REGION, METROPOLITAN STATUS, AND STATE,
1999 AND 2011

	1999	2011	2011–1999 Change
U.S. total	13.1	15.0	1.9
Region			
Northeast	11.4	13.1	1.7
Midwest	10.2	14.0	3.8
South	13.9	16.0	2.1
West	13.0	15.8	2.8
Metropolitan area status			
Metropolitan areas	11.8	14.6	2.8
Central city	17.6	20.0	2.4
Suburbs	8.4	11.3	2.9
Nonmetropolitan areas	14.6	17.0	2.4
State			
Alabama	16.1	19.0	2.9
Alaska	9.4	10.5	1.1
Arizona	13.9	19.0	5.1
Arkansas	15.8	19.5	3.7
California	14.2	16.6	2.4
Colorado	9.3	13.5	4.2
Connecticut	7.9	10.9	3.0
Delaware	9.2	11.9	2.7
District of Columbia	20.2	18.7	−1.5
Florida	12.5	17.0	4.5
Georgia	13.0	19.1	6.1
Hawaii	10.7	12.0	1.3
Idaho	11.8	16.5	4.7
Illinois	10.7	15.0	4.3
Indiana	9.5	16.0	6.5
Iowa	9.1	12.8	3.7
Kansas	9.9	13.8	3.9
Kentucky	15.8	19.1	3.3
Louisiana	19.6	20.4	0.8
Maine	10.9	14.1	3.2
Maryland	8.5	10.1	1.6
Massachusetts	9.3	11.6	2.3
Michigan	10.5	17.5	7.0
Minnesota	7.9	11.9	4.0
Mississippi	19.9	22.6	2.7
Missouri	11.7	15.8	4.1
Montana	14.6	14.8	0.2
Nebraska	9.7	13.1	3.4
Nevada	10.5	15.9	5.4
New Hampshire	6.5	8.8	2.3
New Jersey	8.5	10.4	1.9

New Mexico	18.4	21.5	3.1
New York	14.6	16.0	1.4
North Carolina	12.3	17.9	5.6
North Dakota	11.9	12.2	0.3
Ohio	10.6	16.4	5.8
Oklahoma	14.7	17.2	2.5
Oregon	11.6	17.5	5.9
Pennsylvania	11.0	13.8	2.8
Rhode Island	11.9	14.7	2.8
South Carolina	14.1	18.9	4.8
South Dakota	13.2	13.9	0.7
Tennessee	13.5	18.3	4.8
Texas	15.4	18.5	3.1
Utah	9.4	13.5	4.1
Vermont	9.4	11.5	2.1
Virginia	9.6	11.5	1.9
Washington	10.6	13.9	3.3
West Virginia	17.9	18.6	0.7
Wisconsin	8.7	13.1	4.4
Wyoming	11.4	11.3	-0.1

SOURCES: 2011 U.S., region, and metropolitan area status figures are from DeNavas-Walt, Proctor, and Smith 2012. Figures for 1999 are from U.S. Census Bureau 2000. The 2011 state figures are from U.S. Census Bureau 2012g.

South, at 17.9 percent, was about double that in the Northeast (8.6 percent), and it was also much higher than poverty rates in the Midwest (9.6 percent) and West (10.4 percent).[33] However, the slow decline of manufacturing, which was once concentrated in the Northeast and Midwest, has taken its toll, helping to narrow these historical differentials over time. As shown in table 3, metropolitan areas have lower poverty rates than nonmetropolitan areas. Within metropolitan areas, central cities continued to have considerably higher poverty rates than suburbs, though here there was a small narrowing of the gap over the decade.

Some researchers have noted that there are some persistently poor and economically depressed rural areas, such as in the Mississippi Delta, Appalachia, the lower Rio Grande Valley, and the Great Plains.[34] Between 1980 and 2009, 706 U.S. counties experienced persistently high child poverty; 81 percent of these were nonmetropolitan counties.[35] These are areas where educational levels have traditionally been low and job opportunities scarce. Rural workers also tend to earn lower wages than urban workers.[36] Poor rural areas are often characterized by spatial isolation, inadequate physical infrastructure, such as under-funded public transportation and schools, and limited social support services.[37] While the poor in Appalachia are predominantly white, the poor in other rural pockets tend to be minorities, such as African Americans in the South, Mexican-origin inhabitants in the South and West, and Native Americans on reservations. Researchers Daniel Lichter and Martha Crowley have noted, "Many Americans assume that disadvantaged minorities are concentrated exclusively in urban ghettos, but some of the most impoverished American minorities live in isolated, economically depressed rural areas."[38]

Concentrated Urban Poverty

What is so important about concentrated poverty? It is significant because many problems, such as crime, welfare dependency, drug use, out-of-wedlock births, and unfavorable health and educational outcomes, are most prevalent in high-poverty areas. Poor people living in these neighborhoods are often isolated from mainstream society both spatially and socially. Their families therefore must often cope not only with their own poverty, but also with the problems that come from hundreds of other poor families living near them.[39]

The spatial concentration of poverty in American cities gradually increased in the twentieth century. Social historians who have reconstructed urban neighborhoods describe how in the nineteenth century the poor were generally clustered into pockets and alleyways near the homes of the affluent, although there were some exceptions in large cities.[40] Class and racial segregation, especially in Northern cities, began increasing in the first decades of the twentieth century as the black population began to swell with the Great Migration North of Southern blacks. At the same time, improvements in transportation and the rise of the automobile industry made the suburban lifestyle more accessible. After World War II, suburbanization surged dramatically; early suburban migrants were overwhelming white and middle class.[41]

It was not until the 1960s and 1970s that people began to talk about sharp increases in "ghetto" or "barrio" poverty, the rise of the "under-class," and increases in "concentrated" poverty. The term *ghetto* or *barrio poverty* connotes both economic and racial and ethnic population concentrations. The term *underclass* typically refers to "nonnormative" behaviors present in many high-poverty neighborhoods, such as dropping out of school, having children out of wedlock, receiving welfare, having low attachment to the labor force, and abusing drugs and alcohol. Concentrated poverty refers more strictly to neighborhoods with high poverty rates. By the 1980s and 1990s, the popular press, pop culture, and academic research were paying considerable attention to the explosive growth of inner-city poverty in large metropolitan areas and its accompanying problems. In particular, they focused on poor and—implicitly or explicitly—dysfunctional black communities.[42] The early 1990s, for example, saw the release of popular movies *Menace II Society, Boyz N the Hood,* and *New Jack City,* each of which described (and some might say glorified) the life of gangsters living in the ghetto, perhaps as the movie *The Godfather* did for the Italian mafia of an earlier generation.

High-poverty neighborhoods are typically defined by researchers as those where over 40 percent of the population is poor, though 20 and 30 percent thresholds have sometimes been used. Qualitative research suggests that neighborhoods where 40 percent or more of the residents are poor tend to have a "threatening appearance, marked by dilapidated housing, vacant units with broken or boarded-up windows, abandoned or burned-out cars, and men 'hanging out' on street corners."[43] Here I focus on concentrated poverty statistics using the 40 percent cutoff.

Research has confirmed that concentrated poverty increased rapidly during the time of growing interest in, and concern about, this issue. Although overall metropolitan area poverty rates were relatively stable between 1970 and 1990, the number of people in high-poverty neighborhoods nearly doubled, from over four million to eight million, over the same period. Nearly half of the people living in these areas were themselves poor.[44] Whites, African Americans, and Hispanics all had increases in their numbers living in high-poverty areas over the period from 1970 to 1990. For whites and Hispanics, the biggest increases occurred in the 1980s. For blacks, it was fairly evenly spread over the 1970s and 1980s.[45]

Since the early 1990s, however, the intense interest in concentrated poverty has dimmed a bit. Not coincidentally, analyses of the 2000 census showed a rather dramatic pivot: between 1990 and 2000, after decades of growth, the number of people living in high-poverty neighborhoods declined by 24 percent. Concentrated poverty declined among all racial and ethnic groups, with the largest decline among African Americans.[46]

Nevertheless, in the wake economic downturns in the 2000s, it appears that concentrated poverty once again increased, with the

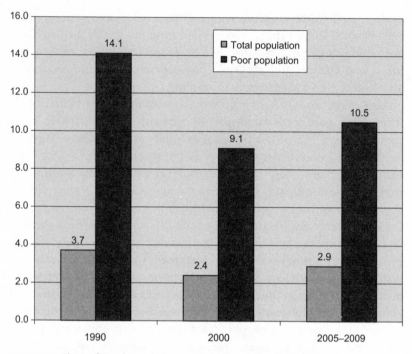

FIGURE 6. Share of Total Population and Poor Population in High-Poverty Neighborhoods, 1990 to 2005–2009. SOURCE: Kneebone, Nadeau, and Berube 2011, figure 1, p. 6.

population living in high-poverty neighborhoods rising by a third between 2000 and the 2005–9 period. By the end of the period, 10.5 percent of poor people in the United States lived in high-poverty neighborhoods, up from 9.1 percent in 2000 but significantly below the 14.1 percent rate in 1990 (see figure 6). The share of individuals in higher-poverty neighborhoods who are black slightly declined over the period, so that in 2005–9, 17 percent of the people living in high-poverty neighborhoods were white (an increase from 11 percent in 2000), 45 percent were black (down from 46 percent), 34 percent were Latino (down from 37 percent), and the remaining were of some other race. Notably, concentrated poverty nearly doubled in midwestern metropolitan areas in the 2000s (where manufacturing declined significantly), and the population in extreme-poverty neighborhoods rose more than twice as fast in the suburbs as in central cities.[47] Thus, concentrated poverty is less of an inner-city black phenomenon than it used to be.

People in high-poverty areas fare worse along a number of social and economic indicators. Nearly a third of adults aged twenty-two to sixty-four in high-poverty neighborhoods are out of the labor force, compared to 14 percent of such adults in the population as a whole.[48] About a third of the adult population twenty-five years of age and over in high-poverty tracts are high school dropouts, compared with 10 percent of the comparable adult population in low-poverty neighborhoods. Similarly, while 14 percent of families in low-poverty neighborhoods are headed by a female householder without a spouse, near half (46 percent) of families in high-poverty neighborhoods are headed by a female householder.[49] Nevertheless, while many residents in high-poverty areas face multiple disadvantages, these neighborhoods are far from homogeneous. A majority of those living in high-poverty areas are not recipients of public assistance and do participate in the labor market, albeit in lower-skill occupations and for fewer hours and lower wages than people living in other areas.[50]

What factors account for the increase in concentrated poverty from 1940 to 1990 and the decline thereafter? The increase likely resulted from several factors, including past government policies, racial and ethnic discrimination, residential segregation, economic changes and employment dislocations, and the movement of prosperous residents to the suburbs. In terms of government policies, some federal housing policies, such as the building of low-income projects in already poor inner-city neighborhoods in the post–World War II period, contributed to poverty concentration. Federal assistance to highway construction and mass transit also accelerated the suburbanization of the middle and upper classes. Infrastructure and tax policies, such as investment tax credits favoring construction of new plants and facilities—often built in the suburbs—over rehabilitation also facilitated suburbanization.[51]

With respect to discrimination, Douglas S. Massey and Nancy Denton describe how real estate brokers, speculators, developers, and banks, acting on racial animosity within the population, preserved racial divisions in housing markets. The official policy of real estate agents in the Detroit area, for example, was expressed in the Code of Ethics of the National Association of Real Estate Boards, which explicitly banned racial mixing in neighborhoods through the 1940s, and later did so tacitly.[52] Segregation served to concentrate black poverty, especially during a time when economic changes limited the opportunities available to low-skill workers.

Other theories put greater emphasis on economic changes. Two of these are referred to as the "spatial mismatch" hypothesis and the "skills mismatch" hypothesis. According to spatial mismatch theory, the increase in the concentration of the inner-city poor was directly linked to the elimination of low-skill manufacturing jobs and the deconcentration of employment from central cities to the surrounding suburbs.[53] A related economic process, the emergence of the service economy, resulted in a lack of well-paying jobs that matched the skills of inner-city residents—a skills mismatch.[54] Many of the new jobs in the cities were either high-paying service jobs that required high levels of education or low-skill and low-wage service jobs that were unattractive as lifetime employment opportunities. The result was increasing poverty in the inner cities and growing affluence in the suburbs.

William Julius Wilson, in *The Truly Disadvantaged,* built on the mismatch hypothesis, arguing that, because of economic restructuring and the accompanying flight of blue-collar jobs from the city, many middle-class blacks with sufficient money left their inner-city neighborhoods. As a consequence, the neighborhoods they left became even poorer. The result was neighborhoods whose people were increasingly socially isolated and faced a shrinking job market, resulting in concentrated poverty.

Others have asserted that welfare policy and changes in norms have contributed to concentrated poverty.[55] They argue that welfare makes people less self-reliant and provides incentives for out-of-wedlock births, which spurred the increase in the number of female-headed households. Crime also rose in cities and elsewhere because the criminal justice system decreased sanctions against aberrant behavior. Government policies that discouraged personal responsibility, combined with social isolation and an ingrown expectation of failure among the poor, led to increasing dependency in poor areas. A culture of poverty based on aberrant norms and behaviors emerged in the ghetto, where the poor did not take advantage of new opportunities that may have arisen.[56] Arguing against the primacy of this perspective, however, William Julius Wilson contends, "Cultural values emerge from specific social circumstances and life chances and reflect one's class and racial position. Thus, if underclass blacks have limited aspirations or fail to plan for the future, it is not ultimately the product of different cultural norms but the consequence of restricted opportunities, a bleak future, and feelings of resignation resulting from bitter personal experiences."[57]

Researcher Paul Jargowsky, in his book *Poverty and Place,* tentatively concludes that, of these factors, limited economic opportunity at the metropolitan level (e.g., deindustrialization and the loss of jobs) was probably the most important factor leading to increases in concentrated poverty up to 1990, while neighborhood sorting processes, such as residential segregation and the growing economic segregation among African Americans, also played important roles.[58]

There is no definitive explanation for the decline in concentrated poverty after 1990, but a few factors likely played a role. First, poverty declined in general in the 1990s, especially during the period of robust economic growth in the middle and latter years of the decade. This general decline in poverty served to push the poverty rate down among those living in what were previously high-poverty neighborhoods. The black poverty rate in particular fell considerably during the decade, from 31.9 percent in 1990 to 22.5 percent in 2000.[59] The rapid suburbanization of the black population in the 1990s also meant that many African Americans moved out of higher-poverty inner-city neighborhoods to neighborhoods in the suburbs that had lower poverty, even if only slightly lower.[60]

The increase in concentrated poverty in the 2000s is likewise probably a function of increasing poverty overall in that decade. This is consistent with the finding that concentrated poverty increased particularly in the Midwest, the region hit hardest by continued industrial declines. For example, cities such as Detroit, Toledo, and Dayton all experienced economic difficulties in the 2000s.[61] The 2000s also saw the continued suburbanization of the U.S. population, as well as the suburbanization of concentrated poverty. For example, although the proportion of the population living in high-poverty tracts increased by 16 percent in central cities between 2000 and the 2005–9 period, the corresponding figure for the suburbs was 37 percent.[62] Thus, the traditionally stark difference between central cities and suburbs has declined over the past few decades.

SUMMARY

Some basic patterns emerge from a number of national surveys:

Declines in poverty in the United States more or less stalled by the early 1970s, and then poverty noticeably worsened in the wake of the severe economic recession in 2007–9. Poverty is more pervasive among some groups, such as children, minorities, high school dropouts, and female-headed families.

A significant percentage of Americans report various hardships, such as difficulty paying bills or experiencing food insecurity, yet both poor and nonpoor Americans report having basic consumer items such as TVs and refrigerators.

A high proportion of Americans experience a bout of poverty at some point in their lives. Although a majority of people who fall into poverty remain poor for only a short time, many families frequently move into and out of poverty.

Poverty varies widely across states. Although concentrated neighborhood poverty increased rapidly from 1970 to 1990, it declined dramatically in the 1990s before once again moderately increasing in the 2000s. Concentrated poverty is no longer primarily an inner-city phenomenon.

CHAPTER 4

Global Poverty

Examining poverty in countries around the world provides greater insight into the nature and extent of poverty in the United States. A look at poverty in developing countries, for example, highlights the difference between extremely deep deprivation in poor countries and relative poverty in rich ones, as well as the role of globalization in shaping patterns of poverty. An investigation of poverty in other rich countries provides insight into how different policy orientations contribute to different economic outcomes. Two distinct patterns emerge from this analysis. First, in absolute terms, poverty in the United States qualitatively differs from that in the developing world, where poverty is still often measured in terms of having sufficient resources to stay alive. Second, despite high general standards of living, the United States suffers from considerably more poverty and inequality than most other developed countries with similar standards of living. These two themes are now explored in turn.

POVERTY IN THE DEVELOPING WORLD

The world population stands at about 7 billion people, with 5.7 billion of them living in developing countries. China and India alone have 1.4 billion and 1.2 billion people, respectively, compared to just 312 million people living in the United States.[1] Countries across the globe have vastly different average income levels and standards of living. Robert Kates and Partha Dasgupta provide the following apt composite description of poverty in developing countries: "In the world of the poor, people don't enjoy food security, don't own many assets, are stunted and wasted, don't live long, can't read or write, don't have access to easy credit, are unable to save much, aren't empowered, can't ensure themselves well against crop failure or household calamity, don't have control over their own lives, don't trade with the rest of the world, live in unhealthy surroundings, suffer from 'incapabilities,' are poorly governed."[2]

In short, much more so than in rich countries, poverty in the developing world is about basic subsistence and survival. It involves extreme vulnerability to adverse events (e.g., draught and disease) and a general inability to control one's circumstances.

Although levels of global inequality are high, as is the incidence of grueling poverty in many low-income countries, one piece of good news is that absolute poverty has been declining in many developing countries in recent decades. Of the world's population living in developing and transition economies, about 1.4 billion, or 25 percent, lived on less than $1.25 a day in 2005, down from 52 percent in 1981 (see figure 7). These declines are roughly in line with Millennium Development Goals (MDGs) proposed by the United Nations. Specifically, the group's aim was to halve, between 1990 and 2015, the proportion of people whose income was less than $1 a day. A U.N. report analyzing progress toward meeting poverty reduction goals notes that the global economic crisis of 2008–9 slowed progress, but the world is still on track to meet the poverty reduction target.[3]

Nevertheless, poverty is especially severe in South Asia, where 40 percent of the population subsists on less than $1.25 a day, and in sub-Saharan Africa, where 52 percent of the population is poor using this measure. About 43 percent of the total number of poor lived in South Asia and another 29 percent in sub-Saharan Africa in 2005.[4] Nevertheless, South Asia saw gradual declines in poverty over the period (from a high of 59 percent in 1981 to a low of 40 percent in 2005). In contrast, poverty rates in sub-Saharan Africa increased in the 1980s and remained stable throughout much of the 1990s before slowly declining thereafter. The 1980s and 1990s were decades of anemic economic growth and political instability in many countries in sub-Saharan Africa.[5] Structural adjustment programs implemented during this time by the International Monetary Fund (IMF) and the World Bank—which set conditions that had to be met by countries in order to obtain new loans (e.g., cutting government expenditures, removing price controls, trade liberalization)—may have helped in some countries but exacerbated poverty in others.[6]

Poverty is considerably lower in East Asia and the Pacific, where the

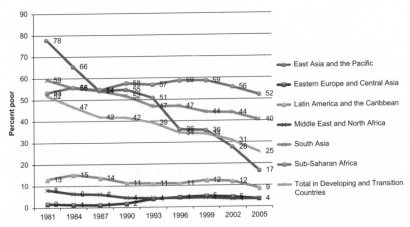

FIGURE 7. Percentage of People Living on Less Than $1.25 a Day, by Region, 1981–2005. SOURCE: World Bank 2012c.

percentage earning under $1.25 a day fell dramatically, from 78 percent in 1981 to just 17 percent in 2005. Large declines in such poverty in China, from 84 percent in 1981 to 16 percent in 2005, helped drive down poverty in this global region.[7] In terms of absolute numbers, the count of those earning under $1.25 fell from 1.9 billion to 1.4 billion from 1981 to 2005 in the developing world during a time when the overall population in this region increased significantly.[8]

What explains the decline in the poverty rate in developing nations? What is the role of globalization in this process? On the one hand, some argue that globalization has made things worse for many developing countries. They point out that Western countries have historically exploited countries in the developing world through colonialism. Today, the argument goes, rich countries preserve their dominance by imposing an international division of labor, with "core" countries focusing on high-skill production and "peripheral ones" concentrating on lower-skill, labor-intensive production and the extraction of raw materials. Profits continue to flow to rich countries because that is where the headquarters of most multinational corporations are located.[9] According to this view, international institutions such as the World Bank and the International Monetary Fund often serve to protect the interests of these rich countries and their wealthy investors by imposing tough loan conditions on poor countries. Conventional wisdom also has it that global inequality is increasing, and this is serving to increase poverty in many parts of the developing world.

However, research indicates that by many measures global inequality has stabilized in recent decades after a period of enormous growth in inequality during Western industrialization from about 1800 to 1950.[10] Some of the most rapid economic growth in recent years has occurred in developing countries such as China and India, both of which also experienced significant declines in absolute poverty.[11] The growth in these and other industrializing nations in the developing world surpasses economic growth rates in Europe, the United States, Japan, and most other rich countries.[12]

There remains considerable debate about whether globalization has improved the lives of people around the world. It is probably fair to say that economic growth in rapidly industrializing countries has been aided by globalization. China's economy, for example, has depended extensively on export-oriented production. Indeed, the market system has now become the organizational model for a majority of rich and poor economies alike. Declines in absolute poverty rates have been accompanied by improvements along other social indicators, such as broad-based declines in infant mortality, a reduction of child malnourishment, and an increase in school enrollment.[13] Industrialization, urbanization, and growing trade played a role in spurring these growing standards of living.

Yet it is important to note that globalization has often contributed to inequality *within* countries, as well as to social and economic exclusion and marginalization.[14] The poorest 20 percent of the global population also has not benefited much from general improvements, and some countries are as poor as they have ever been.[15] Even individual families that escape the lowest level of poverty still sometimes work long hours under difficult conditions for wages that are far below what U.S. workers make. To take just one example, much of the iPhone assembly work is currently done in Longhua, Shenzhen, in China. The manufacturing facility, located in what is known as Foxconn City, has 230,000 employees, many of whom work six days a week and often spend up to twelve hours a day at the plant. Over a quarter of Foxconn's work force lives in company barracks, and many workers earn less than $17 a day.[16] Note that these wages, although low by U.S. standards, are nevertheless much higher than the $1.25 threshold used by the World Bank to measure poverty. Wages are often worse and conditions as bad in countries with poverty rates that are significantly higher than those in China.

Figure 8 illustrates how extreme poverty in poor countries translates into differences in critical outcomes—here, infant mortality. In the thirty nations of the Organization of Economic Cooperation and Devel-

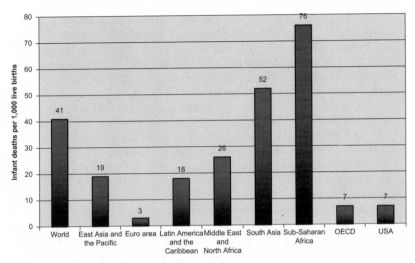

FIGURE 8. Infant Mortality by Region, 2010. SOURCE: World Bank 2012b.

opment (OECD)—which consists of many Western European countries plus other industrialized countries, such as Japan and Australia—7 out of every 1,000 children died before the age of one in 2010, but in sub-Saharan Africa, 76 out of 1,000 die before that age.[17] In the United States, the infant mortality rate is likewise about 7 per 1,000.[18] The world average is 41 deaths per 1,000 live births, but in the poorest countries as many as over 100 in 1,000 children die before the age of one. For example, the highest infant mortality rate in 2010 was 114 per 1,000 in Sierra Leone, as compared with only 2 per 1,000 in a number of countries, including Sweden, Japan, Iceland, and Singapore.[19] Life expectancy at birth in sub-Saharan Africa, at 54 years, is far less than the OECD average, which is 79 years.[20]

New York Times columnist Nicholas Kristof has reported:

> No interview haunts me more than a conversation with a Cambodian peasant, Nhem Yen, in 1996. She was forty years old, though she looked much older, and was living with her family in a clearing in the Cambodian jungle. The area was notorious for malaria, but the family members were ambitious and industrious and figured that it was worth the risk to make more money by cutting wood for sale.
>
> Nhem Yen's eldest daughter, who was twenty-four and pregnant with her second child, promptly caught malaria. There was no money to get medical treatment (effective drugs would have cost less than $10), and so she died a day after giving birth. That left Nhem Yen looking after five children of her own and two grandchildren.

The family had one mosquito net that could accommodate about three people. Such nets are quite effective against malaria, but they cost $5—and Nhem Yen could not afford to buy any more. So every night, she agonized over which of the children to put under the net and which to leave out.

"It's very hard to choose," Nhem Yen told me. "But we have no money to buy another mosquito net. We have no choice."

That is the real face of poverty: it is not so much the pain of hunger or the humiliation of rags, but the impossible choices you face. If you can only afford school fees for some of your children, which do you send? If you must choose between medical treatment for Dad, the breadwinner, or for Daughter, the A student, which is it? Do you use your savings to provide a good dowry so Eldest Daughter can get a decent husband, or do you settle for the drunkard who will beat her and instead invest the savings in a food cart that may help provide an income to send the younger ones to school?[21]

This grimly illustrates how poverty for those with little social support and a weak national safety net are forced to make difficult choices, if there are choices to be made at all.

Globalization and growing pockets of affluence in developing countries can heighten resentment among those who are left behind economically. Describing unrest in many poor countries in Africa, commentator John Githongo writes:

Africa's middle class has grown in recent years, but its members are politically and economically vulnerable and their lives can be overturned by the whims of elites who rule instead of govern. Meanwhile, the poor are assaulted daily by the potent symbols of rising inequality: glitzy malls filled with designer goods and status-enhancing baubles that cost 10 times the monthly minimum wage. . . . Their resentment is only heightened by the tools of the information age, which remind them that they have been excluded from feeding at the trough enjoyed so blatantly by the nouveau riche—a lifestyle that is showcased by the newly minted wealthy on television, Twitter, Facebook and the Web in infuriating detail. Globalization has changed the aspirations of the poor, and their expectations will follow.[22]

Consistent with one of the running themes of this book, we see how the change in one's reference group can change people's views about their economic well-being and satisfaction with life more generally. In decades (and certainly centuries) past, when there was relatively little communication across large distances, people living above subsistence gauged their prosperity by comparing themselves to others in their community. People today, however, are increasingly aware, via communication technology and social media, of the affluence of others and wonder why they do not seem to have the opportunity to participate in this abundance. This contributes to the unrest we see in many parts of the globe today.

How one might address global poverty naturally relies on accurately diagnosing its causes. The reasons for continued poverty vary widely across countries. Jeffrey Sachs, author of *The End of Poverty,* offers some of the following reasons for continued poverty in developing countries, and especially in sub-Saharan Africa:[23]

1. Poverty and fiscal traps. Poverty results in a lack of funds available to invest in future growth. Thus, poverty serves as a reinforcing trap. Many communities in poor countries lack physical infrastructure, such as paved roads and power generators. They also lack educational institutions, such as widely accessible and effective schools, which could serve to build human capital. Those who lack skills often end up depending on subsistence jobs to earn a living. Poor countries may also not have the medical facilities and public health services to maintain a healthy and productive population. It is not a coincidence that epidemics such as AIDS are often felt more acutely in poor countries.

2. Physical geography. Many poor countries are landlocked, are located in mountain ranges, or otherwise lack easy ways to transport goods over long distances (such as rivers or coastlines). Countries in this category include Bolivia and Kyrgyzstan. Other countries, such as some of those in sub-Saharan Africa, have arid conditions and low agricultural productivity. Although it is possible to overcome these factors through technological means, they nevertheless often serve to hinder economic development.

3. Governance failures. This can stem from ineptitude and corruption, which is endemic in many poor countries. In these circumstances the government fails to provide an environment conducive to economic growth. The regulatory environment may be unstable and opaque, or brazen corruption may allow only favored insiders to fruitfully conduct business while everyone else remains shut out of engaging in meaningful entrepreneurial activity.

4. Cultural barriers. Cultural or religious norms can impede the participation of all members of a community in its economic activity. For example, cultural or religious norms may block the participation of women who would otherwise have much to contribute. This may then serve to increase fertility, which often lowers investment in children (see also reason number 6, Demography,

below). Cultural barriers may also affect the opportunities available to religious or ethnic minorities and hamper their access to public services. Outright hostility between groups can lead to internal turmoil and violence.

5. Geopolitics and conflict. Internal political instability or external wars can serve to impoverish communities, such as through the physical destruction of property or by dampening economic activity and trade. Conflict destroys infrastructure and scares away investment, leading to even fewer opportunities.[24]

6. Demography. Developing countries typically have high fertility rates. When poor families have many children, it becomes more difficult to invest in the education of each one of them. In addition, having a large family hinders a mother's ability to join the labor force. Girls and women tend to be more empowered when they are allowed to receive an education and participate in the labor market. These activities can serve to reduce poverty.

Based on his assessment of the causes of poverty in developing countries, Sachs advocates greater financial assistance from rich countries, to be coordinated with efforts from within poor countries to devote more of their national resources to reducing poverty rather than to war, corruption, and infighting.[25] Paul Collier, however, believes that external financial aid is often ineffective. Rather, he claims that what is needed is a coordinated effort between rich and poor nations to adopt preferential trade policies, new laws against corruption, and perhaps even targeted military interventions in failing states.[26] Of note, economic growth in the developing world has surpassed growth in the slow economies of many rich countries for a number of years now, and this may serve to reduce global poverty and inequality over the long run.[27]

In contrast to Sachs's focus on conditions within developing countries, some argue that current global institutions serve the interests of rich countries and the business elite within them, which serves to keep poor countries poor. They decry the "neoliberal" economic order that puts profit over people and thus leaves many behind. As a result, some countries have tried to counter the negative effects of globalization by adopting protectionist practices, such as promoting domestic industry and manufactured goods, limiting imports, heavily regulating or forbidding foreign investment, or nationalizing foreign-owned companies or industries so that profits remain within the country. While globalization and neoliberalism continue to draw many critics, wholesale national efforts to combat the global capitalist system are, on the whole, in retreat, though certainly many countries adopt some policies to protect segments of their domestic economies.

One policy approach that works well *within* the market system and has garnered significant and growing attention in recent years is *microfinance*. Microfinance is the provision of financial services to low-income individuals or groups who traditionally lack access to banking and credit. It is thought that microcredit helps individuals start their own businesses and thus alleviate their poverty. The reason microcredit is thought to be so important is that many people in the world have no access to formal financial services, and the problem is especially acute in developing countries.[28] Although it is difficult to measure the scope of microfinance, one estimate is that microfinance institutions had 155 million clients, more than 100 million of them women, as of December 2007.[29]

Many organizations, such as the World Bank, have promoted microfinance as a way of increasing development, reducing poverty, promoting gender equality and the empowerment of women, reducing child mortality, and improving maternal health. However, some have noted that the impact of microfinance may not always be positive. Although many individuals are undoubtedly helped by having greater access to credit, borrowing can also lead to overindebtedness. For example, unwise (and often predatory) lending was one of the factors that contributed to the rise and collapse of the U.S. housing bubble and the subsequent recession in 2007–9 (see chapter 6). Likewise, many fear that microfinance lenders sometimes exploit vulnerable borrowers. Careful empirical evaluations of the effects of microfinance tend to find that it does reduce poverty.[30] As with many programs, the benefits likely depend in part on the extent to which it is carefully implemented and regulated to prevent abuse. Overall, microfinance efforts remain popular and will likely continue to grow in the coming years.

POVERTY IN WEALTHIER COUNTRIES

Today the United States is the sole superpower, after sharing the position with the Soviet Union from the beginning of the post–World War II era until the crumbling of the Soviet empire in the early 1990s. The United States has the world's largest economy and most powerful military, it is a center of economic and artistic innovation, and it continues to serve as a powerful beacon for immigrants. While many believe that U.S. power may have reached its zenith, and other countries—particularly China—

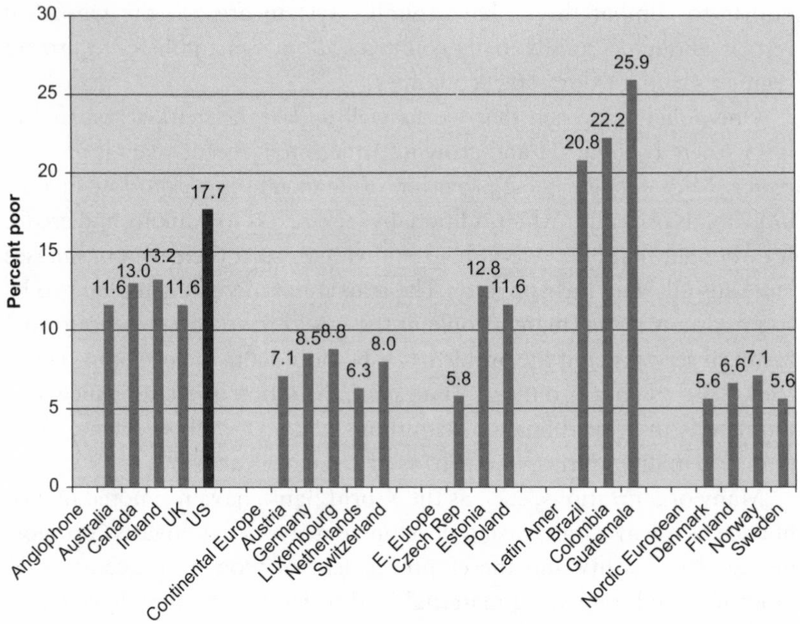

FIGURE 9. Relative Poverty Rates for Selected Countries, Mid-2000s. SOURCE: Gornick and Jantti 2011, table 1. NOTE: The threshold is set to 50 percent of median income in each country.

are presenting challenges in various arenas, the United States is maintaining its preeminent role in the global order for the time being. For many Americans this state of affairs corroborates the notion of "American exceptionalism," which was first described by Alexis de Tocqueville in the 1830s and has been elaborated upon by others since. According to this view, there is a unique American ideology based on liberty, egalitarianism, individualism, populism, and laissez-faire.[31]

Nevertheless, whether because of or despite American exceptionalism, poverty in the United States surpasses that experienced in most other rich countries. So while poverty in the United States, with its high standards of living, is qualitatively different from poverty in most of the developing world, it is still more common than in other countries with similar levels of development.

Figure 9 compares poverty rates for selected countries in the mid-2000s using a relative poverty measure. The measure is relative because it uses poverty thresholds equal to 50 percent of the disposable household median income in each of the countries shown. The poverty thresholds thus take into account national standards of living and are much higher in richer countries than in poorer ones. For example, disposable median income ranged from a high of $35,000 in Luxembourg, $29,210 in the United States, and $28,291 in Switzerland to a low of $2,186 in Colombia, $2,917 in Guatemala, and $4,195 in Brazil. The corresponding median incomes are also fairly low in the Eastern European countries (averaging just over $9,000), but they are generally in the $20,000s in most of the remaining developed countries shown.[32]

The relative poverty rate in the United States (17.7 percent) is higher than that in all of the countries except those in Latin America. Income inequality has long been high in Latin America, where many countries have a small (if growing) middle class and a number of people living in poor rural areas or working in the informal economy in urban areas.[33] Relative poverty rates are particularly low in Nordic countries such as Denmark and Sweden (5.6 percent in both), but they are also fairly low in a variety of other countries, such as the United Kingdom (11.6 percent), Germany (8.5 percent), and Estonia (12.8 percent).

These findings might not be altogether surprising, as inequality is known to be relatively high in the United States compared to Europe. Perhaps less expected is that *absolute* poverty rates are also higher in the United States than in a majority of other developed countries, even though the U.S. median income is substantially higher. Figure 10 compares poverty rates in the same set of countries using a poverty line that does not vary across place. Specifically, Gornick and Jantti used the official U.S. poverty line and converted it into the currency of the country in question using purchasing power parity (PPP) exchange rates.[34]

The absolute U.S. poverty rate of 9.4 percent is surpassed only by Australia (14.7 percent) among the Anglophone, continental European, and Nordic countries in figure 10. The lowest poverty rates are in Luxembourg (only 0.9 percent), Denmark (2.9 percent), and Switzerland (3.4 percent). However, we can see that applying the U.S. poverty threshold in countries with substantially lower standards of living yields very high poverty rates in those countries, topping out at well above 80 percent in all three Latin American countries. It also results in high poverty rates in Eastern Europe. In these countries the U.S. poverty line would not be considered a reasonable one because of their substantially lower standards of living overall.

Why is the U.S. poverty rate (both absolute and relative) higher than those in many of the richest developed countries? It does not appear to be due primarily to differences in family structure. Even when considering only single-parent families, poverty rates in the United States are higher than in other well-to-do countries. Rather, the main culprit is

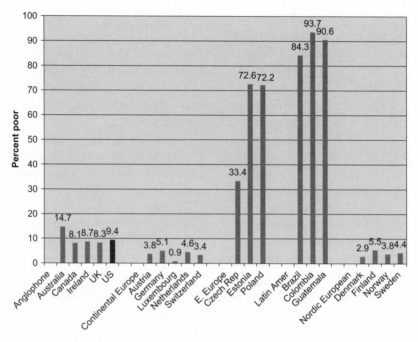

FIGURE 10. Absolute Poverty Rates for Selected Countries, Mid-2000s. SOURCE:
Gornick and Jantti 2011, table 1. NOTE: The U.S. threshold is used in each country's
poverty calculation.

lower government transfers to low-income families in the United States.
If we were to consider pretransfer poverty rates (i.e., those based on the
market incomes earned by families through salaries, wages, and self-
employment), U.S. absolute and relative poverty rates are among the
lowest. For example, the absolute poverty rates in the United States
when considering only market income is 20.6 percent, higher only than
poverty in Luxembourg (19.5 percent) and Switzerland (20.3 percent).[35]
Countries with lower posttransfer poverty rates thus rely significantly
on government programs such as universal child allowances, food assistance, and more generous guaranteed child support for single parents.[36]
Indeed, government expenditures on social welfare programs as a percentage of gross national product are considerably higher in Western
European countries than in the United States.[37]

One caveat about these findings is that studies looking at hardship
outcomes find that poor Americans have more consumer durables and
larger houses than the poor in other rich countries, such as Sweden,
Germany, and Canada. Poor Americans may own more consumer dura-

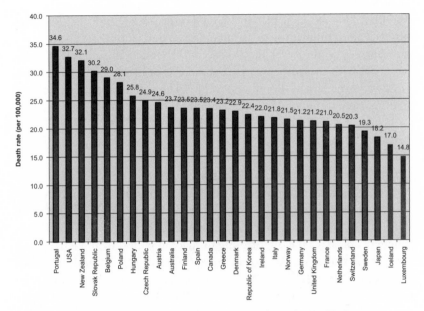

FIGURE 11. Death Rates among Children 1–19 Years of Age, by OECD Country, Mid-2000s. SOURCE: National Center for Health Statistics 2011, figure 26.

bles than the poor in other countries because of unmeasured wealth, the greater availability of credit in the United States, or differences in tastes among the poor, where the possession of consumer goods may receive higher priority in the United States than other countries.[38]

Nevertheless, many find the generally high rates of relative poverty in the United States troubling. Amartya Sen conceptualizes poverty as "capability failure," or the inability to participate fully in society. He argues that people with little political voice, modest physical and economic security, and little opportunity to better their lives lack basic capabilities. Although goods and services are valuable, they are so only because of their instrumental value—what they can do to help people lead satisfying lives. In highly unequal societies, those at the bottom often lack the power to do so. According to this way of thinking, poverty can be more intense than it appears when measured using family income.[39]

This thinking is consistent with other intrinsically important measures of well-being. Figure 11, which compares child mortality rates across OECD countries, shows that of the 28 countries, only Portugal has higher child mortality (34.6 deaths per 100,000 children 1 to 19 years of age) than the United States (32.7). The child mortality rate is less than half the U.S. rate in Luxembourg (14.8), and also lower in other sizable countries such as Japan (18.2) and Germany (21.2). Child mortality rates are lower than those in the United States even in some countries with considerably lower standards of living, such as Hungary (25.8) and the Slovak Republic (30.2).[40] These general patterns extend to other similar outcomes, such as infant mortality and life expectancy.[41]

ECONOMIC MOBILITY

These health indicators notwithstanding, some have argued that income inequality and poverty in themselves may not be troubling if a society provides sufficient opportunity and economic mobility. One core American belief is that the United States is a vibrant meritocracy, where people have the opportunity to succeed with skill and hard work. Numerous stories testify to this, such as that of Henry Ford, who was born on a Michigan farm before becoming the founder of the Ford Motor Company. More recently Steve Jobs, who was raised by working-class parents in Cupertino, California, achieved astounding success as a founding member and later head of Apple Computer. Although the United States clearly affords such opportunities, some research has called into question whether, at least for the typical person, economic mobility is greater in the United States than in other countries.

Figure 12 shows estimated correlations between the earnings of fathers and sons. A high correlation would indicate that one's parental background is a good predictor of the child's earnings. In a fully stratified society where there is no economic mobility, the correlation would be 1.0. The U.S. estimate is 0.47, which means that nearly half of parental earnings advantages are passed onto sons. The U.S. correlation is surpassed only by that of the United Kingdom (0.50), whereas the correlations are substantially lower in Germany (0.32), Canada (0.19), and all of the Nordic countries.[42] The same kind of ordering occurs for women in an analysis of a selected number of countries, though the differences across countries are smaller.[43]

Another way to look at mobility is to examine the probability that a child will be in the same earnings quintile as his or her parents. Table 4 shows this for fathers and sons in a few selected rich countries. Consistent with findings above, we see that in the United States the probability is relatively high (0.42) that a son whose father had earnings in the bottom quintile of the earnings distribution (i.e., low earnings) will also have earnings that will place him in the bottom quintile. This 0.42 figure is higher

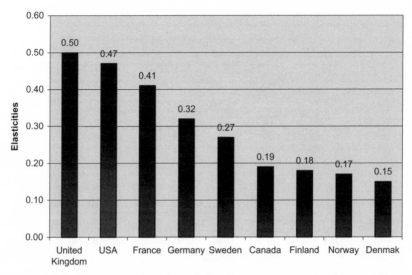

FIGURE 12. Father-Son Earnings Elasticities, by Country. SOURCE: Corak 2006, table 1.

than in the five other countries shown, which range from 0.25 (Denmark) to 0.30 (United Kingdom). While the U.S. probabilities for staying in the same quintile are generally higher across the earnings spectrum, the difference is greatest for the bottom quintile. In other words, while Americans in the middle and top of the distribution are nearly as intergenerationally mobile as those in other countries, the lowest American earners seem to have the greatest difficulty in moving up. In all countries there is some stickiness at the top; upper quintile parents seem more able to confer their privilege to their children than parents in most of the other quintiles.

A few factors might explain the relative lack of mobility for the lowest earnings quintile in the United States. The extent of income inequality and the depth of poverty in the United States, which leaves poor children starting well behind others, likely play a role. Inequality is in turn affected by tax policy and the strength of the social safety net. Overall, countries with higher levels of income inequality (such as the United States) generally have lower intergenerational social mobility.[44] Another explanation could be the high variation in educational quality and student performance in the United States, combined with high economic returns to receiving higher education. Indeed, parental background plays a larger role in predicting how students do in the United States than in many other countries—perhaps because schools, which rely considerably on the local tax base, often vary considerably across

TABLE 4   INTERGENERATIONAL MOBILITY ACROSS THE EARNINGS DISTRIBUTION

Probability that the son will be in the same quintile as his father

	Denmark	Finland	Norway	Sweden	United Kingdom	United States
1st quintile	.25	.28	.28	.26	.30	.42
2nd quintile	.25	.22	.24	.23	.23	.28
3rd quintile	.22	.22	.22	.22	.19	.26
4th quintile	.22	.23	.22	.22	.25	.25
5th quintile	.36	.35	.35	.37	.35	.36

SOURCE: D'Addio 2007, table 1.

American communities.[45] Racial inequality in the United States and the greater incidence of single-parent families may also play some role.[46] These findings taken as a whole challenge the notion of American exceptionalism in economic mobility.[47]

There are some important caveats to these findings. First, the studies above measure relative mobility, or the likelihood that children will share their parents' place in the general income distribution. Some people prefer to examine absolute mobility, which focuses on whether children have higher incomes than their parents more generally, regardless of their place in the income distribution. As discussed in chapter 3, at least two out of three (and possibly as many as four out of five) Americans have higher incomes than their parents. This occurs because standards of living (as indicated by rising median household incomes) have risen over time in the United States.[48] There is no comparable study done on absolute mobility patterns across countries.

The studies reviewed above also omit immigrants (who have only been in a country for one generation), and they and their children are thought to be quite mobile. Greater income compression (which reflects less income inequality) in some of the other countries may also play a role. For example, a Danish family can move from the tenth percentile to the ninetieth percentile with $45,000 of additional earnings, while an American family would need an additional $93,000.[49] And although there is moderately less income mobility in the United States than in these other countries, there still is substantial movement, as a majority of people born in any given quintile move to a different one as adults. In terms of occupational mobility, Americans rank somewhere in the middle.[50]

Studies of economic mobility of individuals across their lifetime (rather than across generations) indicate that the Unites States has rates of relative mobility that are fairly similar to those of other countries when measured over a five- to ten-year span. In terms of absolute changes in income, one study found that full-time workers in the United States generally experience more absolute growth in earning and income than in Europe, though low-income workers in particular experience somewhat less growth. This provides additional evidence of low levels of mobility at the bottom of the American income ladder.[51]

While Americans tend to be less concerned about income inequality as a social issue than are Europeans, economic mobility has long been considered important. The recession, however, has hampered such mobility, at least in the short term. The Occupy Wall Street protests beginning in 2011 were indicative of the feeling that the playing field was no longer even, and that the "1 percenters"—the very rich—had rewritten the rules to favor their continued accumulation of wealth.

As commentator Fareed Zakaria noted during the protests, "I think underlying their sense of frustration is despair over a very un-American state of affairs: A loss of social mobility. Americans have so far put up with inequality because they felt they could change their own status. They didn't mind others being rich, as long as they had a path to move up as well. The American Dream is all about social mobility—the sense that anyone can make it." He goes on to add, with some justification given the findings from the studies described above:

> We talk a lot about the genius of Steve Jobs these days, and justifiably, because he was a genius. But he also grew up in an environment that helped. He graduated from high school in 1972 at a time when the California public school system was ranked first in the country and American public education was the envy of the world. The public school he went to in Cupertino was high quality, with excellent programs in science as well as the liberal arts. Today, California's public schools are a disaster, and the state spends twice as much on prisons as it does on education.[52]

In short, while many Americans might not be that concerned by some measure of income inequality in society, the finding that economic mobility may not be as common as it once was is more troubling.

SUMMARY

In comparisons of poverty in the United States with poverty around the world, research indicates that poverty in developing countries—because it is so widespread and severe—differs qualitatively from that in the United States and other developed countries. Being poor in a poor country makes it difficult to meet the most basic of needs, makes one vulnerable to adverse events (e.g., unexpected illness), and generally hampers the ability to control one's circumstances. As a consequence, infant mortality rates are much higher in developing countries and life expectancies lower. Globalization has likely lowered absolute poverty rates worldwide, especially in rapidly industrializing countries such as China and India. However, globalization has increased inequality within some countries, done little for people in some countries that continue to have very high poverty rates, and has, through technological means such as the Internet, heightened people's awareness of existing inequalities. Some countries remain poor because of poverty and fiscal traps (it is hard to invest in the future if you have no money in the first place), physical geography (e.g., being landlocked), governance failures in the form of corruption, cultural barriers, geopolitics and conflict, and demography (e.g., high fertility rates and a lack of investment in children). Anemic economic growth in rich countries and rapid growth in many developing ones in recent years is serving to reduce global inequalities between countries.

A second theme of this chapter is that, despite the fact that the United States has virtually the highest GNP per capita in the world, it has higher levels of both absolute and relative poverty than other rich countries in Northern and Western Europe. It also has higher levels of relative poverty than an even broader set of countries. The higher U.S. poverty rates are a function of fewer government transfers to low-income families. In contrast to conventional wisdom, the United States also has lower levels of economic mobility than many other rich countries in Europe, such as Sweden, Germany, and Denmark. Economic mobility also seems particularly low for the low-income population. Growing levels of economic inequality combined with moderate levels of economic mobility may be contributing to recent expressions of apprehension and unease among many Americans.

CHAPTER 5

Causes of Poverty

It is commonly believed that individual failings or wayward values propel people into poverty. In the 1960s, anthropologist Oscar Lewis wrote, "By the time slum children are age six or seven they have usually absorbed the basic values and attitudes of their subculture and are not psychologically geared to take full advantage of changing conditions or increased opportunities which may occur in their lifetime."[1] When asked about causes of poverty, about half of Americans say that poverty is the fault of individuals, while nearly the same proportion feel that circumstances play the principal role. Affluent people are more likely to believe that poor people are not doing enough to help themselves, while the poor are more likely to point to circumstances. About two-thirds of Americans believe that the poor have the same values as other Americans, and about a fifth think they have lower moral values.[2]

Economists often focus on individual traits by emphasizing the role of *human capital* in people's economic well-being. Human capital refers to people's knowledge, skills, personality, and experiences that help them do a job well. Many studies have indeed shown that people who invest in their education and skills can expect higher incomes. However, this emphasis on individual characteristics as the main determinant of poverty often overlooks the roles that social, economic, and political systems play in affecting people's well-being.[3] In this chapter I discuss the underlying structural cause of poverty, including why poverty is more prevalent among some groups than others. I begin with a brief discussion of general sociological theories of social stratification. I then examine the role of the economy and low-wage work in explaining patterns of poverty, analyze changing patterns of racial and ethnic stratification, and, finally, discuss gender norms, family structure, and culture and their impact on poverty.

SOCIAL STRATIFICATION

The term *social stratification* here refers to a set of social and economic institutions that generate inequality and poverty. Inequalities have played themselves out in various ways in different social systems over time. David Grusky posits that modern industrial societies have egalitarian ideologies that run contrary to extreme forms of stratification found in caste, feudal, and slave systems. Nevertheless, inequality continues to be a prominent feature in most societies.[4]

Many of the concepts used to understand stratification today come from sociological theorists of the nineteenth and early twentieth centuries. Karl Marx focused on the role of economic systems in producing inequality. Briefly, he argued that stratification in industrial societies is generated by the conflict between two opposing classes, the bourgeoisie and proletariat. The former are the owners of the means of production—the capitalists—and the latter are the workers.[5] The bourgeoisie exploit the proletariat by keeping the surplus value—the profit—generated by their work.[6]

Max Weber, whose main body of work dates to the early twentieth century, held that the concept of class alone was not enough to understand stratification. He proposed a triumvirate of concepts: class, status groups, and parties. He defined status groups as communities, often distinguished by a specific lifestyle and value system. If the line between groups is rigid, a status group is a closed "caste." Status groups gain power through the monopolization of goods or control of social institutions. The third concept, parties, refers to political power. Weber makes the distinction between the three concepts in the following way: "Whereas the genuine place of 'classes' is within the economic order, the place of 'status groups' is within the social order . . . [and] 'parties' live in a house of 'power.'"[7]

The concepts of class, status, and party continue to have resonance in discussions of the causes of poverty today. Below I discuss the role of the market system (factors relating to "class") in generating prosperity and poverty and social forces ("status") that produce unequal outcomes among different groups. The effect of policy ("party") is discussed in chapter 7.

The Effect of Economic Processes on Poverty

Economic processes affect trends in poverty in two ways. First, economic growth determines absolute increases and declines in average standards of living. Second, economic inequality affects the distribution of income. A common analogy is that economic growth determines the size of the pie, while inequality affects the size of each slice. I now discuss the impact of each of these on poverty in more detail.

Economic growth here refers to increases in overall levels of national income. Economic growth is a function of changes in the size of labor supply, human and capital investment, and technological improvements. The U.S. economy experienced increases in all three over the last two centuries. First, the country's population grew from under 4 million in 1790, to 76 million in 1900, to 309 million in 2010.[8] As a country grows, usually its economy grows as well. Second, we have seen increases in human capital investment over time. For example, whereas only 25 percent of people twenty-five years and older had four years of high school in 1940 (the first year in which the Census Bureau collected these figures), 85 percent had achieved this level by 2006–210.[9] Greater human capital is associated with greater productivity and hence growth. Third, technological shifts in the form of the industrial revolution and more recent advances in computing and associated technology have also contributed to improvements in productivity and growth.

Figure 13 shows the trend in both poverty rates, using an absolute poverty standard, and the gross domestic product (GDP)—the output of goods and services produced by labor and property located in the United States—over the period 1947–2011.[10] As expected, the figure shows a negative correlation between GDP growth and poverty, particularly in the 1947–73 period. In 1947, by one estimate, the poverty rate was well over 30 percent. By 1973 it had declined to 11.1 percent. Over that period the GDP rose from 1.8 trillion to 4.9 trillion, in constant 2005 dollars. Note that when we observe slight dips in the GDP, as during the recessions of 1973–74, 1981–82, and 1991–92, we see corresponding spikes in the poverty rate. Evidence from developing countries around the world also indicates that there is a very strong relationship between economic growth and absolute poverty rates.[11]

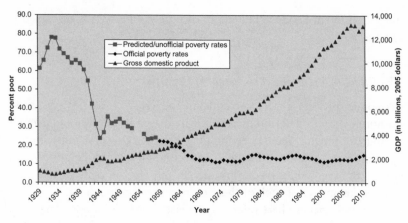

FIGURE 13. Poverty Rates and the Gross Domestic Product, 1929–2011. SOURCE:
GDP data are from the Bureau of Economic Analysis 2012. Poverty rates from 1947 to
1958 come from Fisher 1986, as reprinted in Plotnick et al. 1998, Appendix D. Poverty
figures for 1959–2011 come from U.S. Census Bureau 2012j.

The figure also suggests that the relationship between income
growth and poverty weakened beginning in the 1970s. Some believe
that growing inequality may have played a role in persisting high rates
of poverty after 1970.[12] Even through much of the 2000s, while GDP
grew, poverty remained remarkably flat. It was only with the sharp
decrease in GDP during the Great Recession in the latter part of the
decade that we see a noticeable response in poverty. Perhaps more
important than GDP growth alone is the effect of unemployment. It has
been estimated that a 2-point rise in the unemployment rate leads to a
0.9-point rise in the poverty rate over time.[13] This relationship held
during the latest recession as well.

One caveat about these findings is that the association between economic growth and poverty, using a relative or subjective poverty standard, is less straightforward than when we use the absolute poverty
standard discussed here. When using relative poverty measures, we find
that as general living standards rise, so do the poverty thresholds, resulting in a much weaker association between income growth and poverty.
Inequality therefore tends to have a larger association with trends in
relative poverty rates.[14]

Income inequality results from economic systems that foster the
accumulation of money and assets in one segment of society, often at
the expense of another. To paraphrase Marx, business owners favor
having inexpensive labor to maximize their profits (to reap surplus

value). However, it should be noted that the market is not necessarily a zero-sum game; economic growth potentially benefits large segments of society. Average standards of living rose in the United States dramatically over the twentieth century (as measured by per capita income), as have life expectancies. Still, stratification and inequality generated by the market are phenomena that continue to cause concern among many observers in the United States and abroad. While some people remain unconcerned with inequality—believing, for example, that equality of opportunity is much more important than equality in outcomes—others contend that any economic system needs to be able to restrain inequality in order to retain its popular support and legitimacy.

Aside from the issue of how capital is distributed, economic disruptions, which are common in the market system, can also help produce economic instability and inequality. In the early 1940s economist Joseph Schumpeter popularized the idea of "creative destruction" inherent in capitalism. The term refers to the notion that capitalism prizes innovation that often disrupts the traditional order.[15] For example, in the nineteenth century the United States was largely rural, and a majority of people were engaged in farm-related activities. Industrialization, accompanied by urbanization, changed this; many workers in the countryside and small towns, such as farmers, unskilled laborers, and skilled craftsmen, were displaced by the mechanization of agriculture and the mass production of other goods. These workers, left with few relevant skills, often searched in vain for steady employment. One consequence was widespread poverty in many American cities and towns.[16]

At the turn of the twentieth century, economic instability in the United States continued. This was the era of the consolidation of large corporations. Although these corporations provided stability for many workers in core industries, such as the automobile industry, workers involved in more marginal industries were particularly susceptible to low wages, unemployment, and poverty.[17] The conflict between capital and labor reached a fever pitch in the United States early in the twentieth century. Workers in many manufacturing industries tried unionizing to bring about higher wages and better working conditions, and they were bitterly opposed by business owners.

Reformers such as President Theodore Roosevelt were dismayed by the concentration of wealth and power among prominent industrialists and giant corporations and favored a more equitable distribution of resources among the population. While World War I shifted the focus

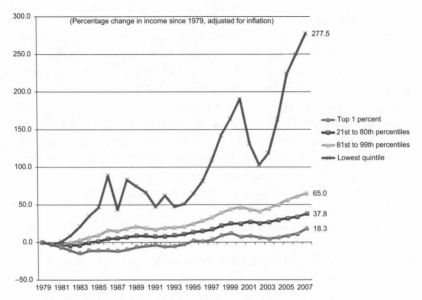

FIGURE 14. Cumulative Growth in Average After-Tax Income, by Income Group, 1979–2007. SOURCE: Congressional Budget Office 2011.

of politics to other issues, these basic tensions between capital and labor simmered through the first half of the twentieth century. Slowly, however, labor unions gathered wider acceptance, and membership grew.[18] In addition, most segments of the population shared in the economic boom that followed World War II.[19]

By the 1970s, the situation had changed once again. In addition to the slowing of economic growth, inequality began to increase. Figure 14 examines the growth in average after-tax income, by group, from 1979 to 2007. The lowest income quintile saw a modest increase in income—18 percent—over the period. Meanwhile, the middle-income group saw a 38 percent increase, the highest quintile a 65 percent increase, and the top 1 percent a full 278 percent increase in income over the period. As a result, income inequality grew substantially.[20]

This is further illustrated in figure 15, which shows the change in shares of income by each quintile. Whereas 7.1 percent of all income was held by the bottom quintile in 1979, by 2007 this share fell to 5.1 percent. The four bottom quintiles showed a drop in their share of income. In contrast, the 81st to 99th percentile of the income distribution saw a very slight increase in its share, from 35.1 to 35.6 percent, while the top 1 percent of households experienced an enormous increase

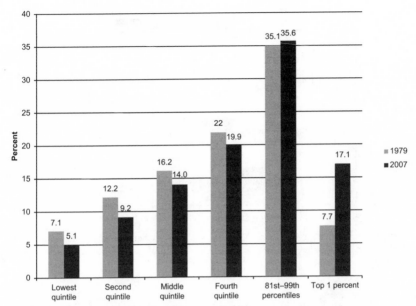

FIGURE 15. Shares of Income after Transfers and Federal Taxes, 1979 and 2007.
SOURCE: Congressional Budget Office 2011.

in its share of national income, from nearly 8 percent to over 17 percent over the period.[21] Recent data indicate that although income inequality may have dipped briefly at the start of the recession in 2007, it continued its long-term upward march in the few years afterward.[22] /

Why, more generally, after decades of decreasing inequality throughout the middle of the twentieth century, did inequality rise in the last quarter of the century? There are several, often overlapping, reasons, including the increasing demand for high-skill workers due to technological changes, globalization and international trade, the decline in unionism, the rising salaries for people who are considered "superstars," and changes in government policies that favor the rich at the expense of the poor. These are now discussed in turn.

Changes in the structure of the economy that have favored more-educated workers over less-skilled ones clearly have played a role in recent increases in inequality. Specifically, some have argued that technological advancements in the 1980s led to "skill-biased technological change" (SBTC), where workers were increasingly called upon to be familiar with computers or high-tech equipment and machinery. The increased demand for more-skilled workers drove up wages for people

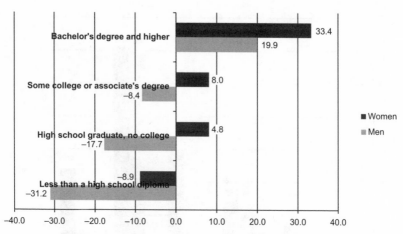

FIGURE 16. Percentage Change in Median Usual Weekly Earnings, by Educational Attainment and Gender, 1979–2010. SOURCE: Bureau of Labor Statistics 2011, chart 3.

with those skills during a time when demand for less-skilled workers also fell.[23] Thus, a much higher proportion of jobs now require, or are most suitably filled by, college graduates than before.

Much of the evidence for this hypothesis comes from the growing differences in employment and wages by level of education. Although about 90 percent of men with at least some college were in the labor force in both 1979 and 2007, labor force participation rates among those with only a high school diploma declined from 92 percent to 83 percent, and the rate among those without a high school diploma fell from 79 percent to 73 percent. Among women, the pattern differed somewhat, with women of all educational levels increasing their labor force participation from 1979 to 2007, though the increases were highest among the most educated women.[24]

Likewise, weekly wages among less-skilled men declined by 31.2 percent between 1979 and 2010, during a time when weekly earnings grew by 19.9 percent among men with a bachelor's degree or higher (see figure 16). Among women, the decline among high school dropouts was less pronounced (an 8.9 percent decline), and the increase among those with a bachelor's degree or more was even higher than among men (33.4 percent increase).[25]

Globalization and international trade may have contributed to growing wage inequality. U.S. workers increasingly compete with workers around the world. Highly skilled U.S. workers often have a comparative advantage in the global economy because of both the high quality of postsecondary education in the United States and because the headquarters of many multinational corporations, to which profits flow, are located in the United States. Conversely, many less educated American workers are at a disadvantage given the lower costs and wage levels in other parts of the globe.[26] This has at least in part contributed to the continued deindustrialization in the United States that began in the second half of the twentieth century.[27] Many of these jobs have moved to locations outside the United States where wages are lower.[28]

Apple, for example, employed 43,000 people in the United States and 20,000 overseas in 2012. This, however, is a small fraction of the more than 400,000 workers General Motors employed in the United States in the 1950s. An additional 700,000 people work for Apple's contractors to engineer, build, and assemble various Apple products, such as iPhones and iPads. Nearly all of these jobs are in Asia, Europe, and elsewhere outside the United States.[29] A *New York Times* article illustrated why many of these jobs went overseas:

> Apple executives say that going overseas, at this point, is their only option. One former executive described how the company relied upon a Chinese factory to revamp iPhone manufacturing just weeks before the device was due on shelves. Apple had redesigned the iPhone's screen at the last minute, forcing an assembly line overhaul. New screens began arriving at the plant near midnight.
>
> A foreman immediately roused 8,000 workers inside the company's dormitories, according to the executive. Each employee was given a biscuit and a cup of tea, guided to a workstation and within half an hour started a 12-hour shift fitting glass screens into beveled frames. Within 96 hours, the plant was producing over 10,000 iPhones a day.
>
> "The speed and flexibility is breathtaking," the executive said. "There's no American plant that can match that."[30]

Moreover, wages at these factories, at $17 a day, were a fraction of what U.S. employees would be paid for this kind work. Not only is low-skill work increasingly done abroad, but many middle-class jobs, such as much of the engineering work done for Apple products, are also being done abroad. The article on Apple cited above also gives the example of Eric Saragoza, a former employee of Apple:

> The first time Eric Saragoza stepped into Apple's manufacturing plant in Elk Grove, Calif., he felt as if he were entering an engineering wonderland.
>
> It was 1995, and the facility near Sacramento employed more than 1,500 workers. It was a kaleidoscope of robotic arms, conveyor belts ferrying circuit boards and, eventually, candy-colored iMacs in various stages of

assembly. Mr. Saragoza, an engineer, quickly moved up the plant's ranks and joined an elite diagnostic team. His salary climbed to $50,000. He and his wife had three children. They bought a home with a pool.

"It felt like, finally, school was paying off," he said. "I knew the world needed people who can build things."

At the same time, however, the electronics industry was changing, and Apple—with products that were declining in popularity—was struggling to remake itself. One focus was improving manufacturing. A few years after Mr. Saragoza started his job, his bosses explained how the California plant stacked up against overseas factories: the cost, excluding the materials, of building a $1,500 computer in Elk Grove was $22 a machine. In Singapore, it was $6. In Taiwan, $4.85. Wages weren't the major reason for the disparities. Rather it was costs like inventory and how long it took workers to finish a task.

"We were told we would have to do 12-hour days, and come in on Saturdays," Mr. Saragoza said. "I had a family. I wanted to see my kids play soccer."[31]

Not unrelated to this trend toward jobs going overseas, the decline of unions also likely contributed to inequality in the United States over the past few decades. The proportion of the workforce that is unionized has been falling since the 1950s, and it accelerated after the mid-1970s.[32] A mere 12 percent of workers were in unions in 2011, down from 29 percent in 1975.[33] Nonunionized workers are typically paid lower wages and have less job security than unionized ones.[34] There has been a lot of controversy about whether immigration has contributed to inequality, but, on the whole, studies suggest that immigration has served to depress the wages of native low-skill workers by only a modest amount.[35]

Why the incomes of the top 1 percent in particular have surged in recent years is not altogether clear. It seems that "superstars," such as actors, athletes, and musicians, make more than they used to, perhaps because improving standards of living and globalization have increased consumer demand and related profits. Changes in the governance and structure of executive pay, the general increase in the size and complexity of businesses, and the increasing scope of activities in the financial sector may also have played a role.[36]

A final factor contributing to inequality more generally is that the equalizing effect of government transfers and taxes on household income has been smaller in recent years than in the past. For example, the wealthy pay substantially less in taxes than they did a generation ago. This effect of government policies on poverty is discussed in more detail in chapter 7.[37]

SOCIAL STRATIFICATION: RACE, ETHNICITY, $p.89-99$
GENDER, AND CULTURE

While the economic forces described above determine overall levels of economic growth and inequality, social stratification across social ("status") groups determine, in a world of finite resources, *who* becomes poor. The main status groups in today's society are defined by the intersection of ethnic, gender, and class affiliations.[38]

Social stratification across status groups occurs when social groups seek to maximize their rewards by restricting others' access to resources and opportunities. Max Weber noted that one social group usually "takes some externally identifiable characteristic of another group—[such as] race, language, religion, local or social origin, descent, residence, etc.—as a pretext for attempting their exclusion."[39] Caste systems are an extreme form of closed stratification systems; this system, such as in the form of Jim Crow segregation, prevailed in parts of the United States until the middle of the twentieth century.

The process of stratification is usually a cumulative one. A person may begin life at a disadvantage, and disadvantages may be augmented at each stage of the life cycle, such as through the discriminatory restriction of educational opportunities, then job opportunities, and so on.[40] When stratification is so deeply ingrained in society, reducing its effects becomes very difficult. The analysis of trends in poverty that follows indicates that, although social stratification across racial, ethnic, and gender lines inhibits opportunities and serves to increase poverty among some groups, the degree of stratification across these groups diminished substantially over the last half century in the United States.

Racial and Ethnic Stratification

Several minority groups fare worse than whites according to a number of social and economic indicators. On average, minorities are more likely than whites to have lower levels of education, employment, and wages, and they are more likely to have chronic health problems—all characteristics associated with higher poverty rates.[41]

Discrimination against minority group members has historically played a critical role in producing social inequalities. More generally, discrimination arises out of competition for scarce resources and serves to protect group solidarity.[42] In the educational system, discrimination has contributed to school segregation, classroom segregation, and unequal access to high-quality facilities.[43]

Societies characterized by high levels of discrimination also usually have highly segregated labor markets where wages for the same kind of work differ across groups.[44] Disadvantaged group members may be excluded altogether from many better-paying jobs and thus have to settle for less desirable jobs, whose wages are in turn driven lower by higher levels of competition from others in a similar situation.[45]

A less overt but perhaps more common type of bias in the labor market is statistical discrimination, which refers to the tendency of employers to use generalizations in their hiring practices. Employers basically lower their cost of searching for employees by using easily identifiable characteristics, such as sex or race, to predict job performance instead of determining an individual's actual skill. This reliance on stereotypes is inherently unfair because individuals are judged not according to their ability but based upon their appearance. Shelly Lundberg and Richard Startz note that this can lead to actual differentials in skills if minority group members invest less in their education or training because they feel this type of investment would not be rewarded.[46]

Racial and ethnic minority groups in multicultural nations around the globe often struggle to obtain equal access to resources, such as jobs, education, and health services. In the United States these conflicts have a long history, though their scope and nature have changed over time. African Americans, Asian Americans, Hispanics, Native Americans, and even many white ethnic groups, such as Jews and the Irish, have all had to cope with limited opportunities, though their experiences have qualitatively differed. Below I discuss the experiences of some of these groups in more detail.

African American Poverty

The official poverty rate among African Americans was 27.6 percent in 2011, up from its historical low of 22.5 percent in 2000. This 2011 figure was substantially above the national poverty rate of 15.0 (see figure 17). The relatively high black poverty rate is a function of lower black employment levels, wages, and differences in family structure (the last is discussed below). The black unemployment rate in January of 2012, for example, was 13.6 percent—nearly double the white unemployment rate of 7.4 percent.[47] The median earnings of black men and women working full time were $633 and $592 in 2010, respectively—considerably lower than the earnings of white men and women working full time, at $850 and $684.[48] Disparities in wealth are even starker.

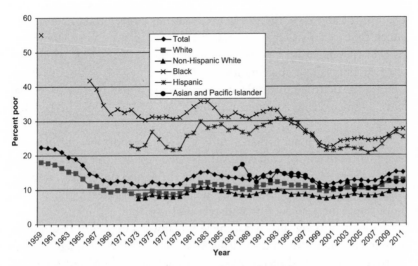

FIGURE 17. Official Poverty Rates by Race and Hispanic Origin, 1959–2011. SOURCE: U.S. Census Bureau 2012f.

The median net worth of white households was $113,149 in 2009; for blacks, it was only $5,677.[49]

African Americans, who comprised close to 13 percent of the U.S. population in 2010, historically had to contend with acute forms of discrimination, including a severely constrained labor market throughout the nineteenth century and into the twentieth. After the abolition of slavery during the Civil War, blacks in the South often worked as sharecroppers, primarily because they were barred by law or custom from most other full-time jobs outside the black community. In addition, under the Jim Crow system, most blacks who lived in cities were employed as common laborers or as domestic and personal servants. Opportunities for promotion and advancement were uncommon, if not nonexistent, for African Americans in these and other occupations.[50]

William Julius Wilson, among others, has argued that the traditional patterns of interaction between African Americans and whites in the labor market have fundamentally changed in recent decades, and that economic class position is now more important than race in determining success among African Americans.[51] From the antebellum period through the first half of the twentieth century, racial oppression was deliberate, overt, and easily observable, ranging from slavery to segregation. By the latter half of the twentieth century, many traditional barriers were dismantled as a result of the political, social, and economic changes of the civil rights era. Wilson emphasizes that it is not so much that racial segregation and discrimination have been eliminated as that they have become less rampant, whereas economic conditions play an increasingly important role in determining black disadvantage. He argues that deindustrialization and class segregation in particular have hampered the economic mobility of less-skilled blacks in the labor market.[52]

Glenn Loury asserts that although discrimination in *contract*—the unequal treatment of otherwise similar people based on race in formal transactions—has declined drastically in the period since 1965, discrimination in *contact* remains more prevalent. The latter highlights the importance of associations and relationships that are formed among individuals in social life as a vehicle for upward mobility. Discrimination in contact means that African Americans are not included in many of these useful social relationships, leading to lower levels of the social capital that is often crucial to achieving economic success.[53]

Empirical studies tend to show that the economic penalty of race—and of being African American in particular—has declined since the 1960s. Occupational mobility has increased, as has wage parity.[54] But because the level of employment discrimination is difficult to measure and quantify, it is difficult to say precisely to what extent discrimination still directly contributes to racial income disparities and poverty. Studies tend to indicate that discrimination still occurs in labor markets and in other areas. For example, paired-test studies, in which minority job applicants were paired with white applicants with similar backgrounds and trained to be as similar as possible in behavior, have shown that minorities, particularly African Americans and foreign-sounding Latinos, were less likely to receive job interviews and offers, at least in the low-wage labor market.[55] Economists have estimated that perhaps one-quarter of the black-white wage gap is due to prejudice, suggesting that racism continues to contribute to African American economic disadvantage.[56]

Other factors—some related to race and others nonracial in origin—have also contributed to relatively high levels of African American poverty. One of the former is racial residential segregation. Douglas Massey and Nancy Denton have argued that segregation, interacting with economic forces, reinforces minority poverty by limiting minority individuals' access to the potentially broad range of metropolitan area employment opportunities.[57] Since a significant portion of school funding comes from local taxes, segregation can serve to reinforce educational inequalities as well. High levels of segregation may contribute to ethnic stereotypes that give rise to discrimination in employers' hiring patterns and contribute segregated job referral networks.[58] Declining levels of black segregation in recent decades and rapid black suburbanization have likely reduced the effects of segregation in contributing to racial inequalities over the past couple of decades. However, many cities—particularly some in the Northeast and Midwest such as Chicago, New York, Detroit, and Milwaukee—still have very high levels of black segregation.[59]

Two economic factors less directly associated with race that have contributed to black disadvantage are the decline in the strength of unions and deindustrialization. Black women had benefited from public sector unionism in particular, and black men benefited from industrial unionism in the post–World War II period.[60] African Americans have been especially affected by deindustrialization because, as late as the 1968–70 period, more than 70 percent of all blacks working in metropolitan areas held blue-collar jobs at the same time that more than 50 percent of all metropolitan workers held white-collar jobs.[61]

Another factor that contributes to higher poverty rates among African Americans is human-capital skills differentials. This refers to differences in average levels of education, quality of educational opportunities, and subsequent work experience and skills. The gap in average levels of education has declined over the past few decades. Nevertheless, the quality of schooling received by children in the United States varies widely, and African Americans are more likely to attend inferior schools with fewer resources. Lower employment levels among young African Americans subsequently contribute to earnings differentials. High black incarceration rates (black men are eight times more likely to be incarcerated than white men) means that a relatively high proportion of young black men enter the labor force with a criminal record, which further hinders their employability.[62]

Thus, some have emphasized that poverty often persists across generations because of *cumulative disadvantages*. This means there is no single "cure" for poverty, and this also helps explain why poverty among African Americans has been slow to decline.[63] Even as race has become less important in American society, economic inequality and class background have become more important. As a result, although we have seen considerable growth in the black middle class in recent decades,[64] the economic challenges faced by poor African Americans remain daunting.

Poverty among Other Minority Groups

Some of the factors that have hampered African American economic well-being, such as discrimination, segregation, and human capital differentials, have historically also affected other minority groups, including Latinos, Asian Americans, and Native Americans.

Hispanics have a long history in the United States, dating at least as far back as the annexation of territory in Florida in the early 1800s and, in 1848, huge swaths of land from Mexico extending from Texas westward to California. Mexican Americans were often treated as second-class citizens in these territories. In more recent decades, there has been a growth in the population of Hispanics from other areas of Latin America, including Puerto Rico, Cuba, and the Dominican Republic.

Asians historically suffered discriminatory treatment in immigration policies limiting their arrival. The 1882 Chinese Exclusion Act barred the immigration of Chinese laborers, and immigration from Japan was completely halted in 1924. By the early decades of the twentieth century, Japanese and Chinese immigrants were denied citizenship and voting rights and were prevented from joining most labor unions. Through intimidation and discrimination, whites limited the economic achievement of Asian Americans.[65] Asians today have many origins, including China, the Philippines, India, Vietnam, and Korea.

Latinos and Asian Americans thus share certain commonalities: both have historically been discriminated against, both experienced substantial increases in their population due to immigration since the 1960s, and are both very heterogeneous in terms of their national origins. The increase in immigration from non-European countries—and especially from Asia and later Africa—is a direct consequence of the passage of the Immigration and Nationality Act of 1965, also known as the Hart-Celler Act. This act eliminated the discriminatory national quota system that favored Northern and Western Europeans and opened immigration to a wider variety of countries. A surge of immigration from Asia followed the passage of the act. Immigration from a wide array of countries and from Africa also broadened some years later. Latin American immigration, which was never subject to formal quotas until the passage of the act, nevertheless gradually increased in the post–World War II period, and this increase continued through the 1960s and the decades after.[66]

As a consequence, the percentage of all immigrants who were from Europe was only 12 percent in 2010, down from 86 percent in the 1900–1920 period. The share of immigrants from Asia grew from

4 percent to 28 percent and from Latin America from 10 percent to 53 percent over the same time period. Although the percentage of all immigrants from Africa in 2010 was relatively small (4 percent), the number of African immigrants has nevertheless been growing rapidly in recent years.[67]

As was indicated in figure 17 above, poverty rates vary widely across these racial and ethnic groups. The Latino poverty rate of 25.3 percent was twice as high as the Asian poverty rate (12.3 percent) in 2011. Differences in the characteristics of the immigrants coming to the United States and in the levels of education of immigrants and native-born people of each of the two groups explain many of these differences. Immigration plays a large role for both Asians and Hispanics because nearly two-thirds of Asians are foreign-born, as are about 40 percent of Hispanics.[68] Many more are of the second generation.

Immigrants typically have different labor force outcomes than natives. On the one hand, immigrants are often a "select" group of people who frequently possess qualities such as ambition and eagerness to learn that are helpful in achieving economic success. On the other hand, limited language proficiency and unfamiliarity with American customs and the labor market considerably hinder immigrant economic mobility, especially in the years immediately after arrival. Overall, immigrant families are at greater risk of poverty than nonimmigrant families. Yet over time and subsequent generations, labor market barriers become less important. Immigrants and then their children become more similar to the native-born population in terms of their employment, earnings, English-language fluency, fertility, and poverty the longer they have been in the United States.[69] This process is often termed "assimilation." The fact that levels of immigration have been quite high in recent decades has put a modest upward pressure on national poverty rates, at least in the short run, because of high poverty rates among immigrants themselves. Immigration may have also put some downward pressure on the wages of less-educated natives (those without a high school diploma) through labor market competition, though immigration has had little effect on the wages of others.[70]

Table 5 illustrates patterns of poverty by race/ethnicity and nativity. While the overall poverty rate in 2011 was 15.0 percent, it was moderately lower among the native born (14.4 percent) than the foreign born (19.0 percent). We see considerable variation among the foreign born by citizenship status: the poverty rate among naturalized citizens was only 12.5 percent, versus 24.3 percent among noncitizens.[71] Naturalized citizens

TABLE 5   POVERTY RATES BY NATIVITY AND RACE AND HISPANIC ORIGIN, 2011

	Percent poor
Total population	15.0
Native born	14.4
Foreign born	19.0
Naturalized citizen	12.5
Not a citizen	24.3
White	12.8
Native born	11.9
Foreign born	20.8
Naturalized citizen	13.5
Not a citizen	25.8
Black	27.6
Native born	28.0
Foreign born	23.5
Naturalized citizen	19.8
Not a citizen	26.9
Asian	12.3
Native born	11.6
Foreign born	12.7
Naturalized citizen	8.1
Not a citizen	18.2
Hispanic (of any race)	25.3
Native born	25.8
Foreign born	24.4
Naturalized citizen	15.6
Not a citizen	28.7

SOURCE: U.S. Census Bureau 2012a.

have low poverty rates for a few reasons. They have lived in the United States for at least five years (often considerably longer) in order to become citizens, and thus they are much more likely to be acculturated to the English language, American customs, and the workings of the U.S. labor market. Their poverty rates are lower than even among the native born, perhaps because, like immigrants more generally, they often possess qualities such as ambition and eagerness to learn that are helpful in achieving success. In addition, immigrants who become naturalized citizens have higher levels of education than the native-born population. For example, while 30 percent of the native population twenty-five years old and over had a bachelor's degree or more in 2010, the corresponding figure among naturalized citizens was 35 percent. In contrast, noncitizen poverty rates are higher than others because many of them are recent immigrants and still unaccustomed to the United States, and they may not have the legal status to access the full range of economic opportunities and government benefits available to citizens. They also have lower levels of education: only 24 percent had a bachelor's degree or more in 2010.[72]

These general patterns hold especially for Asians and Hispanics, where noncitizens have the highest poverty rates and naturalized citizens have the lowest. The main difference between the two groups is that Hispanic poverty rates are considerably higher than Asian ones among all subgroups. The pattern by nativity and citizenship differs only slightly for whites, where the native born have a slightly lower poverty rate (11.9 percent) than naturalized citizens (13.5 percent). However, the pattern for blacks differs. As with Asians and Hispanics, foreign-born blacks who are naturalized citizens have a lower poverty rate (19.8 percent) than noncitizens (26.9 percent). However, among blacks, even noncitizens have a lower poverty rate than native-born blacks (28.0 percent). Among other factors that could be at work here, black immigrants have higher levels of educational attainment and are much less likely to be in a single-parent family than native-born blacks, and this serves to lower poverty among the foreign-born black population.[73]

Back to the general issue of differences in poverty across racial/ethnic groups, these figures suggest that immigrants from Asia tend to comprise a more "select" group than immigrants from Latin America. Immigrants from Korea, India, and the Philippines exhibit higher average levels of education than both Latinos and native-born whites. For example, four-fifths of immigrants from India have a bachelor's degree or more, compared with 6 percent from Mexico.[74] One factor explaining these differences is that while many immigrants from Asia become eligible to migrate to the United States because of their work-related skills, a larger proportion of immigrants from Latin America immigrate because they have relatives who are U.S. citizens.[75]

It is of course important to note that poverty also varies considerably by country of origin among immigrants; not all Asian and Hispanic subgroups are similarly advantaged or disadvantaged. Among foreign-born Hispanics, for example, poverty rates in 2007 (before the spike in poverty rates in the Great Recession) were high among Dominicans (28 percent) and Mexicans (22 percent) but more moderate among Cubans (16 percent) and Colombians (11 percent). Among Asian immigrant groups, poverty rates were a little higher for Koreans (17 percent) and lower for immigrants from Japan (9 percent), India (7 percent), and the Philippines (4 percent).[76] Many of these differences are likely rooted in the average characteristics of the immigrants themselves (especially educational attainment), though each group has a unique history of immigration to the United States.

As discussed above, initial disadvantages tend to persist over time and across generations. Native-born Hispanics obtain on average higher levels of education than immigrant Hispanics, but their educational levels still lag behind those of native-born whites, largely because of their lower initial level of family resources.[77] In contrast, native-born Asian Americans tend to have high levels of education, which translate into better jobs, higher incomes, and less poverty. In 2010, the median income of Asian households was $64,208—considerably higher than the median household incomes of non-Hispanic whites ($54,620), Hispanics ($37,759), and blacks ($32,068).[78] Asian Americans have also gained greater access to high-tier technical and professional occupations. Once family characteristics are taken into account, there is little difference in the poverty rates between native-born Asians and native-born non-Hispanic whites.[79] Latinos, however, are less likely to have a college degree and tend to work in lower-skill, lower-wage jobs.

The research literature does not offer a definitive answer as to the extent of racial/ethnic discrimination faced by Asians and Latinos in the labor market. For Asians, it is probably safe to say that discrimination is not widespread enough to significantly affect their levels of poverty. For Latinos, especially lighter-skinned individuals, it is likely that family background characteristics (such as education and income) play the most prominent role and ethnicity a more minor one. Race appears to continue to play a significant role in explaining lower wages and higher poverty among blacks and perhaps darker-skinned Latinos.[80]

The experience of Native Americans differs from that of all of the other groups. In addition to historically being forcibly removed from their land to reservations, Native Americans have had to overcome a dearth of job opportunities in and around reservations as well as low levels of educational attainment. The poverty rate among Native Americans in 2011 was 29.5 percent, a little higher than African American and Latino poverty rates.[81] Some evidence indicates a decline of the net negative effect of being Native American on wages over the last half of the twentieth century.[82] However, Native Americans still have lower levels of educational attainment and earnings than otherwise comparable whites. It is not clear whether it is discrimination or other difficult-to-observe factors correlated with being Native American that explain these differences.[83] Quantitative research on Native Americans tends to be more limited than that on other groups, in part due to the relatively small Native American population. Additional research on Native Americans, not to mention the other groups, would help shed further light on the complex interrelationship between race and poverty.

Overall, we see significant differences in poverty by race/ethnicity. Some of the continuing differences, particularly among blacks and perhaps Native Americans, can be explained by prejudice, stereotypes, and discrimination. However, most research has indicated that the importance of race alone in determining life chances has declined substantially in recent decades. The civil rights movement abolished legal forms of racial and ethnic discrimination, and whites are less likely to express blatantly racist attitudes than they did in past decades.[84] Nevertheless, as the salience of race has declined, the importance of socioeconomic background has increased. For example, although the black-white reading gap was substantially larger than the rich-poor reading gap in the 1940s, by the 2000s the reverse was true.[85] Unfortunately, the increasing importance of socioeconomic background serves to slow progress in reducing racial disparities, as initial disadvantages among groups have a way persisting across generations (see chapter 3 for more on the intergenerational transmission of poverty).

Gender and Poverty

The term *feminization of poverty* was coined by Diana Pearce in a 1978 article in which she argued that poverty was "rapidly becoming a female problem."[86] The term gained further currency in the 1980s and early 1990s. Women's poverty rates were 55 percent higher than men's in 1968, then peaked at 72 percent higher in 1978. The differential has gradually narrowed, such that by 2011, the female poverty rate (16.3 percent) was only moderately (20 percent) higher than the male poverty rate (13.6 percent). Women comprised from 57 to 58 percent of the poverty population over the 1966 to 2000 period, before declining to 56 percent in 2011.[87] Overall, the empirical claim for an accelerating "feminization of poverty" is weak, though female poverty rates do remain higher than those of men.[88]

Women tend to have higher poverty rates than men for two main reasons: 1) their employment levels and wages are lower, and 2) they are more likely to be the heads of single-parent families (discussed below).[89] Elderly women are also more likely to be poor than elderly men because of fewer economic resources—such as less Social Security income—but also because of higher female life expectancies, which make elderly women more likely to live alone than men.[90]

Many have argued that women's lower economic status reflects the unequal distribution of power in society. Men have historically excluded women from many kinds of jobs and limited women's social roles more generally. Labor market discrimination is a manifestation of unequal power. First, discrimination occurs when men are paid more than women for the same work. Second, discrimination contributes to occupational sex segregation—where men and women are highly concentrated in different types of jobs. The result is that women's work is typically accorded both lower status and lower earnings than occupations with high concentrations of men.[91]

Inequality in the labor market may also occur due to common social practices or discrimination prior to a person's entrance into the labor market, such as in the education system or in the family. For example, girls have traditionally been socialized into family-oriented roles, while boys and young men have been expected to build careers that pay enough to support a family.[92]

Gender norms have changed over time. The women's rights movement that took flight in the 1960s pressed for more equal treatment in the workplace, such as in the form of equal pay for equal work, and for the easing of gender roles that limited women's opportunities in society at large. Until that time women were rarely in positions of power—whether in private business or politics—nor were they represented in a wide range of professional occupations, such as lawyers, judges, doctors, professors, or scientists. For a while, progress in reducing inequalities seemed slow. Figure 18 shows the change in the female-to-male ratio of earnings since 1960. It relies upon a common indicator of the gender wage gap, women's median annual earnings as a percentage of men's among full-time, year-round workers. While the ratio of earnings did not budge (remaining at close to 60 percent) over the period from 1960 to 1980, it finally began to increase thereafter. By 2011 such women earned 77 percent of what men earned.[93]

Why does some gap still remain? In contrast to the blatant gender discrimination that occurred in the past, the gap today is probably best explained by gender socialization and women's resulting weaker attachment to the labor market. A greater percentage of women than men still

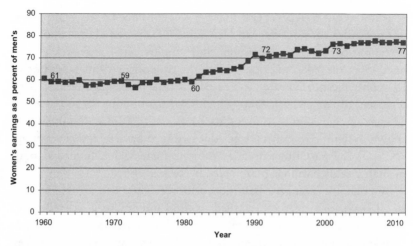

FIGURE 18. Women's Median Annual Earnings as a Percentage of Men's Earnings for Full-Time, Year-Round Workers, 1960–2011. SOURCE: U.S. Census Bureau 2012n.

tend to leave the labor force for childbirth, child care, and elder care. As of 2009 about a quarter of married-couple households with children had a stay-at-home mother, down from 44 percent in 1969.[94] Stay-at-home dads have until recently been viewed as oddities, and this arrangement is still relatively rare. This leads to a lower accumulation of human capital and hence lower pay for women. Similarly, working mothers tend to value workplaces that have "family-friendly" policies; many of these offer less pay, if perhaps better fringe benefits. One study estimated that once many of these factors are taken into account, the gender wage gap is reduced to between 4.8 and 7.1 percent (rather than about 20 percent).[95] It is not clear what explains the remaining difference; it could, of course, reflect continued gender discrimination in the labor market or other harder-to-measure factors.

It is important to note that studies have noted that wage parity is also greater among younger women and men than among older workers. For example, one study found that women 16 to 34 years old make somewhere between 91 and 95 percent of what men make, even without taking into account the wide array of factors described above. In contrast, women above 35 years old earned between 75 and 80 percent of similarly aged men.[96] Some of the movement toward gender inequality has been the result of a gradual process of "cohort replacement," where younger women are taking on new roles and earning more in the labor market than their mothers.[97]

Some recent trends suggest that we will continue to see a narrowing of the gender earnings gap. In fact, some have raised alarms about the deterioration in the educational and employment outcomes among men. Over the 1969 to 2009 period, the proportion of men ages 25 to 64 who were not working increased by 11.8 percentage points (from 6 percent to 18 percent). Among high school dropouts, the increase was 23 percentage points (from 11 to 34 percent).[98] In addition, as was shown in figure 16, only college-educated men have seen their earnings rise over the past three decades. Among male high school dropouts, median weekly earnings plummeted by 38 percent.

Women now comprise half the workforce. They also earn 58 percent of all bachelor's degrees awarded in the United States, as well as 59 percent of master's degrees and about half of the doctoral degrees. Women are likewise awarded about half of law and medical degrees. The general educational advantage among women occurs among all racial and ethnic groups, but it is largest among blacks, where, for example, women earn 66 percent of all bachelor's degrees awarded.[99] These trends strongly suggest that women's relative economic position will rise in the coming years.

Family Structure and Poverty

Family arrangements have become more diverse (and often more complicated) over the past several decades, as have the life course trajectories of individuals. Getting married before having a baby is no longer particularly normative. Whereas in 1940 only 2 percent of births were to unmarried women, by 2009 this figure had risen to 41 percent (see figure 19). Moreover, more than half of births to young women— those under 30—occur outside marriage. These percentages have been growing for all racial and ethnic groups. The proportion of all white births to unmarried women increased sharply over the past two decades, from 20 percent in 1990 to 36 percent in 2009. Among black women, increases occurred earlier; from 1970 to 1990 the percentage of births to unmarried black women jumped from 38 to 67 percent before gradually continuing to drift upward to 72 percent in 2009. In 2009, over half of Hispanic births (53 percent) were to unmarried women. Only among Asians is the corresponding figure is much lower; in 2009, it was 17 percent.[100] Indicative of the rising importance of class background in U.S. society, there is even greater variation by levels of education than by race: about 92 percent of women with a bachelor's degree or more

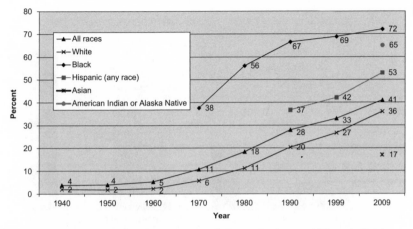

FIGURE 19. Percentage of Births to Unmarried Women by Race and Hispanic Origin, 1940–2009. SOURCE: Ventura and Bachrach 2000; Martin et al. 2011.

are married when they give birth, compared with 62 percent of women with some post-secondary schooling and 43 percent of women with a high school diploma or less.[101]

Complicating the picture, however, is the fact that much of the rise in nonmarital births in recent years has occurred among cohabiting couples. In fact, more than half of nonmarital births occur within cohabiting relationships, compared with 29 percent in the early 1990s.[102] Thus, the actual percentage of families headed by single women living alone (without a coresident partner of one sort or another) has not changed much since about 1995. As of 2010, 26 percent of all families, 21 percent of white families, 29 percent of Hispanic families, and 55 percent of African American families were headed by a single woman living with no other parent present in the household (i.e., no spouse or cohabiting partner).[103] While cohabiting couples in many ways resemble married families, such unions are nevertheless more than twice as likely to dissolve than marriages. About two-thirds of cohabiting couples split by the time their child turns ten, compared with 28 percent of married couples.[104]

The contribution of single parenthood to higher levels of poverty among African American families was discussed by E. Franklin Frazier in 1932 and 1939, Gunnar Myrdal in 1944, Daniel Patrick Moynihan in 1965, and many others since.[105] In recent years there has growing alarm at the growing number of children born to unwed white women as well, most notably in the 2012 book *Coming Apart* by conservative

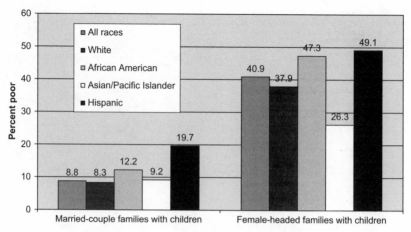

FIGURE 20. Poverty Rates of Families by Family Structure and Race and Hispanic Origin, 2011. SOURCE: U.S. Census Bureau 2012e.

commentator Charles Murray.[106] Numerous reasons have been offered for changing family formation patterns, including changes in social norms and the declining economic fortunes of men, issues that are discussed in more detail in the following section.

The crux of the problem with this general trend is that single-parent families with children headed by women are considerably more likely to be poor. While the poverty rate among married-couple families with children was 8.8 percent in 2011, it was 40.9 percent among female-headed families with children (see figure 20).[107] Poverty rates also vary by ethnicity, ranging from 8.3 percent among white married-couple families to 49.1 percent among Hispanic female-headed families with children. The poverty rate for people in female-householder families has declined—from 60 percent in 1959 to 44 percent in 1970 to a low of 33 percent in 2000 before edging up thereafter.[108]

Poverty is high among female-headed families for several reasons. Single mothers (and fathers) often face the challenge of supporting a family on one income, as well as finding and paying for child care while they work and running a household alone when they do not. Children add to living costs but usually do not contribute to family income. Lower average levels of education among women who head such families also contribute significantly to their lower earnings.[109] Furthermore, as discussed above, women tend to earn less than men, and mothers tend to accumulate less experience than other workers.[110] Finally, many such families do not receive sufficient child support from the children's absent fathers.[111] However, research tends to show that even if all families received the full amount of child support due them, poverty rates would decline only a little. While many fathers deliberately evade their child support obligations, others simply earn too little to pay much.[112] It should be noted that even cohabiting couples also have significantly higher poverty rates than married-couple families, mainly because they have lower levels of education and are younger. For example, one study reported that while the poverty rate among children living with their married biological parents was 7.6 percent, among children living with cohabiting biological parents the poverty rate was 23.2 percent.[113]

Low-income single parents (if not all low-income families) often have to make trade-offs. Child care in particular often raises daunting challenges. Some single parents handle this by taking jobs that allow them to work primarily at home or take their children with them. As one respondent reported in an ethnographic study by Kathryn Edin and Laura Lein:

> I had a better job, an office job, but I left it for a job as a salesperson for a chemical manufacturer's rep—it was a perfect job because I didn't have [supervision]. My boss was in Atlanta, and I was here. So when the kids were real sick, I would stay home with them. If they were medium sick, I could take them with me in the car and drive around. When they started school, I was here to meet their bus everyday. Whatever paperwork or anything, I did at night. It didn't pay well, about $5, but it gave me an opportunity not to have my kids feel abandoned.[114]

Similarly, in his book on the working poor, David Shipler describes the challenges faced by Caroline, a low-income woman with a daughter, Amber:

> After a month the [temporary employment] agency tempted Caroline with a job back at the Tampax factory for $10 an hour, the most she had ever earned. She took it, but there was a problem: Proctor & Gamble had organized the factory on rotating shifts. One week she left the house at 5:30 a.m. and got home at 2:30 p.m., the next week she left at 1:30 p.m. and was home by 10:30 p.m., and the third she left home at 9:30 p.m. and returned at 6:30 a.m. Putting aside the question of sleep, stamina, and the basic requirements of an orderly life, the "swing shifts," as they were called, raised havoc with Caroline's arrangements for Amber. She had rented rooms to boarders occasionally or taken in homeless families so Amber wouldn't be alone. But these situations never lasted long; Caroline found the people intrusive or bossy or dishonest. . . . Without the boarders, though, Caroline had nobody to look after Amber, so she very reluctantly left the girl home alone during her evening and nighttime shifts. While Caroline was running the machines that put tampons into boxes, she was worrying about Amber, and with good cause.[115]

Some studies suggest that changes in family structure played a significant role in growing child poverty rates from the early 1970s through the mid-1990s due to the aforementioned declines in the proportion of children living in married-couple families during that time.[116] Yet the poverty rate among female-headed families declined in the 1990s, mainly because of very substantial increases in the employment of single mothers. The greatest rise in employment among such mothers occurred in the 1990s, coinciding with changing welfare policies that make it more difficult to receive benefits without working. The employment rate of never-married mothers, who were the most likely to have little education or job experience and long stays on welfare, rose from 43 percent in 1992 to 65 percent in 1999.[117] However, reflecting more recent increases in poverty rates among female-headed families, the percentage of single mothers who were employed fell from 76 percent in 2000 to 73 percent in 2007, and then to 68 percent in 2009 in the wake of the Great Recession.[118]

Cross-national comparisons suggest that while single-parent families are more vulnerable to poverty than others, their poverty rates are nevertheless not inherently extremely high. Using a relative poverty line equaling 50 percent of the national median income, the poverty rate in the mid-2000s for children in single-mother families in Sweden, for example, was 10.4 percent. For children in single-father families it was 5.9 percent, and in two-parent families it was 3.3 percent. The corresponding figures in the United States using this relative measure were 50.5 percent, 19.5 percent, and 13.1 percent.[119] High employment rates among women, lower general wage inequality in the labor market, and generous government transfer policies help explain these low poverty rates in single-parent families in Sweden.[120] Nevertheless, in the twenty countries included in this study, poverty rates in single-mother families tended to be considerably higher than among two-parent families. Relative poverty rates in single-parent families in Anglophone countries (Australia, Canada, Ireland, the United Kingdom, and the United States) averaged 41 percent, compared to 10 percent in two-parent families. Even in lower-poverty countries in continental Europe (Austria, Germany, Luxembourg, the Netherlands, and Switzerland), relative poverty rates among single-mother families averaged 27 percent, compared to 8 percent among two-parent families.[121] What, then, explains the rising prevalence of single-parent families in the United States, and indeed in many rich countries around the world? We now turn to this debate.

Culture and Poverty

Culture is often a politically loaded term in discussions of poverty. It has at times been invoked to "blame the victim," or to blame poor people for their poverty because of their supposed wayward values and lifestyles, such as their sexual promiscuity, criminal behavior, or drug use. Culture is hard to define and likewise difficult to measure. Today, the view that cultural behavior contributes to poverty differentials tends to be associated with conservative commentators, though this has not always been the case.

In the 1920s, a number of sociologists from the University of Chicago and their students began to focus more systematically on the effect of social disorganization on poor people. Poverty was thought to result from temporary "cultural breakdown" that occurred in many immigrant and, in the case of African Americans, migrant communities in urban and industrial cities. The breakdown of social controls and customs led to increased crime, out-of-wedlock births, family breakup, and economic dependency.[122]

Following the lead of Booker T. Washington (in 1902), sociologists such as Gunnar Myrdal (1944) and E. Franklin Frazier (1932, 1939), in adopting these arguments, were debunking the idea that the poor—and poor African Americans in particular—were genetically inferior.[123] They traced the roots of racial inequality to a wide range of factors, including racism and discrimination, which helped produce a deviant cultural response. Frazier, for example, saw "Negro matriarchy" as an accommodation to slavery and black male joblessness, and therefore a common feature of lower-class culture and poverty.[124] Similarly, other progressives at the beginning of the twentieth century deemphasized the notion that southern and eastern European immigrants were genetically inferior by arguing that immigrants needed to be Americanized and adapt to mainstream American values and culture.[125]

In the two decades after World War II, however, there was greater discussion of a culture of poverty without reference to broader social and economic conditions. These arguments echoed nineteenth-century beliefs about the "undeserving" poor. Oscar Lewis, quoted at the beginning of this chapter, was a strong promoter of the culture of poverty thesis. Lewis believed that the poor contribute to their own impoverishment and identified seventy behavioral traits that distinguish the poor.[126] In the late 1950s, Edward Banfield asserted, "The lower-class person lives from moment to moment, he is either unable or unwilling to take into account the future or to control his impulses . . . being improvident and irresponsible, he is likely also to be unskilled, to move frequently from one dead-end job to another, to be a poor husband and father."[127]

Recent observers who have adopted this view—that the poor are essentially different, governed by their own code of values and behavior—tend to emphasize that wayward government policies aimed at helping the poor are often responsible for their degraded position. The argument goes that in the post–Great Society era of the 1960s, high welfare benefit levels provided work disincentives and encouraged dependency. The resulting culture of poverty consists of an eroded work ethic, dependency on government programs, lack of educational aspiration and achievement, increased single parenthood and illegitimacy, criminal activity, and drug and alcohol abuse.[128] Policy did not reward good behavior and did little to penalize harmful behavior. All of these problems in turn have an adverse effect on patterns of income and poverty, producing a vicious cycle of multigenerational dependency, especially in neighborhoods with high poverty levels. Charles Murray has been the most effective proponent of this view, and the debate of these issues contributed to the passage of welfare reform in the mid-1990s, which ended a system of guaranteed cash transfers to poor female-headed families as long as they remained poor.[129]

The debate on this issue is far from over. At the risk of oversimplification, there are two basic camps. On the one hand are those who continue to invoke the preeminence of culture in explaining high rates of single motherhood, and thus disadvantage, among a large swath of Americans. In his most recent book, *Coming Apart: The State of White America, 1960–2010*, Charles Murray focuses on whites, in part to avoid a potentially racially tinged debate and to focus on fairly striking recent trends in births to unmarried white women (see figure 19 above). He argues that cultural norms in America have sharply diverged since the early 1960s.

Specifically, today we have a group consisting of affluent, highly educated whites who overwhelmingly decide to get married before having children and who live in residential enclaves surrounded by like-minded people. They value marriage, diligence, honesty, and religiosity, and this allows them to enjoy secure and affluent lives. Their choices are also a function of their higher cognitive abilities, which allow them to plan ahead and envision the consequences of their actions. The second group is the less-educated lower class, which has experienced an erosion of family and community life, and where having children outside marriage has become the norm. Murray attributes the declining fortunes of the lower class to the corresponding decline in traditional values that emphasize marriage, honesty, hard work, and religiosity. This population finds itself at or near the bottom of the economic ladder because its members, on average, have less cognitive ability—and are thus more poorly equipped to resist the lure of the sexual revolution and doctrines of self-actualization. They live in different neighborhoods than the elite and therefore lack appropriate role models. They thus succumb to higher rates of family dissolution, nonmarital births, nonwork, and criminality. Murray further takes liberal elites to task because they do not do enough to publicly defend and affirm the traditional values to which they personally sub-scribe, and this has served to both exacerbate growing class divisions in society and will lead inexorably to America's decline unless this unhealthy dynamic is reversed.[130]

There are those who vehemently disagree with Murray's analysis and instead focus on economic trends as underpinning the growth in non-marital births. Specifically, marriage has historically been an economic or social arrangement between families (rather than just individuals), often to ensure their survival. The modal family arrangement in indus-trialized countries in the nineteenth and much of the twentieth century was one of specialization: the husband earned his wage working outside the home while the wife focused on home production, taking care of household work and raising the children.[131]

In recent decades, this line of thinking asserts, the decline in job opportunities for low-skill workers—a consequence of deindustrializa-tion, globalization, and the decline in unionism—is the main driver of declining marriage rates and growing income inequality in America, not changes in culture. Less educated men, whose wages have indeed declined substantially in recent decades, have been particularly harmed by the transformation of the economy. This has led to a reduction in the number of "marriageable" men. Women, whose educational attain-ment and labor force participation has continued to increase, see fewer reasons to get married.[132]

In elucidating this view—and as a response to Murray—columnist Nicholas Kristof writes:

> Eighty percent of the people in my high school cohort dropped out or didn't pursue college because it used to be possible to earn a solid living at the steel mill, the glove factory or sawmill. That's what their parents had done. But the glove factory closed, working-class jobs collapsed and unskilled laborers found themselves competing with immigrants. . . . So let's get real. A crisis is

developing in the white working class, a byproduct of growing income inequality in America. The pathologies are achingly real. But the solution isn't finger-wagging, or averting our eyes—but opportunity.[133]

A fair reckoning of these two arguments—one economic and one cultural—is that both have elements of truth to them. Below I draw extensively from an excellent review of the social scientific literature on the reasons behind the rise in nonmarital births by longtime family researcher Pamela Smock and her coauthor Fiona Rose Greenland.[134] They note that unmarried couples with children articulate at least three perceived obstacles to marriage: concerns about financial stability, relationship quality, and fear of divorce, with financial concerns often the paramount issue.[135] Women (and men) value marriage and aspire to it, but, because of fears about divorce, they believe that marriage should occur after financial stability is achieved. Low-income women, because of their low earnings expectations, have less to lose by having children early and outside marriage; they also place a very high value on children as adding meaning to their lives.[136] In addition, good mothering is seen by this group as something that does not require tremendous resources, as it basically involves being there for the children—an approach to parenting that differs from that of the middle class.[137]

Sociologist Andrew Cherlin has noted that the symbolic importance of marriage has increased over time, and it now represents achievement and signifies prestige. Americans also expect more from marriage in the form of emotional fulfillment and as a means of self-actualization than they did previously, when it was generally seen as an arrangement for practical support. In essence, whereas economic struggle during the early years of marriage was a normative assumption in an earlier era, nowadays there is a widespread perception that marriage should occur after financial goals have already been reached, perhaps to help ensure its stability in a era of high divorce rates. As a result, low-income women generally view marriage as something to which to aspire, whereas parenthood is attainable regardless of financial stability or marital status.[138] The declining economic fortunes of low-skill men, and indeed the growth of income inequality, has made marriage seem less attainable.

Smock and Greenland also note that cohabitation offers a marriage-like relationship with many of the same advantages of marriage, such as companionship, shared expenses, sexual access, childbearing, and child rearing. With cohabitation available as an increasingly normative option, the incentive to get married has declined. This helps explain rapid increases in cohabitation in recent years.

A news story on rising nonmarital births in the United States offered the following anecdote that would seem to support this view, and which highlights the importance of both economic conditions and the role of values and norm, and hence culture:

> Over the past generation, Lorain lost most of two steel mills, a shipyard and a Ford factory, diminishing the supply of jobs that let blue-collar workers raise middle-class families. More women went to work, making marriage less of a financial necessity for them. Living together became routine, and single motherhood lost the stigma that once sent couples rushing to the altar. Women here often describe marriage as a sign of having arrived rather than a way to get there.
>
> Meanwhile, children happen.
>
> Amber Strader, 27, was in an on-and-off relationship with a clerk at Sears a few years ago when she found herself pregnant. A former nursing student who now tends bar, Ms. Strader said her boyfriend was so dependent that she had to buy his cigarettes. Marrying him never entered her mind. "It was like living with another kid," she said.
>
> When a second child, with a new boyfriend, followed three years later— her birth control failed, she said—her boyfriend, a part-time house painter, was reluctant to wed.
>
> Ms. Strader likes the idea of marriage; she keeps her parents' wedding photo on her kitchen wall and says her boyfriend is a good father. But for now marriage is beyond her reach.
>
> "I'd like to do it, but I just don't see it happening right now," she said. "Most of my friends say it's just a piece of paper, and it doesn't work out anyway."[139]

In short, many studies indicate that there has been a cultural shift in Americans' views of marriage and especially nonmarital childbearing. Although single parenthood is generally not something people aspire to—most would like to be in committed, fulfilling unions—it is nevertheless generally socially accepted when it occurs. There is greater emphasis today on self-expression and self-actualization than on community and conformity. Nevertheless, the decline in marriage and increase in nonmarital childbearing is also rooted in economic changes that have served to decrease the employment and earnings of men with less than a college degree at the same time as the employment and earnings of women have increased. The traditional economic foundations of marriage seem less applicable today than in the past. Thus, while people of all income levels still value marriage, for many—especially those who are poor or otherwise struggling financially—it seems out of reach.

CONCLUSION

All too often people assume that personal traits are the sole determinants of economic well-being, and they overlook the impact of the social and economic environment. This is not surprising given that it is often difficult to recognize how structural forces affect our daily lives. Sociological concepts such as class, status (social group differences), and party (policy) are helpful for understanding how stratification systems evolve. This chapter focused on the first two concepts by examining how economic and social factors determine levels and patterns of poverty in the United States.

Economic growth tends to drive down absolute poverty rates. As standards of living rise, more people earn incomes above the poverty line. However, income inequality—which often results both from the ordinary workings of a market system in which the accumulation of assets is the goal and from economic shifts and instability—may at times impede the positive impact of economic growth. If only the rich benefit from growth, then growth will have little impact on poverty. Increasing inequality since the 1970s has inhibited progress against poverty since that time.

Social stratification by race and gender helps explain why some groups of people are more likely to be poor than others. Notably, however, the effect of social stratification along these group lines declined significantly over the last half century, due in large part to a decline in discrimination, especially in its overt forms. Today, past poverty, economic dislocation, wealth differentials, and family instability are barriers at least as important as racism and discrimination in producing higher poverty rates among African Americans, Hispanics, and Native Americans. (The poverty rate among Asians is similar to the white poverty rate.) Nevertheless, despite this progress, racial and ethnic antipathy and discrimination—particularly toward African Americans—have not disappeared altogether. Moreover, the simple lifting of many barriers to opportunity does not mean that equality is immediate or automatic given the growing importance of family socioeconomic background on one's life chances.

Changing patterns of family formation also affect trends in poverty in the United States. Female-headed families are more likely to be poor because women who are householders face the challenge of supporting a family on one income and often must pay for child care while they work. Lower levels of education among women who head such families also contribute to their lower earnings. Furthermore, women tend to earn less than men, and mothers tend to accumulate less experience than other workers. Finally, many such families do not receive sufficient child support from the children's absent fathers. Cultural shifts in American society and the declining fortunes of men have both contributed to the decline in marriage, rise in cohabitation, and increase in nonmarital childbearing in recent decades.

CHAPTER 6

The Great Recession

The Great Recession of 2007–9 has officially been over for some time. Unfortunately, however, this recession was unlike other recent ones. First, it lasted eighteen months, making it the longest recession since the Great Depression of the 1930s.[1] Second, the unemployment rate rose more sharply in this recession than in previous ones. In December 2007—at the start of the recession—unemployment stood at 5.0 percent. By October 2009, unemployment had doubled, peaking at 10.0 percent. The change in the unemployment rate from start to peak was thus 5.0 percentage points, whereas the change in the previous four recessions ranged from 2.0 to 4.2 percentage points.[2] Third, the pace of recovery was slower after the recent recession than after some of the previous ones, with very high unemployment persisting for quite some time. Many people have had trouble reentering the labor market, with serious consequences for their lifetime earnings and the well-being of their families. This chapter reviews the causes of the recession and its consequences.

CAUSES OF THE GREAT RECESSION

The Great Recession was the worst economic downturn since the Great Depression. The 2007–9 recession had many causes, the most important precipitating one being the bursting of a large housing bubble that rocked the banking system and nearly caused a complete economic meltdown. There were a number of underlying structural causes of the

2007 crisis, and I focus on three: rising inequality, the loosening of bank lending rules and the corresponding rise in consumer debt, and the rise of mortgage securitization with too little regulatory oversight. The latter two are intimately intertwined, so I discuss them together below.

The first structural cause of the crisis, rising inequality, was summarized by Raghuram Rajan in his insightful book *Fault Lines*.[3] Of particular interest here is that the incomes of the top quintile of American households (and especially the top 1 percent) rose rapidly in recent decades even as the earnings of much of the rest of the middle class only drifted slowly upward. A recurring theme I have emphasized in previous chapters is that relative poverty matters: people see the living standards of those around them and seek to emulate them. For the American middle class, this meant trying to keep up with the consumption patterns of those whose incomes were surging ahead. The average size of a house, for example, grew 15 percent, to 2,277 square feet, in only ten years, between 1997 and 2007.[4] Large open-concept houses with impressive foyers, superfluous bathrooms, and granite kitchen countertops were the rage. Many people who decided to stay in their homes rather than purchase new ones borrowed money for expensive home renovation projects. In turn, housing prices grew at a steady clip during this time. This further pushed up the domestic demand for credit, as people needed larger bank loans to afford these houses.[5]

The second cause of the crisis was the loosening of bank lending rules and the corresponding rise in consumer debt. One of the political responses to rising inequality—although perhaps it was not consciously articulated in these terms—was to expand lending to households, especially low-income ones, so that they could attain a middle-class standard of living. It had not always been easy to buy a house in the United States. Before the Great Depression of the 1930s, people seeking to buy homes faced variable interest rates, high down payments, and a short time horizon (such as five years) before payment on the entire loan was due. The housing market crash during the Great Depression, when property values declined by 50 percent, was an impetus for reform. The federal government became involved in the housing finance market, by, among other things, creating the Home Owners' Loan Corporation (HOLC). HOLC purchased defaulted mortgages from financial institutions and then reinstated the mortgage loans, changing them to fixed-rate, long-term (twenty-year) ones so that families could better afford to pay them back. HOLC disbanded in 1936. Two years later, Fannie Mae (officially the Federal National Mortgage Association) was chartered to provide a secondary market for Federal Housing Administration (FHA) loans to virtually guarantee the supply of mortgage credit that banks could supply to homebuyers.[6]

In the post–World War II period, the FHA sought to stimulate housing construction by liberalizing the terms of mortgages. The maximum term of a mortgage rose to thirty years, and loans were allowed to increase in size relative to the purchase price of the home, but there remained a fixed interest rate for such loans. Over the next few decades, homeownership rose rapidly, from 44 percent in 1940 to 64 percent by 1980.[7] High, and often variable, inflation beginning in the 1960s and extending to the early 1980s made traditional fixed-rate home loans less agreeable to banks, which were not sure if customer payments on fixed-rate mortgages would yield sufficient interest over the long run to produce much of a profit. In other words, banks need interest payments rates to surpass the rate of inflation in order to be profitable.

Starting in the 1980s, considerable deregulation took place in banking with the passage of, among others laws, the 1982 Garn–St. Germain Depository Institutions Act, which once again allowed adjustable rate mortgages. Later on, the 1999 Gramm–Leach–Bliley Act allowed commercial and investment banks to merge. This series of acts allowed once stodgy commercial banks—that is, those who issued home loans—to get increasingly involved in much riskier investments traditionally reserved for brokerage firms, such as those on Wall Street. During the 1980s and 1990s commercial banks also expanded into higher-risk loans with higher interest payments.

These changes helped lay the groundwork for the third factor contributing to the recession: the growth of mortgage securitization with little regulatory oversight. The actions of Fannie Mae and Freddie Mac (the latter created in 1970) exacerbated the situation. Recall that Fannie Mae supported the mortgage market by buying mortgages from banks in order to boost bank lending. In 1968 Fannie Mae was converted into a private corporation, and after 1970, both Fannie Mae and Freddie Mac were given the option of assembling a pool of mortgages and issuing securities backed by the mortgage pool (known as "securitization"). Those securities would be sold to investors, who saw them as safe investments because Fannie Mae and Freddie Mac are both sponsored by the government (though they are privately managed). The two organizations thus had both a public mission, supporting the mortgage market, and a private one, maximizing returns on these securities for shareholders. These missions had the potential to conflict at some point, as private gains do not always coincide with the provision of a public good. In any case, their public mission to increase homeownership in the United States also received strong support from the Clinton and George W. Bush administrations.[8] They instructed the Fair Housing Authority to lower standards on guaranteed loans, such as by dramatically cutting the minimum down payment required from a borrower and increasing the maximum size of the mortgage it would guarantee.

As Rajan asserts, "Unfortunately, the private sector, aided and abetted by agency money, converted the good intentions behind the affordable-housing mandate and the push to an ownership society into a financial disaster."[9] The loosening of lending rules led to the rapid expansion of the subprime lending market. Subprime loans are typically made to people who may have difficulty maintaining a repayment schedule. These loans have higher interest rates and less favorable terms in order to compensate for the higher credit risk. In short, "the time-tested 30-year fixed-rate mortgage, with a 20 percent down payment, went out of style."[10]

By the early 2000s the housing boom was in full throttle and housing prices rose rapidly. Average housing prices in 2006, for example, were 60 percent higher than in 1997—an unprecedented increase in such a short time.[11] Businesses continued to sell the ever-growing volume of mortgages and create new forms of mortgage-backed securities. There was an expanding global demand for these mortgage–backed securities that offered apparently solid and secure returns. Investors around the world clamored to purchase securities built on American real estate, seemingly one of the safest bets in the world. In 2003 the mortgage business represented a $4 trillion industry. In the same year, the financial sector, comprising about 10 percent of the labor force, was generating 40 percent of the profits in the American economy.[12] Wall Street firms such as J.P. Morgan, Bear Stearns, and Lehman Brothers were making money hand over fist on the fees generated from selling mortgage securities. Many individual investors knew that many of the mortgage securities were risky. Nevertheless, the compensation system in finance too often rewarded short-term gains yielded by large sales, in the form of annual bonuses to investment brokers, rather than question whether these investments were in the long-term interest of the company, not to mention the economy and country.[13]

Meanwhile, with easy credit available and ever-rising prices, buying a house seemed like a good deal. Under the leadership of Alan Greenspan, the Federal Reserve did much to keep interest rates low. This made buying a house seem more affordable, as it kept monthly payments made by individual borrowers to banks low. Buying a home certainly seemed to be a better investment than earning the low interest paid by having a safe savings account or a certificate of deposit (CD). This led to a gold rush mentality during the housing boom. As described in a report issued by the Federal Commission that investigated the causes of the financial crisis, Angelo Mozilo, the longtime CEO of Countrywide Financial, testified:

> Housing prices were rising so rapidly—at a rate that I'd never seen in my 55 years in the business—that people, regular people, average people got caught up in the mania of buying a house, and flipping it, making money. It was happening. They buy a house, make $50,000 . . . and talk at a cocktail party about it. . . . Housing suddenly went from being part of the American dream to house my family to settle down—it became a commodity. That was a change in the culture. . . . It was sudden, unexpected.[14]

Some of the subprime loans had complicated repayment schedules. For example, they may have appeared affordable to home buyers by requiring only low monthly payments for two or three years, but then requiring a balloon payment thereafter. Between 2003 and 2007, the proportion of new mortgages that were subprime increased from 30 percent to almost 70 percent of the total.[15] Some borrowers may not have understood the terms, others may have been duped by scheming predatory lenders, and yet others assumed that they could restructure the repayment schedule (i.e., refinance) as the value of their home continued to rise. Indeed, with rising housing prices, many people took out loans on their home equity (the estimated value of one's house minus the amount of it owed to the bank). In short, many people went on a debt-fueled consumption binge.

Meanwhile, the typical investor was perhaps only vaguely aware of the risks carried by mortgage securities, which consist of many mortgages bundled together. Different mortgage securities were supposed to carry different levels of risk, but in practice many were jumbled together. The credit rating agencies, such as Moody's, played a key role in the crisis too. They evaluated many of the securities as safe investments when in fact they contained subprime loans at high risk of default, and investors often blindly relied on these evaluations. The credit rating agencies did such a poor job because of flawed computer models, the pressure from financial firms that paid for the ratings (which often posed a conflict of interest), the lack of resources to do a thorough job (despite record profits), and the absence of significant public oversight.[16]

As mortgage defaults climbed (that is, as many people could no longer pay their monthly mortgage bills), investors could no long ignore that housing prices could not continue to increase at the same torrid pace and that, in fact, homes were overpriced and demand was flagging. In 2006, by the time the rise in home prices slowed dramatically, the default rate on subprime mortgages stood at 20 percent.[17] Likewise, it became clear that many of the mortgage securities themselves were far overvalued given the fact that many contained junk mortgages. Some large companies that held these overvalued securities were in deep trouble, as they often had little cash on hand available to cover their losses. Thus, at the end of 2007, Bear Stearns, one of the companies that had purchased many mortgage-backed securities, had $11.8 billion in equity and $383.6 billion in liabilities.[18]

The crisis finally came to a head in September 2008 with the bankruptcy of Lehman Brothers and the impending failure of many other companies, including the insurance giant American International Group (AIG). Panic spread throughout the financial industry and confusion reigned as people tried to sort out who owed how much to whom. There was a tremendous concern that if too many companies—especially larger ones deemed "too large to fail"—went bankrupt the economy would go into free fall. As it was, the credit markets seized up. No one could borrow money from anyone else, as many banks and businesses wanted a lot of cash on hand to cover their own potential losses, and lending to other teetering businesses was a tremendous risk. As a result, trading ground to a halt, the stock market plunged, and the economy tumbled into a deep recession.[19]

At this point the government, in the waning months of the George W. Bush administration, decided to step in. Congress passed legislation known as TARP (Troubled Asset Relief Program), which authorized the use of up to $700 billion to support many companies considered too large to fail, such as banks, large insurance companies, and the automobile industry. This effort was on the whole fairly successful, as most economists agree that it prevented an even deeper crisis and recession. Moreover, the ultimate cost of TARP will likely be assessed at less than $30 billion after all money is paid back from institutions that obtained funds under the program. Much of the remaining losses are from money provided to the auto industry, which might have become irrevocably bankrupt without government intervention.[20]

A subsequent general economic stimulus package, the American Recovery and Reinvestment Act of 2009, injected an estimated $787 billion dollars into the economy in the form of spending in a variety of areas, such as infrastructure, education, health care, and tax credits. Many believe that the economic stimulus, like TARP, helped stem the severity of the recession. For example, in spite of the sharp decline in state and local tax revenues, state and local governments were able to maintain their prerecession employment levels for many months into the recession. Government benefits helped boost the spending of the unemployed and poor, and lower taxes helped soften the blow of a loss of wealth from home equity declines for many middle-class families.[21] Economists Alan Blinder and Mark Zandi estimate that the stimulus added 3.4 percent to 2010 GDP and boosted employment by 2.7 million jobs in that year.[22]

Nonetheless, the public remained skeptical whether the stimulus did much to help the economy or whether the money was wasted.[23] The economic downturn was bad enough, so it is difficult to imagine how much worse the situation would have been without the stimulus. Among other people, there was (and is) a deep distrust of government action more generally. There is still an open question about whether those most responsible for the recession were properly held accountable. Many feel that average Americans have paid the price for these misdeeds—such as through unemployment, limited support for families facing foreclosure, and of course taxes needed to cover the stimulus—while the rich quickly recovered as the stock market rebounded and CEO pay reverted to prerecession levels. As Gary Burtless and Tracy Gordon note, "Unfortunately for the policymakers who sponsored or supported the stimulus programs, 'It could have been worse' is rarely a winning slogan in a political campaign."[24]

CONSEQUENCES OF THE GREAT RECESSION

The Great Recession had a broad effect on the well-being of individuals and families in the United States. Below I review the effects of the recession on unemployment, poverty, and associated measures of well-being, such as wealth, food security, and family formation patterns. The last section discusses the politics of the Great Recession and the movements it helped spawn.

Macroeconomic Effects of the Recession

The effects of the recession were not confined to the financial sector or to those who unwisely took out large mortgage loans. Michael Hout and his coauthors describe the ripple effects of the mortgage and banking crisis as follows: "The 'housing bubble' burst, Wall Street stumbled, banks stopped lending, construction workers lost their jobs, sales of building materials and appliances plummeted, truckers and dockers lost their jobs, shops and restaurants suffered, tax revenues fell, governments furloughed police and teachers, and the downward spiral spun even lower."[25] The nation's output (GDP) declined by 8 percent from the end of 2007 to mid-2009. Households lost one-quarter of their wealth over the two-year period, and a third of those losses were attributable to declining home values (homes are the most valuable asset for many families).[26] The nation's economy lost 8.5 million jobs from a peak of 138.1 million jobs in December 2007 to a low of 129.6 million jobs in February 2010.[27] The unemployment rate peaked at 10.0 percent. Even by August 2012 it had decreased only to 8.1 percent.[28]

Men were initially hit hard by the recession because they outnumbered women in declining industries such as construction, transportation, and manufacturing. For example, in November 2010, 80 percent of prime-working-age men were employed, down from 88 percent before the recession. The immediate effects of the recession on women were a little smaller because women are more likely to be employed in expanding sectors of the economy such as health care, and women also have more education on average than men of the same age. However, employment recovered more quickly for men than women as the country slowly emerged from recession, so that by 2012 the effect of the recession did not differ much by gender.[29]

The slow decline in unemployment even after the official end of the recession meant that many families experienced extended bouts of hardship. This has both material and psychological consequences. As a 2012 Associated Press story reported:

> J. R. Childress is up before the sun, bustling about in the French colonial brick house he built. He helps pack his wife's lunch, downs some eggs or cereal for breakfast, pores over online and newspaper job listings and hopes—even prays—this will be the day when his fortunes turn around.
>
> He's determined to stay busy, job or no job, for sanity's sake. Maybe he'll help a neighbor. Exercise. Or check out computer blueprints of construction projects around Winston-Salem, N.C., to stay connected to the world where he thrived for three decades. Childress has been laid off twice since late 2009, most recently for 10 months.
>
> "Every day is a struggle," he says in a soft drawl. "The struggle is the unknown. You've worked your way up the ladder and you get to a point in life and a position in work where you're comfortable . . . then all of a sudden

everything goes away. It's like being thrown into a hole and you're climbing to get up, but it's greased. There's no way of getting out."[30]

Despite the fact that unemployment in 2012 was at its lowest levels in three years, there were still 5.6 million fewer jobs early in that year than there were when the recession began in late 2007. More than 40 percent of the unemployed had been jobless more than six months.[31]

Effect of the Recession on Poverty

Most demographic groups have felt the effects of the recession, but the impact was by no mean uniform. Table 6 shows poverty rates for 2006, a full year before the beginning of the recession in late 2007, and in 2011, two years after the end of the recession. The table also shows the percentage change in poverty for different groups.

Overall, we see that official poverty rose from 12.3 percent in 2006 to 15.0 percent in 2011, a 22 percent increase. All racial/ethnic groups felt the poverty increase. Both children and working-age adults experienced similar increases in poverty (26 to 27 percent increases), with the elderly being the only group shown in the table that experienced a decline in poverty. Many of the elderly received fixed incomes from Social Security or pensions, which were less affected by the recession. As described above, although men were initially hurt by the recession more than women, the effect had evened out by 2011. The effects of the recession were felt by both the native and foreign born as well as by all educational groups. The effects of the recession were smaller in the Northeast and South, and the West was the hardest hit. The states with the highest levels of unemployment in December 2011, for example, were Nevada (12.6 percent) and California (11.1 percent).[32]

Poverty would have been substantially higher in 2011 without government action. Specifically, the federal government implemented six temporary initiatives in 2009 and 2010 with goals of stimulating the economy and reducing hardship: expansions in the Earned Income Tax Credit (EITC) and Child Tax Credit (CTC), the Making Work Pay tax credit, expansions in the duration and level of unemployment insurance, and expansions in Supplemental Nutrition Assistance Program (SNAP) benefits. Five of these six programs (all except unemployment insurance) are not captured by the official poverty statistics cited above because of flaws in the measure described in detail in chapter 2 (the official measure does not count noncash transfers and tax credit income).

TABLE 6 POVERTY RATES BY GROUP, BEFORE AND AFTER THE GREAT RECESSION, 2006–2011

	2006	2011	Percent change in poverty
Total	12.3	15.0	22
Race			
White	10.3	12.8	24
White, not Hispanic	8.2	9.8	20
Black	24.3	27.6	14
Asian	10.3	12.3	19
Hispanic (of any race)	20.6	25.3	23
Age			
Under 18 years	17.4	21.9	26
18 to 64 years	10.8	13.7	27
65 years and over	9.4	8.7	−7
Sex			
Male	11.0	13.6	24
Female	13.6	16.3	20
Nativity			
Native born	11.9	14.4	21
Foreign born	15.2	19.0	25
Education (for people 25+ years old)			
No high school diploma	22.9	25.4	11
High school, no college	10.6	14.9	41
Some college, less than 4-year degree	7.5	11.1	48
4-year degree or higher	3.6	5.1	42
Families with children, by type			
Married-couple families	6.4	8.8	38
Male householder, no wife present	17.9	21.9	22
Female householder, no husband present	36.5	42.9	18
Region			
Northeast	11.5	13.1	14
Midwest	11.2	14.0	25
South	13.8	16.0	16
West	11.6	15.8	36

SOURCE: U.S. Census Bureau 2012c. Education data are from U.S. Census Bureau 2012b.

Using a version of the poverty measure recommended by the National Academy of Sciences, researcher Arloc Sherman finds that these six initiatives kept 6.9 million people, including 2.5 million children, above the poverty line in 2010. Figure 21 shows the effect of government assistance more generally and these six initiatives in particular on poverty rates. If we were to exclude all types of government assistance from

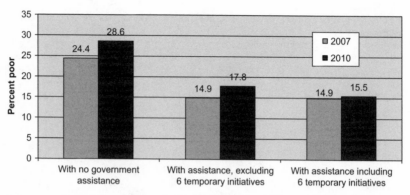

FIGURE 21. Poverty Rates, Using the National Academy of Sciences Poverty Measure, with and without Government Assistance, 2007 and 2010. SOURCE: Sherman 2011, figure 2.

families' incomes, 28.6 percent of families would be considered poor in 2010, up from 24.4 percent in 2007. However, if we include government transfers (both cash and noncash) but exclude the six temporary initiatives, poverty rates were considerably lower, at 17.8 percent in 2010. If we take into account the temporary initiatives, the poverty rate goes down by another 2.3 percentage points to 15.5 percent in the same year. Overall, then, the increase in poverty from 2007 to 2010 was only 0.6 percentage points (from 14.9 percent to 15.5 percent) when all government transfers are included, indicating that the extra benefits were important for dampening the negative effects of the recession on people's well-being. Of these initiatives, extending unemployment insurance kept 3.4 million people out of poverty, the three tax credits kept 3.1 million people out of poverty, and expanded SNAP kept another 1 million out of poverty.[33]

Despite some help provided by the safety net, people's well-being declined according to a number of measures. For one, food insecurity rose. In the fourth quarter of 2011, 19.4 percent of families answered affirmatively to the question "Have there been times in the past twelve months when you did not have enough money to buy food that you or your family needed?" This is up from 16.3 percent in the first quarter of 2008, shortly after the beginning of the recession.[34] Food hardship rose even though from 2007 to 2011 the number of people receiving SNAP increased by 70 percent. One in seven Americans received SNAP benefits in 2011, with as many as one in five in Michigan, Mississippi, New Mexico, Oregon, Tennessee, and the District of Columbia.[35]

The recession considerably reduced the wealth of Americans. Households saw an average decline of 39 percent in their home equity from 2007 to 2009. Minority households were harder hit: African American and Hispanic households saw their home equity decline by 48 percent and 45 percent, respectively (compared to a still substantial 37 percent decline among whites). Many homeowners also saw the value of their home equity become negative, meaning that they owed more to the bank in loans than their house was worth. Somewhere between 16 and 20 percent of homeowners were in this situation by the end of 2009. As a result, 5 percent of homeowners were delinquent on their mortgage in 2009. Among whites, blacks, and Hispanics, the respective numbers were 3, 11, and 15 percent. The share of households experiencing a foreclosure rose fourfold from 0.5 percent in 2006 to 2 percent in 2009, with numbers likely still rising thereafter.[36]

Workers nearing retirement were also hurt by the recession. Declines in the stock market led to marked declines in pension wealth, particularly 401(k)s. Retirement accounts declined by 34 percent from 2007 to 2009, though the value of these accounts has rebounded since then as the stock market has recovered.[37] More generally, in the three years spanning 2008 through 2010, more than one in five Americans saw their available household income fall by a quarter or more and lacked enough financial resources (such as savings) to manage this decline.[38]

The Great Recession also had a significant effect on fertility and family formation patterns. After steady increases in fertility from 2003 to 2007, fertility fell modestly in 2008 and 2009 by 2 to 5 percent. This decline was likely a result of people's insecurity about their jobs or finances. A survey of women during this period found that many women reported that they wanted to reduce or delay their childbearing because of the economy.[39] The recession did not appear to have had a large effect on marriage or divorce. Both marriage and divorce rates had been slowly declining before the recession, and these trends more or less continued into 2008 and 2009. Similarly, the gradual increase in cohabitation before the recession continued through 2008 and 2009 as well.[40]

However, there was a rise in the proportion of young people living with their parents during the recession. This is consistent with the notion that the difficult job market led more younger people to return home (or never leave home) and co-reside with kin in order to get through the tough economic times.[41] More specifically, between 2007 and 2011 the number of young adults ages 25 to 34 living at home rose from 4.7 million to 5.9 million. This increase was driven mainly the growing share of young men living at home. In 2011, 18.6 percent of men 25 to 34 lived with their parents, up from 14.2 percent in 2007. For women, the share held steady at about 10 percent over the period.[42]

While one might think that the Great Recession might have had a profound effect on people's attitudes toward business, government, and fairness in society, one study suggests that the effects were moderate. The proportion of people saying they had "hardly any confidence in major companies" went up only a few percentage points, though the proportion who expressed less confidence in banks and financial institutions in particular spiked rather sharply from a little over one in ten before the recession to about four in ten after. People's attitudes toward government soured in the 2000s in general, but there was not much change during the recession itself. Nor did the recession appear to have much of an overall effect on people's perceptions of fairness in society. People had mixed opinions on whether the government could and should do more to alleviate hardship. They did approve of government action in general, but there was no specific support for policies that enhanced opportunity, supported the poor, or supported redistribution of wealth.[43]

Statistics on the effects of the recession on people's health are as yet hard to come by, but it is not difficult to find anecdotes that suggest that for some individuals the effects, certainly on mental health, were substantial. Jerome Greene doesn't mince words when he describes life without a steady paycheck for more than three years.

> "It's been like hell," he says. "It's very hard to see people leave and go to work in the morning and come home every night. It's hard to see people spending money, going out and having fun and you can't. It's very stressing. But there are people in worst [sic] situations than I have and I feel sorry for them."
>
> Greene, about to turn 50, worked for 16 years as an Oracle software developer, most recently at a Pennsylvania company that made electronic components for cars. When he was laid off in June 2008, the recession was just taking hold, and he still had job interviews. By fall, with the economy in free fall, his phone stopped ringing.
>
> Greene hoped the downturn would be brief and he'd weather it with unemployment benefits.
>
> But the jobless rate hovered above 9 percent and Greene's 99 weeks of unemployment expired. He had trouble sleeping. Depression set in. Without health insurance, he took precautions—carrying hand sanitizer and his own pen when doing errands to avoid getting sick and having to pay $65 for a doctor's visit.
>
> "There's no room for error," he says. "There's no extra money."[44]

The Politics of the Great Recession

Two noteworthy political movements arose in the wake of the Great Recession on opposite sides of the political spectrum: the Tea Party and Occupy Wall Street movements. The views aired by the participants of each are not particularly new, but the events and conditions spawned by the economic crisis seem to validate aspects of their views, and thus gave each greater resonance among the public.

The Tea Party movement arose in the aftermath of the 2008 Republican Party defeat in the presidential election, which also gave Democrats a majority in both houses of Congress. The movement grew throughout 2009 and achieved substantial success in the 2010 midterm elections, which vaulted many Tea Party candidates into Congress and gave Republicans the majority in the House of Representatives. The Tea Party ideology represents a long-standing strand of U.S. conservatism. Tea Party supporters are generally against "big government." They resent taxes and government regulation of business. They vehemently opposed Obama's health care reform plan (passed by Congress in 2010), which aimed to expand health insurance coverage to a greater number of Americans and the federal government's role in its provision. Tea Party supporters were not opposed to all government spending, as many were older (and mostly white) Americans who received Social Security and Medicare and did not favor dismantling these programs. Tea Party supporters tended to make distinctions between programs perceived as going to hard-working contributors to society and "handouts" perceived as going to undeserving people.[45]

Many Tea Party supporters thus viewed the price tag of the Wall Street bailouts and the subsequent economic stimulus with alarm. The beginning of the Tea Party movement is sometimes linked to an on-air tirade in February of 2009 by CNBC reporter Rick Santelli against the Obama administration's mortgage plan, whose aim was to assist people facing foreclosure. As he reported on the floor of the Chicago Mercantile Exchange, he shouted, "The government is promoting bad behavior!" Some moments later he turned away from the TV camera and asked the people on the floor, "How many of you people want to pay for your neighbor's mortgage that has an extra bathroom and can't pay their bills, raise your hand? [boos from the audience] President Obama, are you listening?!"[46] Support for the Tea Party movement likely crested in 2010, though many aspects of its ideology remain popular among conservatives.[47]

The Occupy Wall Street (OWS) movement is politically associated with the left. It started as a protest in September 2011 in Zuccotti Park, located in New York City's Wall Street financial district, before spreading to other cities. Participants protested against social and economic inequality, greed, corruption, and the undue influence of corporations, and particularly the financial sector, on government. These protests echoed those against corporations and crony capitalism of a hundred years ago.[48]

The more recent roots of the OWS movement were stagnant family incomes and growing income inequality. When the economic crisis hit, unemployment soared and many young people seeking to enter the labor market saw economic opportunities vanish. They also resented that the large banks at the center of the crisis got bailed out. Sixty-one percent of Americans surveyed in 2011 agreed with the statement "The economic system in this country unfairly favors the wealthy."[49] Corporations continue to pour billions of dollars into lobbying, not to mention presidential and congressional campaigns, increasing skepticism and cynicism about the fairness of the political system.

In addition, although many Americans accept some measure of inequality in society, there is a feeling that economic mobility is limited, and perhaps now harder to achieve than in the past. One of the primary vehicles for economic mobility has been obtaining a college degree; however, the cost of college has increased far beyond inflation in recent years. As a result, many of those attending college wind up with considerable student debt. OWS participants maintained that more fairness and accountability were needed in our political and economic institutions. Although the movement effectively shone a light on these issues, it was less successful in articulating specific aims or solutions. The OWS protests ebbed by the end of 2011, but, as with the Tea Party, its general goals still resonate among many Americans.

CONCLUSION

The Great Recession resulted from the bursting of the housing bubble and the subsequent crisis in the banking industry in 2007–9. These shocks reverberated throughout the economy such that by October of 2009, the national unemployment rate had doubled to 10 percent. The recession was officially over by the end of 2009, but high unemployment declined only very slowly in the subsequent months and years. The root causes of the Great Recession were rising inequality (which made it more difficult for many families to attain a middle-class life-style), the loosening of bank lending rules and the corresponding rise in consumer debt, and the rise of the mortgage securitization industry with relatively little regulatory oversight. Government bailouts of many companies deemed "too large to fail" and a subsequent economic stim-ulus package, though viewed with suspicion and resentment by many, likely served to prevent an even larger economic calamity.

Other consequences of the recession include higher poverty, greatly reduced wealth (especially home equity), greater food hardship, and more young adults living with their parents. Political responses to the crisis have varied widely, ranging from, on the conservative side of the political spectrum, the rise of the Tea Party movement in 2009 and 2010 to, on the liberal side, the Occupy Wall Street movement in 2011. Although these specific movements may have ebbed, their underlying philosophies live on and continue to inform political debates on poverty.

CHAPTER 7

Poverty and Policy

The struggle between providing aid to those in need while not promoting socially "undesirable" behaviors is a central one in current debates on poverty. This debate is not a new one. Over a century ago, in 1904, Emil Munsterberg described this dilemma:

> The conduct of society toward poverty continues to oscillate between two evils—the evil of insufficient care for the indigent, with the resulting appearance of an ever-increasing impoverishment . . . and the evil of a reckless poor-relief, with the resulting appearance of far-reaching abuses, the lessening of the spirit of independence. . . . The history of poverty is for the most part a history of these constantly observed evils and of the efforts to remove them, or at least to reduce their dimensions. No age has succeeded in solving this problem.[1]

The set of policies historically employed in the United States toward the poor reflect both its market orientation and its individualistic ethos. Compared with other developed countries, the emphasis of policies has tended to be on stimulating economic growth rather than ensuring income equality and on promoting individual liberty over collective well-being. Policies also generally do not guarantee aid to all people with low income, and they usually require them to work in order to be eligible to receive aid.

This chapter examines the origins of current policy debates in the United States, describes existing policies toward the poor, reviews evidence on the effect of government transfers on poverty, and finally discusses how competing goals and values drive ongoing deliberations on the size, scope, and direction of the American welfare state.

HISTORICAL ORIGINS OF CURRENT U.S. POLICY DEBATES

Colonial American policies toward the poor drew heavily from English poor laws. The Elizabethan Poor Law of 1601 in England brought together, in a single statute, many years of previous legislation that established a civil system of locally financed and administered relief. According to this system, whose major features were adopted in many colonies, assistance included direct aid to the unemployable, a policy of apprenticeship for the young, and work relief for able-bodied adults. It gave local governments responsibility for helping the poor, who were often thought of as falling into one of three groups: children, able-bodied adults, and incapacitated, helpless, or "worthy" poor.[2]

The law had some features that would be considered unusual or harsh by today's standards. Not only were parents legally liable for children, but children were also liable for needy parents and grandparents. Vagrants refusing work could be committed to a house of correction, whipped, branded, put in pillories and stoned, or evicted from the community. Potential recipients also had no way of appealing these decisions.[3] The poor in some places could even be auctioned off to the lowest bidder or placed in an asylum, if the town had one.[4]

Residency requirements for the receipt of public assistance were common in American villages and towns. Each town often expelled nonresident vagrants and strangers. There was little social welfare for American Indians or African Americans during the colonial period. Black slaves were the responsibility of their masters, as were sometimes newly freed blacks, while the treatment of other free blacks varied.[5] In some places, such as Pennsylvania, African American paupers were the responsibility of their legal county of residence,[6] while in others they were denied assistance and forced to rely on their own self-help methods. Overall, colonists tended to accept responsibility for those they viewed as their community members, but not for others.[7]

By the early 1800s the country was growing rapidly, and the beginnings of industrialization and urbanization were evident in a few areas. Growing social tensions and disarray brought by these changes raised concerns about how to handle poverty. Residency rules (whereby people were required to live in a community for a particular amount of time before being eligible for aid) were thought to interfere with labor mobility, and many believed that poor laws might make the poverty problem worse by fostering dependency. It was also thought that money spent to support the poor took money away from industrious workers in the form of taxes. Rugged individualism was the ideal, and able-bodied poor people were thought to be lazy and morally degenerate.[8]

Thus there was a growing belief that "outdoor" relief, which did not require recipients to enter institutions, aggravated these problems. Paupers were proof that a modest life could be had without hard labor. By the 1820s, the movement toward "indoor" relief was underway. Indoor relief involved the widespread use of institutions, such as almshouses, workhouses, orphanages, and mental hospitals. They remained a part of the policy landscape until the Great Depression in the 1930s, even though other types of relief supplanted them well before.[9]

These institutions were meant to reform, rehabilitate, and morally educate the poor. Conditions in poorhouses varied widely. Some were places of degradation, disease, and near starvation, while others were not. Most were actually used for temporary shelter during times of personal crisis or economic distress rather than as places for permanent or long-term residence.[10] These institutions were increasingly funded by states rather than localities, even if they were still run at the county level.[11] In part because so many poorhouses were dismal places, poorly managed and underfunded, over time they failed to meet the goals predicted by their sponsors, that is, they failed to serve as efficient places for moral education, reform, and work, and eventually they lost general support.[12]

During this period outdoor relief continued, some of which was supplied by private charities. Even at the height of indoor relief, more people were often served outside poorhouses than within.[13] African American communities in some cities often ran their own mutual aid societies. In Philadelphia in the early 1800s, for example, there was a rapid increase in the number of black mutual aid societies, which collected dues from many adult African Americans and distributed benefits to those in need.[14]

During the Civil War and immediately after, the federal government played a role in aiding freed black men and women through the work of the Freedmen's Bureau and by implementing policies aiding Union veterans. The Freedmen's Bureau served as an employment agency and was also a significant source of relief for African Americans in the South before it was dissolved in 1872;[15] however, some have argued that in its effort to increase employment, it also had the negative effect of essentially tying freed slaves to plantations as sharecroppers.[16]

For the most part, African Americans were treated separately from the white poor and usually in an inferior manner. With the end of Reconstruction (1867–76), public welfare programs for blacks began petering out, forcing them to turn to self-help, mutual aid, or private Negro benevolent societies.[17] On the positive side, Civil War benefits were offered to millions of disabled and elderly Union war veterans, including African American veterans. By 1910 more than a quarter of all elderly American men were receiving regular payments from the federal government.[18]

Aside from benefits for veterans, by the 1870s many cities and localities reduced public outdoor relief, and "scientific charities" grew in importance.[19] This represented the trend of coordinating the administration and supervision of aid into larger charities that were professionally and privately managed. The organized charity movement aimed not only at eliminating fraud and inefficiency in the administration of relief, but also at devising a constructive method of treating poverty. It involved having "friendly visitors" look into each case to diagnose the cause of poverty. Investigation was the cornerstone of treatment, followed by personal contact between the rich and the poor, which was aimed at passing on advice and moral training. The philosophy behind the movement rested upon the notion that poverty was an individual and moral problem. In the late 1800s Josephine Shaw Lowell, founder of the New York Charity Organization Society, stated, "Human nature is so constituted that no [working] man can receive as a gift what he should earn by his own labor without a moral deterioration. No human being . . . will work to provide the means of living for himself if he can get a living in any other manner agreeable to himself."[20]

The scientific charity societies, however, were criticized by some as being too uncomprehending of the causes of poverty, too paternalistic, and sometimes cold and cruel. It was assumed that the poor wanted the moral guidance of the friendly visitors, which was rarely the case. The societies also failed to fully recognize the multifaceted causes of poverty, which included not only individual failings but also such factors as accidents, poor health, low wages, and involuntary unemployment. Yet the professional orientation of these societies encouraged good record keeping and the collecting of information about the causes of poverty during the visits. This contributed to the development of a technique of social service and research—casework—and, with it, the growth of social work as a profession.[21]

The early years of the twentieth century were a time of continued rapid industrialization, urbanization, and immigration. Economic insecurity and deprivation were widespread. Some reformers felt that the complex problems associated with these processes required greater monetary support than private charities could provide. Between 1909 and 1920 forty-three states passed legislation that required employers to provide workman's compensation for employees hurt on the job. This was one of the first organized and sustained social insurance programs in the country.[22] A number of programs to help mothers, such as mothers' pensions, and children also arose in this period.[23] In 1912 the U.S. Congress established the Children's Bureau, whose mission was to collect and exchange ideas and information on child welfare. At the bureau's urging, Congress passed the 1921 Sheppard-Towner Act to fund health education programs for mothers with babies.[24]

Other legislation in this period supported extending aid to widows with children, a segment of the "deserving" poor. Thirty-nine states had such statutes in place by 1919, and all but two did by 1935. Widow pension laws marked a turning point in the welfare policies of many states because they removed the stigma of charity for a large number of welfare recipients. The early twentieth century also saw the continued professionalization of charity; by the 1920s charity workers were becoming "social workers," and the number of schools of social work began to grow. The volunteer "friendly visitor" gave way to the paid, trained caseworker.[25]

The stock market crash in the fall of 1929 and the subsequent depression vastly changed the economic, social, and political landscape. Between 1929 and 1933 the unemployment rate climbed from 3.2 percent to 24.9 percent. The nation's private charity agencies simply lacked the means to meet the growing need across the country. It became quite evident that at least some of the new poverty resulted from social and economic factors that the needy could not control.[26] President Herbert Hoover approached the economic crisis timidly, and, as conditions failed to improve, he lost the 1932 election to Franklin Delano Roosevelt.

Roosevelt adopted a proactive approach by instituting a large federal relief program to help restore public confidence in the nation's institutions. In the 1930s, a number of measures were taken, including the creation of the Works Progress Administration, which provided jobs for the unemployed; the National Labor Relations Act, or Wagner Act, which gave unions guarantees of their right to organize; the Farm Security Administration, which aided small farmers and migratory workers;

and the Wagner-Steagall Act, which established the U.S. Housing Authority to provide low-interest loans to local officials building public housing. The Federal Emergency Relief Act, signed into law in 1933, opened up the era of federal aid by making $500 million of federal funds available to distribute as grants-in-aid to states. African Americans tended to receive less economic assistance than whites due to discrimination and exclusion. Nevertheless, the New Deal programs represented a notable departure from the past in that they officially tried to prohibit discrimination, and they did end up helping a number of African American families.[27]

One of the most momentous pieces of legislation was the Social Security Act, which became law in 1935. It provided both social insurance, in the form of pensions for the aged and unemployment insurance for workers, and public assistance, in the form of Aid to Dependent Children (ADC, later known as Aid to Families with Dependent Children, or AFDC) and assistance to disabled children. Over time the social insurance portions of the act have tended to be more popular and less controversial than the public assistance portions.[28] Old Age Insurance (OAI) was eventually expanded to cover just about all retired employees and provide benefits to survivors and disability protection as well. The Social Security Act marked the beginning of federal aid to the states on a permanent basis. It introduced the ideas of entitlement into national policy and made the federal government assume responsibility for the welfare of its citizens.[29] In 1932 the federal share of public aid was 2.1 percent; by 1939 it had risen to 62.5 percent.[30]

World War II brought back full employment and rising incomes for most Americans. The GI Bill of 1944 offered a comprehensive set of disability services, employment benefits, educational loans, family allowances, and subsidized loans for homes, businesses, and farms to sixteen million World War II veterans.[31]

The late 1940s and 1950s were years of general prosperity, and the general image of the nation was that of an affluent society with the highest standard of living in the world. Despite these advances, poverty remained. Moreover, there were groups of people among whom poverty was widespread and who, for the most part, had been left out of the mainstream of American life: unemployed southern blacks who had migrated to northern cities, some rural whites, Mexican Americans, Native Americans on their reservations in the West and Southwest, and Puerto Ricans. The civil rights movement brought national attention to the condition of these socially, economically, and politically marginalized groups, many of whom had benefited only modestly from past policy measures. The urban violence and social disarray of the 1960s shattered the image of America as a classless or relatively homogeneous society.[32]

The Kennedy administration advocated a number of new policies aimed at reducing poverty and inequality, such as the 1962 Public Welfare Amendments to the Social Security Act, which increased federal support to the states for providing services to public assistance recipients. Kennedy's successor, Lyndon Johnson, made reducing poverty a centerpiece of his domestic agenda with the launching of the War on Poverty. Legislation supporting this effort included the Economic Opportunity Act, which, among other things, created the Job Corps for school dropouts; Operation Head Start, a project to give preschool training to children; the Legal Services Corporation; and the Community Action Program (CAP), which supported the creation and operation of community action agencies to combat poverty. The last of these, CAP, was designed to address problems in "disorganized" communities with high poverty by providing aid directly to local community organizations, often bypassing local elected officials. CAP programs ultimately failed because of widespread opposition and resistance from these officials. Much of the money allocated never made it to those who needed it.[33]

Other legislation during the period that created programs well known today include the Food Stamp Act (1964), which provided funds for low-income families to purchase food (known today as the Supplemental Nutrition Assistance Program, or SNAP); Medicare (1965), which provided health insurance for the elderly; and Medicaid (1965), which did the same for low-income families. Between 1963 and 1966 federal grants to the states for social services more than doubled. In addition, approximately 1 million new public assistance cases were added to the welfare rolls, especially the AFDC program, and another 3.3 million would be added by 1970.[34] In 1974 the Supplemental Security Income program federalized benefits available to the blind, disabled, and elderly.

Despite some efforts in the 1960s that attempted to give communities greater power (such as CAP), the general trend in the administration of policies for the poor since the 1930s was toward larger bureaucratic structures and increased professionalization. The combination of these two has at times made poverty programs less responsive to actual needs and also harder to reform. Over time this has lead to greater dissatisfaction with these policies and institutions from many parts of the political spectrum.[35]

By the late 1960s a growing number of people were denouncing welfare. In addition, antiwar protests, student upheavals, and social change (such as the women's liberation, civil rights, and welfare rights movements) caused resentment among conservatives. Nevertheless, while Richard Nixon, elected in 1968, criticized federal involvement in services to individuals and communities (preferring self-help), he actually ended up supporting a number of proposals that expanded the scope of social programs designed to help "deserving" needy citizens, including the disabled, the elderly, and the working poor. These programs included the Earned Income Tax Credit (EITC), which provided tax rebates for low-income workers, and the Comprehensive Employment and Training Act (CETA), which subsidized public service jobs for the unemployed.[36]

In the mid-1970s the economy suffered from high unemployment and inflation. By the end of the decade it was clear that the optimism of the 1960s had given way to pessimism and cynicism; liberals and many social programs came under attack, and Ronald Reagan led the subsequent movement to limit welfare and reduce social spending, believing that widespread freeloading plagued the system. Under Reagan military budgets were expanded and taxes cut, as were some social programs, such as CETA. Spending on others, such as AFDC, child care subsidies, unemployment insurance, food stamps, subsidized housing, public and mental health services, and legal aid, was slashed. Reagan also pushed for the transfer of many government functions from the federal level to the states.[37]

Some of these cuts in the early 1980s coincided with a deep recession. Poverty and unemployment soared to their highest rates in years. By the mid-1980s the economic crisis eased, though unemployment and poverty were slow to decline. The next big piece of welfare legislation was the Family Support Act, signed into law by Reagan in 1988, whose centerpiece was the Job Opportunities and Basic Skills (JOBS) program, which required single parents on welfare whose children were older than three years to work in order to receive assistance. If they could not get jobs, they had to enroll in education or job training courses, to be paid for by the states and the federal government. Money was also provided for child care, transportation, and other expenses necessary to enable recipients to work or take part in education or job training.

The early 1990s witnessed another significant recession and a sharp increase in the number of cash welfare and food stamp recipients. Dissatisfaction with the welfare system remained. President Bill Clinton, who had vowed to "end welfare as we know it" in his 1992 campaign, helped do just that, in 1996 signing a bipartisan bill, the Personal Responsibility and Work Opportunity Reconciliation Act (PRWORA). This was a dramatic and controversial measure that brought an end to six decades of federal social policy guaranteeing at least a minimum level of aid to those in poverty. The measure abolished AFDC and replaced it with a system of smaller grants to states, which established rules of eligibility but were required to end welfare to recipients after two years, regardless of whether they had found jobs by that time. It also set a lifetime limit on assistance at five years.[38] A number of other social programs to support the poor remained in place, such as housing subsidies, Medicaid assistance for the disabled, and the Earned Income Tax Credit.

More generally, the basic goal of PRWORA was to "transform the culture of poverty" and reduce dependency.[39] The number of people receiving cash assistance (renamed Temporary Assistance for Needy Families, or TANF, from AFDC) dropped dramatically after its passage, from 5 million families in 1994 to 2.2 million in June 2000.[40] Some of the decline was due to the bill itself, some to the strong economy of the time, and some to the expansion of the EITC, which made work more appealing.[41] The employment rates among single mothers increased from 60 percent in 1994 to 72 percent in 1999—a remarkable jump in such a short time.[42] The earnings and disposable income of single mothers more generally also rose significantly after welfare reform as their receipt of public assistance fell, a trend that continued into the 2000s.[43] However, there remained a significant group of very disadvantaged women with few skills who had difficulty finding work or maintaining employment and who suffered from poor physical and mental health. These women were not helped by welfare reform, and likely did worse after it was enacted.[44]

Since the passage of welfare reform in 1996, the most significant new government program benefitting poor and vulnerable populations was the Patient Protection and Affordable Care Act (ACA), passed by Congress and signed into law by President Barack Obama in March 2010 (sometimes referred to as "Obamacare"). The plan provided for a phased introduction (over a four-year period) of a comprehensive system of mandated health insurance whose main purpose was to reduce the number of people without health insurance in the United States. The plan called for the creation of state-based American Health Benefit Exchanges through which individuals and small businesses could purchase coverage. It also expanded Medicaid to more low-income families and allowed children to stay on their parents' health plans until their twenty-sixth birthday. The law prohibited the denial of coverage and claims by insurers for preexisting medical conditions.

The most controversial element of the proposal was the requirement that all U.S. citizens and legal residents purchase health insurance, subject to a significant penalty.[45] Opponents of the plan saw it as representing too much government intrusion in the provision of health care and, by extension, too much intrusion into people's lives. Some also believed that the plan will end up being prohibitively expensive, as it provides medical benefits to a greater number of people. The individual mandate, however, was thought to be an essential element of the plan because uninsured individuals impose major costs on the rest of society. They are less likely to obtain preventative care and more likely to use expensive emergency room services that are essentially paid for by all taxpayers anyway (emergency rooms cannot deny critical assistance to anyone). In addition, when healthy people opt out of health insurance, prices rise for all those who remain in the pool, making the whole system much more unaffordable and untenable. Because health care reform is being phased in over a four-year period extending into 2014, it is too soon to evaluate its impact. Notably, however, the proportion of people covered by health insurance increased from 2010 to 2011, and it was the first time in ten years that the rate of private health insurance coverage had not decreased.[46]

CURRENT SOCIAL WELFARE PROGRAMS

There are two basic types of government programs that attempt to alleviate or prevent poverty: *social insurance* and *public assistance.* Social insurance policies are broad, "universal" ones that generally do not impose eligibility criteria based on one's income. Social Security and Medicare are perhaps the two most prominent social insurance programs. Public assistance policies specifically target the low-income population. They are "means-tested" or "income-tested," which means that a person or family has to earn below a certain amount of money to qualify. Temporary Aid to Needy Families (TANF) and food assistance (SNAP) are two of the better-known examples of public assistance programs.

Figure 22 shows the trend in government spending on various types of social insurance and income-tested benefit programs. The figure indicates

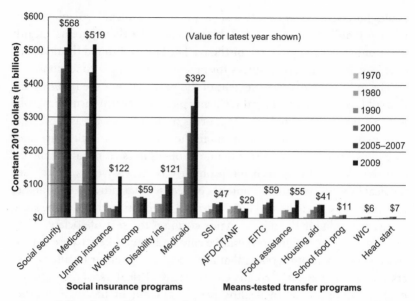

FIGURE 22. Spending on Government Programs, 1970 to 2009. SOURCES: Data for 1970 to 2005–7 are from Scholz, Moffitt, and Cowan 2009, table 8A.1. Data from 2009 are from Ziliak 2011, table 1.

that spending on social insurance programs—social security, Medicare, unemployment insurance, worker's compensation, and disability insurance—tends to be higher than spending on means-test transfers, with the exception of spending on Medicaid. Spending on most programs has increased since 1970 (in constant 2010 dollars). The three largest programs—Social Security, Medicare, and Medicaid—are considerably larger than any of the other programs. Spending on unemployment insurance (UI) is cyclical: it is higher during recessions and lower during periods of low unemployment. The figure bears this out by showing a significant increase in UI spending from 2007 to 2009, when unemployment soared. Among means-tested programs, we see that real spending on cash welfare—AFDC/TANF—declined significantly since 1990 as welfare caseloads plummeted. After Medicaid, the largest programs that help low-income people are the Earned Income Tax Credit and food assistance. Food assistance expenditures in particular rose quickly after the beginning of the Great Recession.[47]

Figure 23 compares federal spending across various broader categories. The three largest program types were Social Security (20 percent), Defense and Security (also 20 percent), and Medicare, Medicaid, and

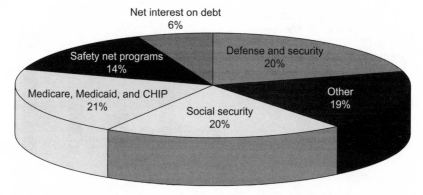

FIGURE 23. Spending on Programs as a Percentage of the Federal Budget, Fiscal Year 2010. SOURCE: The 2010 figures are from the Office of Management and Budget 2012 and the Center on Budget and Policy Priorities 2011.

the Children's Health Insurance Program (CHIP) (21 percent). Note that these numbers represent federal spending only, with states and local governments often chipping in to these and other programs. Federal spending on means-test programs other than Medicaid was relatively modest—comprising 14 percent of the budget. The "other" category in the figure consists of spending on programs such as benefits for federal retirees and veterans (7 percent), scientific and medical research (2 percent), transportation infrastructure (3 percent), education (3 percent), and non-security international spending (e.g., foreign aid) (1 percent).[48] More generally, these figures support the notion that social insurance programs (such as Social Security and Medicare) are larger and more costly (and benefit a greater number of people) than means-tested public assistance programs. This perhaps also reflects the greater popularity of these programs among the general population.[49]

Figure 24 provides a picture of the proportion of people in the United States who received benefits from various programs in 2009, as reported in the Current Population Survey (CPS), a household survey. Although families tend to underreport government benefits in household surveys, figure 24 still provides a rough approximation of receipt.[50] The non-means-tested programs, Social Security and Medicare, are the most used; over a quarter of American households report receiving some income from these programs. As we would expect, other programs are less widely used, ranging from 2 percent of households reporting receipt of TANF cash payments to 19 percent who reported receiving benefits from Medicaid. As would be expected, a much larger percentage of poor house-

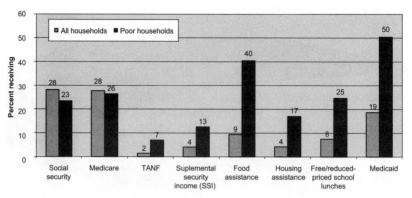

FIGURE 24. Percentage of Households That Report Receiving Income from Selected Programs, by Poverty Status, 2009. SOURCE: U.S. Census Bureau 2010d.

holds receive means-tested programs than nonpoor households. Some nonpoor households receive aid from means-tested programs because, among other reasons, eligibility for receipt is often higher than the poverty line. For example, families with income that is 130 percent of the poverty level are eligible for food stamps. An additional program not listed whose benefits expanded over the 1990s was the Earned Income Tax Credit. In 2009, 27.2 million tax filing units received this credit (representing 19.2 percent of tax returns), with an average credit of $2,195.[51]

Mean amounts of receipt, among those who report receiving them, were highest for Social Security ($17,373 annually) in 2009 and more moderate for others such as Medicare ($7,455), TANF/General Assistance ($3,392), supplemental security income (SSI) ($7,994), food assistance ($2,999), housing subsidies ($2,769), Medicaid ($3,696), and free/reduced-price school lunches ($833), according to CPS data.[52] Although these amounts are significant, they are often not sufficient to push people's income above the poverty line.

Figure 25 provides a careful accounting of the percentage point decline in pretransfer poverty produced by various government programs in 2004 by economist John Karl Scholz and his colleagues. They note that some assumptions have to be made about the extent to which the medical benefits in particular reduce poverty (they are often omitted from calculations, such as those in the previous chapter). For example, say an individual needs a medical procedure that costs $30,000. If Medicare covers that cost, should we consider the entirety of the amount received as contributing to the person's income in that year? It is not clear if it should, as that money cannot be used to meet other basic

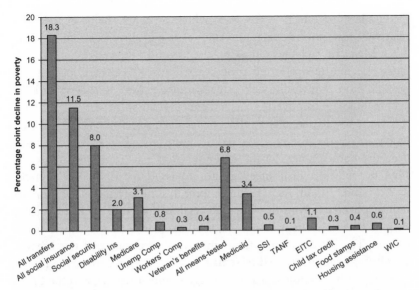

FIGURE 25. Percentage Point Decline in Pretransfer Poverty Produced by Government Transfers (Social Insurance and Means-Tested), 2004. SOURCE: Scholz, Moffitt, and Cowan 2009, table 8.2. NOTES: The pre-transfer poverty rate was 30.3 percent. The poverty rate after all transfers were added was 12.0 percent, for a total reduction of 18.3 percentage points.

needs, such as food, clothing, and shelter. For the calculations in figure 25 then, the value of Medicare and Medicaid is roughly based on the cost of purchasing health insurance.[53] It should also be noted that the calculations in figure 25 only simulate the "marginal effect" of receiving a benefit and do not incorporate the potential behavioral response to that receipt. The receipt of cash welfare, for example, may increase one's benefit income, but it could conceivably reduce other income if, say, a person decides to work less because of the benefit. Potential behavioral responses to government transfers are discussed in more detail below.

With these caveats in mind, figure 25 indicates that government programs serve to decrease pretransfer poverty by 18.3 percentage points, from 30.3 percent to 12.0 percent (if medical benefits were excluded, the posttransfer poverty rate would equal 14.1 percent).[54] Thus, while the American safety net compares unfavorably to those in other rich countries (see chapter 4), it still does much to keep many millions of people out of poverty. Social insurance programs as a whole have a larger impact on poverty (reducing poverty by 11.5 percentage points) than means-tested programs (6.8 percentage points). Social Security is the single most effective program, which of course helps explain the relatively low poverty rates of Americans sixty-five years and older. After Medicaid (which reduces poverty by 3.4 percentage points), the most effective means-tested program was the EITC (1.1. percentage points). Note that traditional cash assistance (TANF) does very little to keep people out of poverty (0.1 percentage points).[55]

On the whole, the relative effect of specific programs has not changed much since 2004 (the year covered by figure 25) because there have not been dramatic changes in the nation's safety net. Many of the provisions of the health insurance legislation passed in 2010 will take effect in 2013 and beyond. As noted in chapter 6, some programs did more to reduce poverty during the Great Recession than they had previously, such as Unemployment Insurance, food assistance (SNAP), the Earned Income Tax Credit, and a few temporary programs and tax breaks. SNAP, for example, served to reduce poverty by 1.7 percentage points in 2010 (rather than just 0.4 percentage points in 2004), and the EITC served to reduce poverty by 2.0 percentages points (rather than 1.1 percentage points in 2004).[56] The increased spending that did occur in the 2000s was a result of changing economic conditions and demographic shifts rather than fundamental policy reforms. Thus, the effectiveness of the safety net has remained fairly constant since 2000.[57]

One notable aspect of the American safety net is that it does a much better job at reducing poverty among the elderly than others. Social Security is responsible for this. Average benefits to retired workers, although often not very high, are still high enough to surpass the official poverty line.[58] One more achievement of policy since the 1970s has been the gradual construction of a work support system that provides a number of benefits for low-income working families. This includes housing subsidies, food assistance, the EITC, Medicaid, the Children's Health Insurance Program, the child tax credit, childcare subsidies, greater child support enforcement, and school lunch and breakfast programs.[59] Detractors, however, still rightfully point out how much less government programs do to help children than the elderly.[60] Others also note that the safety net does a poor job of assisting nonelderly childless families and nonworking families, who have few programs to draw upon other than SNAP.[61]

CURRENT POLICY DEBATES

An evaluation of policy depends on the criteria by which we judge it. Some assess policy on the basis of whether it encourages economic growth and increases average standards of living. Others prefer policy to minimize inequality. Some want policy to promote individual self-sufficiency, while others are most concerned with reducing material hardship. The problem with many policy debates—the source of much confusion on what works and what does not—is that there needs to be greater recognition and discussion of differing underlying aims, priorities, and values.

What should be the basic goals of policy? There are perhaps three areas of broad consensus in the United States. First, Americans generally agree that there is a public responsibility to help those lacking the necessities of life. Second, people should strive to be as self-supporting as circumstances permit; a vibrant society depends on individual industriousness.[62] The tension between the first two goals suggests that most people believe there should be a mutual obligation, one that combines an obligation on the part of the state to provide services and the other on the part of recipients to make efforts to achieve independence through work. Third, policies that promote equity should not unduly hinder economic growth. Such growth determines average standards of living and individual material well-being over the long run.[63] Of course, it should be said that not all Americans subscribe to these goals. There are strident libertarians who believe that government should not be involved in public support at all, and that people are wholly responsible for their own welfare. At the other end of the spectrum there are those who prefer a stronger safety net that does not impose normative values on recipients, or those who deride the focus of capitalism on economic growth and consumerism as ends rather than as a means to well-being. Nevertheless, the consensus on the three goals outlined above is generally broad and strong according to public opinion polls.[64]

In practice, people still diverge in what they believe should be done to reduce poverty. Some people (mostly on the political left) express concern that government benefits are simply too low to help many people out of poverty. That is, the overwhelming majority of means-tested benefits are designed to sustain people in poverty rather than actually help them move out of it.[65] Michael Harrington, author of the well-known book *The Other America: Poverty in the United States,* argues that this reflects poorly on the country's humanitarian efforts: "The poor are the most sorely tried and dramatic victims of economic and social tendencies which threaten the entire nation. . . . In morality and in justice every citizen should be committed to abolishing the other America, for it is intolerable that the richest nation in human history should allow such needless suffering."[66]

Alternatively, those who prioritize the reduction of dependency (usually on the political right) often question the role of government in social and economic affairs. One concern is that welfare programs provide individual disincentives to work. Some supporters of this view assert that disincentives contribute to a "culture of poverty," consisting of an eroded work ethic, dependency on government programs, lack of educational aspiration and achievement, and increased single parenthood.[67] As described earlier, these general views have a long history in debates about welfare. It should be noted that one need not believe that government programs produce a separate subculture to still accept that benefits may indeed provide some disincentive to work among individuals.

Among those who are concerned about economic growth, there is concern about the potential trade-off between such growth and government spending designed to reduce income inequality. In many European countries, for example, where the welfare state has traditionally played a major role, there have been efforts over the past few decades to cut spending on the welfare state. It has been argued that government spending hampers economic efficiency and growth by limiting flexibility and dampening private investment.[68] Cuts in social transfers are advocated on the grounds that they, or the taxes necessary to finance them, distort the working of the labor market.

What does the evidence say on the behavioral effects of welfare and the potential trade-off between government spending and economic growth? The evidence on the first issue—the behavioral effects of welfare—indicates that various programs do have some, generally small, negative effects on economically "desirable" behaviors. The increase in employment among single mothers and the general decline in welfare rolls in the United States after welfare reform supports this notion. In an extensive review of the pre–welfare reform literature on disincentive effects, economist Robert Moffitt concluded, "Econometric studies show that labor supply is reduced by the AFDC and Food Stamp programs, and that the programs affect family structure though usually weakly." A more recent review of the research by John Karl Scholz and his colleagues generally confirmed these conclusions.[69] Thus welfare benefits appear to moderately reduce employment, as does disability insurance.[70] The employment disincentive effects of welfare have also been demonstrated in other countries.[71] With regards to marriage, however, the behavioral effects of welfare are simply not large enough to explain the large long-term declines in marriage rates. Broader economic and cultural shifts likely help explain the long-term trend.[72]

Regarding the second issue—whether public spending inhibits economic growth—some studies suggests that expansive states may have less growth over the longer run, though the evidence is neither definitive nor straightforward. To first review the positive aspect of public spending, more expansive states do, on the whole, have less poverty, particularly relative poverty. The U.S. relative poverty rate is well above the comparable rate in other countries, as described in chapter 4. Even when using the U.S. absolute poverty threshold, the American poverty rate still surpasses those in many European countries, despite the fact that the United States' gross domestic product (GDP) per capita is significantly higher.[73] Much of the difference is due to the smaller size of government transfers in the United States.[74]

Many European countries invest heavily in universal benefits, such as maternity leave, child care, and medical care.[75] In a comparison of selected OECD countries, gross public social expenditures as a percentage of GDP were lower in the United States than in the other eight countries (Denmark, France, Germany, Ireland, Italy, Japan, Sweden, and the United Kingdom) in 2007. For example, the United States spent about 17.1 percent of its GDP on these public expenditures, compared with the thirty-country OECD average of 24.3 percent. At the top of the list of the selected countries were France (33.0 percent), Sweden (32.9 percent), and Denmark (30.7 percent). However, more than many other countries, the United States delivers benefits through tax breaks, and especially private expenditures (such as via employment-based pension benefits and employer contributions to health insurance). When public and private expenditures are combined, social expenditures in the United States are similar to those in Denmark and Sweden. Thus, it is usually public expenditures that do more to reduce poverty than other kinds of transfers.[76]

However, while rich countries with strong welfare states tend to have lower levels of poverty, there is some evidence that countries with greater pay inequality, low tax rates, and weak employment regulations have greater private sector employment growth. Massive public employment can impose a cost burden on government finances, especially when many of the jobs pay more than is justified by their level of productivity.[77] In an effort to reduce costs and work disincentives, a number of welfare states have reduced the generosity of particular transfers or services in recent decades, such as New Zealand and the Netherlands in the 1980s; Denmark, Sweden, and Canada in the 1990s; and Germany in the early 2000s.[78] None of these efforts, however, have involved the wholesale dismantling of their welfare states.

While large and inefficient government programs and overregulation may crowd out private sector activity and reduce economic growth over the long run, there may be some middle ground where public spending to assist the poor does not automatically lead to high unemployment or a significant reduction in growth. It is not always the size of the welfare state per se that matters, but the way in which programs are designed and implemented.[79]

After all, in the wake of the global recession in 2008, the condition of European economies varied widely. Perhaps the worst off was Greece, where government spending far outpaced revenue during the 2000s. The government bureaucracy was bloated, and money was wastefully spent on frivolous projects. The government borrowed until it basically went bankrupt and could not borrow any more.[80] The rest of the European Union, under German leadership, finally decided to bail out Greece, but only if the Greek government agreed to drastically cut public employment and spending. As a result, Greece fell into a deep recession. The unemployment rate in Greece in the third quarter of 2011 was 17.8 percent and climbing. Other countries, like Spain and Ireland, were also suffering, with unemployment rates of 21.5 and 14.7 respectively during the same period, well above the U.S. unemployment rate of 9.1 at that time.[81]

Nevertheless, other European countries were doing satisfactorily and growing at a moderate clip. Unemployment in Germany and Sweden, for example, were 5.8 and 6.8 percent respectively in the third quarter of 2011.[82] Germany has a strong export-based economy that grew at a pace not unlike that of the United States even in the years before the recession. Thus, it becomes difficult to generalize if welfare states are doomed to fail and implode; much depends not just on the size of the government, but also on its efficiency and responsiveness to changing conditions.

Lessons from these cross-national comparisons can be applied to the functioning of government within the United States—its states, counties, and municipalities. On the one hand, it is not hard to find stories of waste, corruption, and general inattention to the bottom line and the hardship these practices impose on the average taxpayer. On the other hand, a government that is too small often has difficulty providing services that the public generally supports and expects. Severe budget cuts in the wake of the Great Recession resulted in a drastic reduction in services in some places. The city of Trenton, New Jersey, for example, laid off 103 policemen. Crime spiked shortly thereafter. Residents of Colorado Springs refused a call by the mayor to raise taxes. As a result, many city lights went dark, openings in the police and fire departments went unfilled, and park services were substantially reduced. Not everyone was happy about these developments, yet many remained reflexively hostile to taxes and to the notion that government can effectively and efficiently deliver basic services.[83]

The Role of Government in Society

The discussion above suggests that many apprehensions about government programs in the United States are motivated less by purely economic concerns than by suspicion of government's role in social affairs. The devolution of public authority from the federal government to the states reflects the distrust of centralized authority. People are often cynical of government efforts to provide social programs, sometimes feeling that individuals can do best for and by themselves. Assistance to the poor (often considered undeserving) is perceived as coming at one's own expense.

What are the limits of social obligation? What do we owe one another? Who provides in times of need: families, charities, employers, or the state? Michael Katz notes that these are questions without definitive answers because they are not objective and cannot be resolved by "looking at the data," so to speak.[84] The consensus embodied in welfare reform policy seems to be one of mutual obligation, where the state provides benefits and the able-bodied recipient works for these services in one way or another.[85] Many conservatives, such as Charles Murray, worry that government programs encroach on self-reliance and are ultimately degrading. These programs serve to undermine what he sees as the essential building blocks of civil society: family, vocation, community, and faith, and he further argues these are the institutions that formed the basis of American exceptionalism.[86]

Others would counter that the welfare state provides essential services for the greater good. Plato recognized that "society originates because the individual is not self-sufficient, but has many needs which he can't supply himself." More recently, philosopher John Rawls defined the common good as "certain general conditions that are . . . equally to everyone's advantage." Public services ensure that individuals, families, and groups have the capability to achieve fulfillment by reducing poverty and vulnerability. A poor person in an affluent country often lacks these capabilities. The welfare state is rooted in values that recognize people's rights and responsibilities, empathy with others, and citizenship and solidarity.[87] Thus, morality, especially in European welfare states, is typically rooted in this kind of secular humanism rather than religion. The thinking is that in modern, affluent societies we have moved beyond subsistence concerns and can afford to help our neighbors, especially if they take the appropriate steps to help themselves as well.

How far should the welfare state go to reduce material hardship if it results in some measure of dependency on the state? In the past there have always been people dependent on one another. Should this kind of dependency simply be relegated back to families and communities, even if they often lack the resources that a larger entity—such as a national government—may have at its disposal to reduce vulnerability and hardship, especially during a deep recession? Even if social transfers do, in fact, distort the working of the labor market (and the evidence on this issue is mixed), we still need to evaluate collectively whether the economic costs are acceptable in terms of social objectives. Markets often enhance risk, while government transfer programs, particularly social insurance ones, are meant to reduce risk.[88]

Reflecting the less expansive welfare state in the United States, social support for welfare programs is lower in the United States than in Europe. In summarizing American public opinion toward business and policies to help the poor, as expressed in social surveys and more in-depth studies, Lane Kenworthy says:

> So what *do* Americans want? . . . Most Americans support capitalism and business. Many believe hard work, rather than luck or help from others, is the key to success. Many feel they have opportunity to get ahead. Many believe income inequality is too high and that high inequality is not necessary for the country's prosperity. At a general level, many are skeptical about government's ability to help. There is only limited support for enhanced redistribution as a remedy for high inequality. Yet Americans do support increased spending on programs perceived to enhance opportunity and economic security.[89]

The partial retreat from expansive welfare states in Europe in the 1990s and 2000s indicates that there may be at least some convergence in attitudes, partly because of the feeling that the state has become too large and inefficient. Public pressure to cut back the European safety net has also arisen out of growing social divisions based on race, ethnicity, and nativity. Sweden, for example, had few non-European immigrants throughout much of the twentieth century. There was also a strong idea that all Swedes were "in the same boat." By 2006, however,

12.9 percent of the Swedish population was foreign-born, and there were many immigrants from Asia, the Middle East, and Africa. In more diverse counties in Sweden, public support for universal spending is significantly lower than in less diverse ones.[90]

The historical fragmentation of society along racial and ethnic lines in the United States has likewise contributed to the lack of a sense of common national community. Reflecting policy in colonial times, when American communities provided help for their own while turning their back on outsiders, the lack of a sense of community today contributes to the decline in national civic engagement. In a 1904 article Emil Munsterberg noted, "No civilized state is without [policies that address poverty]. . . . Their foundation is laid by a feeling of fellowship."[91] Implicit in this argument is that, in the absence of such a collective feeling of fellowship and citizenship, efforts to alleviate poverty are bound to suffer.

LOOKING AHEAD

So where does this leave us? Ideological divisions remain as strong as ever in the United States, and public discourse about pressing problems is as uncivil as it has been in the past half century. Congress is likewise deeply divided and seemingly incapable of passing legislation to address lingering issues such as rising medical costs, structural deficits, and immigration. In early 2012 public opinion polls indicated that only 11 percent of Americans approved of the job Congress was doing.[92] Congressional districts are drawn to be fairly homogeneous; as a result, ideologically "pure" and uncompromising candidates are often elected to office. As I write this, unemployment is declining but poverty remains high relative to where it has been over the past forty years. Inequality is likewise high and still increasing.

With the nation divided, it is unlikely that any large-scale legislation directed at the nation's low-income population will be enacted any time soon. As health care reform legislation passed in 2010 takes effect, we can expect a decline in the number of people without health insurance. Although a significant percentage of Americans would like to do more to help the poor, opposition to any further government expansion is significant enough to prevent broad-based programs directed to reduce poverty.

Despite the challenges of working in a difficult political environment, there are some policy options that could serve to reduce poverty and that are still broadly consistent with the goal of reducing hardship while not increasing dependency or stifling economic growth. As has been discussed above, policy has been more effective at reducing poverty among the elderly than among children in the United States. Despite this fact, low-income children are typically viewed as being among the "deserving" poor because they are poor due to circumstances clearly beyond their own control. There are already a few policies that help children, particularly the children of working parents, including child tax breaks in the tax code and the Children's Health Insurance Program. Nevertheless, many feel that more can be done to reduce child poverty.

Stronger child care programs could provide more support for working parents and also address some of the intergenerational effects of poverty. Current policy in the United States (as specified in the Family and Medical Leave Act of 1993) is that all public agencies and private companies with fifty or more employees must provide twelve weeks of unpaid leave to parents. The United States is one of the very few countries in the world that does not provide paid time off for new parents. In contrast, in the United Kingdom, all female employees are entitled to fifty-two weeks of maternity leave, thirty-nine weeks of which is paid, with the first six weeks paid at 90 percent of full pay and the remainder at a fixed rate. (There are proposals to raise the length of paid leave to fifty-two weeks.) Sweden is even more generous: all working parents are entitled to sixteen months of paid leave per child, with the cost being shared by the employer and the state.[93] It is unlikely that the United States will implement policies that come close to this, but it is not unthinkable that parental leave policies could be strengthened. This would allow parents to stay connected to the labor market while still providing the necessary care for their infants.

Part of the recent strategy to reduce child poverty in the United Kingdom has been to provide universal preschool for children ages three and four. Many of these schools also provide before- and after-school care. Child care assistance to working families has likewise been expanded there. The goal was twofold: first, to support parental work, and second, to invest in young children's education. Some of the cognitive inequalities between children of low- and high-income household are present even by the time children reach kindergarten. High-quality child care has the potential to reduce these gaps.[94] The large combination of policies (including additional tax credits and boosts to education) adopted by the United Kingdom after 1999 to reduce child poverty were quite effective, as the child poverty rate fell by several percentage points over the next ten years. So far those programs do not seem to have had undesirable effects such as promoting unwed fertility or discouraging work.[95] Britain spent about an extra 0.9 percent of GDP for low-income families with children between 1999 and 2003.[96]

Another possibility is the creation of a universal child allowance, a program that has also been adopted by the United Kingdom as well as seventy other nations.[97] Currently, the U.S. tax code allows many families to receive a similar, if modest, allowance in the form of a child tax credit of $1,000 per child. Very low-income families (those who earn less than $3,000 annually) are ineligible for the credit, and families with more than one child are not eligible for the full credit unless their earnings exceed $16,000 annually. Couples with incomes above $110,000 receive a smaller credit, and those with incomes above $130,000 receive no credit at all. Making all low-income families eligible for this credit and increasing the size of the credit would further help reduce material deprivation among children.[98]

One innovative program adopted by New York City to reduce child poverty was $ave NYC. This program offered a matched savings account to low-income tax filers. Program participants receive a 50 percent match of up to $500 if they deposit at least $200 from their tax refund from the Earned Income Tax Credit into a designated account and maintain the initial deposit for one year. By encouraging individuals to save, it can create a path toward longer-term savings and greater financial stability.[99]

Others have proposed even more ambitious programs along these lines. Duncan Lindsey, for example, has outlined a possible approach where at birth, all children, regardless of the economic status of their family, would have a custodial account opened in their name with an initial deposit of $1,000 assured by the government. Each year an additional $500 would be deposited. In essence, the program would work like the 529 college savings plans currently used by many American families. Lindsey estimates that the plan would cost $41 billion annually and suggests that it could be paid for by a small payroll tax by employees and employers. He reiterates that program could do much to provide young people leaving home with an asset base that could expand their economic and educational opportunities (the United Kingdom has such a program in the form of the Child Trust Fund).[100] The advantage of this policy is that it would not seem to foster dependency; quite the opposite, it provides a basis for people to try to invest and plan for the future. The disadvantage is that it is not without a cost, and it represents an expansion of government. As such, the plan would not go far in the current political climate, though perhaps there will be a time when it might receive further consideration, particularly if local approaches (such as the one in New York City) continue to show promise.

Finally, most people would agree that improving education in America for kindergartners through twelfth graders could serve to reduce disparities, help more children reach their potential, and produce a workforce needed to respond to twenty-first-century global economic challenges. The heated debates about school reform are so complex and varied as to be beyond the scope of this chapter. Suffice it to say that appropriately investing in our children's education is one of our nation's most important challenges.

SUMMARY

Over the course of the history of U.S. welfare policy, there has been a constant tension between the goal of giving aid to those in need in a humane manner and that of not undermining people's incentive to work and be self-supporting. Colonial programs tended to provide sufficient benefits to community members, though they were unkind to outsiders and to able-bodied people. As the social and economic system and the communities embedded in them changed and grew, basic outdoor relief proved insufficient. The poorhouses of the nineteenth century ("indoor" relief) attempted to provide basic care while dissuading dependence. These institutions, many of which were poorly managed, were eventually thought to be too inhumane and did little to address the roots of poverty. Scientific charities at the turn of the twentieth century sought to professionalize the provision of aid and dissuade dependence, but they were largely not very successful.

In the 1930s, the Great Depression vividly illustrated how local efforts alone are often insufficient for providing a safety net and how poverty, even among able-bodied individuals, is clearly sometimes a result of broad structural forces rather than individual laziness or other weaknesses. As general standards of living improved in the post–World War II period, some became concerned that not everyone was benefiting from the changes. The 1960s War on Poverty attempted to bring prosperity to those who had previously been ignored by, or had benefited only marginally from, government policies. This movement broadened the American safety net, though many thought that welfare policies had gone too far and did not do enough to prevent dependency. This led to welfare reform in 1996 that ended cash assistance as an entitlement that could be received by all poor people.

Some of the frustrations about high social welfare costs have stemmed from misperceptions about which government programs consume the largest part of the budget. The most controversial programs, such as cash welfare assistance, have for many years consumed only a small part of the budget. The largest part of income-assistance spending is dedicated to relatively popular social insurance programs, such as Medicare and Social Security. The costs of medical benefits, such as Medicare and Medicaid, have risen the most quickly over the last three decades.

Government transfers are often not high enough to actually lift people's income over the poverty line. Social insurance programs, such as Social Security, do the most in terms of reducing poverty, especially among the elderly. The EITC does more to help many working families with low wages.

Government programs that assist low-income families continue to try to strike a delicate balance by simultaneously providing some sort of safety net while also promoting work. The general consensus is that the welfare reform of the late 1990s worked, though many vocal dissenters argue that it did not do enough to check material hardship. In contrast, many hold high hopes that the health care reform legislation that passed in 2010 will help provide more people with better access to health care, while others counter that it represents government overreach. Here again we see the age-old tension between efforts to help those in need versus those who believe that expansive government policies reduce individual industriousness.

Conclusion

The United States is a strong and prosperous nation. It has the world's largest economy and its strongest military. Its per capita GDP is one of the highest in the world. Americans have many freedoms, such as freedom of speech and worship. As exasperating as the political system can be, the United States does have a stable democracy. The United States continues to be a global center of economic and technological innovation. The waiting list for permanent visas is long, and America remains an attractive destination for immigrants.

But we do have a poverty problem. The problem may not be nearly as large as it is in many developing countries, such as Sierra Leone or Bangladesh, or in middle-income countries, like Mexico or Thailand, but neither is it as small as it is in other countries with standards of living similar to ours, such as Germany and Denmark. Some people are not troubled by poverty as long as there is economic mobility. In other words, they consider it acceptable for people to be poor if they have the opportunity to make something of themselves with their sweat and tears. There are indications, however, that economic mobility may have declined in recent years. It remains true that people have the opportunity to become fabulously wealthy in America, but there are some structural conditions that make it difficult for many to achieve substantial upward mobility even if they have the drive. Many Americans intuitively understand this and are dismayed by it.

One of the vehicles for upward mobility in the post–World War II era has been a college education. Indeed, poverty rates are much lower for college graduates than for those with a high school degree or less. Yet the cost of going to college has risen much faster than inflation in recent years, and attendance is now beyond the means of many families. The problem begins even earlier than that. Public K–12 school systems vary widely across the country. Some produce high-achieving, upwardly mobile students, while others simply do all they can to keep their students from dropping out. Many argue that the problem begins even before that, as disparities are seen even as students begin elementary school. Family background—a family's socioeconomic status—plays an important role in determining how well young children are prepared to learn. Poor parents have difficulty investing time and money in their children, and the stress of their often-disorganized lives may be transmitted to their children, who are more likely to act out in school, get poor grades, or drop out.

Growing income inequality since the early 1970s has exacerbated this situation. The affluent are doing well for themselves—their incomes have grown considerably over the last generation—but the rest of the population has struggled. They may have difficulty finding quality day care, paying high health insurance premiums, or buying a house with some of the modern amenities regularly showcased on TV shows. Inequality was one of the root causes of the housing bubble and its subsequent collapse, which precipitated the Great Recession. Politicians seem more motivated to raise money for their expensive reelection campaigns and score cheap political points than to address some of the nation's deepest problems. Compromise is viewed as a moral weakness. In short, there seems much to worry about. So is there something that can be done about our poverty problem?

QUESTIONS REVISITED

It is time to return to the basic questions raised in the introduction to this book. First, why does poverty remain so pervasive? There are a few reasons, including the way we understand and define poverty, economic inequality, and policy choices. The way we understand and define poverty is critical because it establishes the yardstick by which we gauge success. For example, if we define poverty in terms of extremely severe material deprivation—say, in terms of how many people starve to death each year—then we have, for the most part, beaten poverty in the United

States. However, if we define poverty in terms of comparative disadvantage, as is commonly done, then we are doing less well. Many people in America struggle to attain the basic goods that would allow them to participate in mainstream society. It is not enough to live in a mud hut with threadbare clothes at the edge of town, as might be acceptable in some very poor countries. Because the income perceived as sufficient to avoid poverty increases as standards of living increase, achieving inroads against poverty over the long run is difficult.

Economic inequality also contributes to poverty. Although our market system excels at generating economic growth and improving standards of living, a by-product of the system is income inequality. Businesses keep their labor costs down by paying wages that are as low as possible. People may also be laid off from work and have trouble finding employment during times of recession or economic transition. Capitalism is a system of "creative destruction" that nurtures economic innovation but can leave those working in declining sectors in the lurch.

Policy may increase or reduce the harmful effects of inequality. The rise of the welfare state in the 1930s was a response to the hardship of the Great Depression, which exposed some of the weakness of the unregulated market. Earlier still, Theodore Roosevelt sought to curb the power of the corporations and monopolies that threatened to undermine the competitive marketplace. Policy, however, is a tool used by those with competing interests, and it is not always used to promote equality. For example, some seek to make the tax code more progressive by making the rich pay a higher marginal tax rate, while others push for more tax breaks for businesses and high-income investors.

The second question posed in the introduction was "What does it mean to be poor?" As described above, views about poverty are rooted in a particular time and place. The poverty line in the United States is considerably higher than that in developing countries. In poor countries, particularly in South Asia and Africa, a high proportion of the population fails to earn even $1.25 a day. Moreover, even within the United States, the amount of income that people believe is needed to avoid poverty is higher today than it was at the beginning of the twentieth century. This is not to suggest that efforts to define an absolute, subsistence poverty measure are devoid of value; it is informative to gauge changes in the number of people with incomes below a very low, fixed poverty threshold. However, it is also important to be aware that any fixed line is somewhat arbitrary and will eventually need to be updated if it is to continue to be socially meaningful.

While poverty generally refers to material deprivation, it is a multi-faceted experience. Although it certainly involves economic hardship, such as having difficulty paying bills or living in a home that is in disrepair, for some poverty means lacking some of the basic consumer items that their neighbors have, such as a cell phone or a car to get to work. In the United States, a majority of people manage to escape poverty after a short spell of being poor, but a substantial number are economically vulnerable and experience recurrent bouts of poverty.

Our third question is "Are particular groups of people (e.g., ethnic minorities, single-parent families) inevitably more likely to be poor?" For the most part, the answer is no. Today minorities, women, children, and female-headed families are more likely to be poor than others, and in the short run we may see only small shifts in the composition of the poverty population. However, in recent decades we have also witnessed some very significant declines in poverty among these groups (though all these groups experienced increased poverty in the 2000s). The poverty rate among African Americans plummeted from 55 percent in 1959 to 22 percent in 2000 before rising to 28 percent in 2011. The decline in the prevalence of racial discrimination has played a significant role in the falling poverty rate for African Americans over the past half century. Nevertheless, a racial poverty gap remains; high levels of black poverty today are likely a function of past poverty, economic dislocation, wealth differentials, family instability, substandard schooling in lower-income areas, and lingering racism.

Latinos also have a high poverty rate (25 percent in 2011) that virtually matches the African American one. Continued high levels of immigration from Latin American countries make it more difficult to discern what accounts for these high rates. Newly arrived immigrants tend to fare worse than the native population because of language barriers, unfamiliarity with local labor markets, and lower levels of education. Latinos in particular display high employment rates but low wages. However, native-born Latinos have both higher levels of education and earnings than Latino immigrants (though still lower than non-Hispanic whites), suggesting that high poverty levels among Hispanics may be short-lived. The poverty rate among Asian Americans is similar to that of the white population. Asian American educational levels equal or surpass those of whites and other groups, as does their median household income, particularly among the native born.

The poverty rate among women is only slightly higher than among men. Indeed, gender disparities in earnings have narrowed considerably over time, and particularly among younger cohorts. Nevertheless, a gender earnings gap remains among year-round full-time workers, which is difficult to account for. People disagree if it is a result of continuing gender discrimination in the labor market or a function of woman generally having a lower attachment to the labor force because of their greater responsibilities caring for children and parents (which many argue is a result of gender socialization). Regardless, women today attain increasingly higher levels of education than men, and this will likely serve to narrow gender disparities in the future. This growing divergence in educational attainment that favors women could conceivably leave men at a socioeconomic disadvantage at some point in the future.

The poverty rate of single-parent families, particularly female-headed families with children (41 percent in 2011), is substantially higher than that among married-couple families with children (9 percent). Single parents often face the challenge of working and raising children by themselves. Women, who are far more likely to head such families, face the additional obstacle of having lower earnings than men. Despite the greater economic vulnerability of single-parent families, they are not inherently disposed to very high poverty rates. One reason is that increasing levels of employment and rising wages among all women, including female heads, have driven down the poverty rates among such families. Another is that policy can reduce poverty among single-parent families, whether in the form of income or child care support. Countries that provide generous support, such as Sweden, have greatly reduced poverty among these types of families. However, it should be noted that even in Sweden the poverty rate among single-parent families, while low relative to poverty in the United States, is still well above the poverty rate among married-couple families there.

The fourth question asked in the introduction is "What can we expect over the next few years?" The Great Recession of 2007–9 had a deep impact on unemployment and poverty. The recession also occurred after decades of increasing income inequality. Wealthy Americans have seen remarkable increases in their standards of living, but families in the lowest income quartile are struggling harder to maintain theirs. Indeed, while there is still significant economic mobility in the United States, it is lower among people born in the lowest income quintile than among any other segment of the population. Even as the significance of racial and ethnic differences has declined in recent decades, socioeconomic ones have become more important.

If economic growth accelerates in the future, we will undoubtedly see declines in absolute poverty, even if inequality does not change much (though relative poverty won't change much if inequality persists). As I write this, the country is still emerging from a recession and unemployment is declining, but projections for future economic growth are still rather modest. No one is predicting a substantial decline in income inequality in the near future. Thus, while official (absolute) poverty may decline somewhat in the near future, it is currently difficult to envision large declines. I should add that these sorts of predictions need to be taken with a grain of salt because we usually assume that future trends won't break radically from present patterns.

The final question is "What are the limits of policy?" The American public—more so than the public in Western European countries—accepts a certain amount of income inequality as an inherent part of our economic system. At the same time, the American public favors at least some of the income support structures of the modern welfare state. There is wide acceptance of policies such as Social Security and Medicare, which reduce poverty and hardship and provide some degree of income security, particularly for middle-class families.

Spending on government programs depends on public support, and public opinion is currently deeply divided in the United States. The country lacks a broad sense of community, and thus lacks common goals and ideas about civic responsibilities. On the one hand, the size and diversity of the United States is an important strength, as it contributes to the country's economic power and innovativeness. However, the nation's size and diversity also pose challenges to collective action. Among the most important of our divisions are ideological differences in the role the government should play in society.

There are those who argue that government could do more without drastically reducing the incentive to work or stifling innovation. They do not believe, for example, that universal health care will lead to substantial declines in employment. Rather, they consider that such a program will decrease people's vulnerability to adverse events and contribute to the building of a more humane and modern society. In contrast, others are deeply distrustful of government, sometimes for different reasons. In addition to those who believe that government programs serve to dull individual initiative, some think governments are simply not as efficient as private enterprise. However, in the case of health care, which many would view as a public good, it is difficult to induce private insurance companies to provide their product to people who may not be very healthy to begin with. Others feel that government power is not to be trusted, and that governments do not represent them and their interests. There has long been a streak of this kind of libertarianism in American society.

The result of these differences is that future programs that aim to reduce poverty—certainly in the form of collective action—will provide incremental benefits at best. This does not mean that those who are concerned with reducing poverty should lose heart, but rather that the task at hand is to develop modest policy proposals that could make a difference in the current environment. At the same time, it is important to engage in broader discussions that may serve to fundamentally change the framing of the problem of poverty in America and what we can and should do about it.

Notes

INTRODUCTION

1. For a review of these studies, see Lichter and Crowley 2002; Moore et al. 2009.
2. Holzer et al. 2007.
3. U.S. Census Bureau 2010b.
4. National Research Council 1995.

1. EARLY VIEWS OF POVERTY IN AMERICA

1. Patterson 2000, 38.
2. National Research Council 1995, 24.
3. Ravallion, Chen, and Sangraula 2008.
4. Smith 1776, 351–52.
5. Townsend 1993, 10.
6. Katz 1993a, 3–23.
7. Trattner 1994, 22.
8. Trattner 1994, 26.
9. Katz 1996.
10. Sugrue 1993.
11. Burroughs 1835, cited in Katz 1993a, 6.
12. Gans 1995, 15.
13. Kauffman and Kiesling 1997, 439–48; Katz 1996; Kiesling and Margo 1997, 405–17; Monkkonen 1993, 334–65.
14. Katz 1996, 7; Monkkonen 1993, 343.
15. Katz 1996, 8, 10.

16. Sugrue 1993, 93–94.
17. *Second Annual Report of the Children's Aid Society of New York* 1855, 3, quoted in Katz 1993a, 9.
18. Gurteen 1882, 38, quoted in Katz 1996, 76.
19. Sugrue 1993, 95.
20. Katz 1993b, 446.
21. Katz 1996, 10.
22. Sugrue 1993, 91–92.
23. Kiesling and Margo 1997, 409.
24. Hunter 1904, 11.
25. Ryan 1906.
26. Patterson 2000, 10.
27. Jones 1993, 31.
28. Trotter Jr. 1993, 60.
29. Trotter Jr. 1993, 61.
30. DuBois 1899, 171.
31. DuBois 1899, 273.
32. DuBois 1899, 283–84.
33. Trotter Jr. 1993, 58–69.
34. Patterson 2000, 14–15.
35. Sugrue 1993, 97.
36. Patterson 2000, 41.
37. Patterson 2000, 37.
38. Turner, Beeghley, and Powers 1989.
39. Fisher 1997a.
40. Booth 1892–97; Fisher 1997a.
41. Booth 1889, 33, quoted in Fisher 1997a, 3.
42. Fisher 1997a, 5.
43. Fisher 1997a, 7.
44. Hunter 1904, 5–7.
45. Fisher 1995, 7.
46. Fisher 1997a, 22.
47. Fisher 1997a, 48.
48. Fisher 1997a, 30.
49. Fisher 1997a, 32–41.
50. Galbraith 1958, 251.
51. Harrington 1962
52. O'Connor 2001, 152.
53. O'Connor 2001, 154.
54. Orshansky 1963; Orshansky 1965.

2. METHODS OF MEASURING POVERTY

1. Swarns 2008.
2. Munsterberg 1904, 335.
3. Rector and Sheffield 2011, 1.
4. Vanden Heuvel 2011.

5. National Research Council 1995, 31. An interesting discussion of these issues is also contained in Foster 1998.

6. National Research Council 1995, 1, 24.

7. National Research Council 1995, 31. See also Sen 1983, 153–69.

8. National Research Council 1995, 24. For details on the development of the U.S. official measure, see also Fisher 1997b.

9. The food plan also reflected the differing food needs of adults under and over age sixty-five and accounted for family units with only one or two people. Orshansky used different procedures to calculate thresholds for one- and two-person units to allow for their relatively higher fixed costs.

10. Since its adoption the official poverty measure has undergone minor changes. In 1969 the Consumer Price Index (CPI) began to be used to update thresholds to reflect price changes instead of the per capita cost of foods in the Economy Food Plan. Farm thresholds were also raised from 70 to 85 percent of the nonfarm thresholds. In 1981 nonfarm thresholds were applied to all families, thresholds for families headed by women and men were averaged, and the largest category of family size was raised from seven or more to nine or more people.

11. Sen 1983, 159.

12. Fisher 1997a, 26–38.

13. Fisher 1997a, 5–11.

14. For a detailed discussion, see Townsend 1993.

15. For a complete list of items included in the official Census Bureau income definition, see Dalaker and Naifeh 1998.

16. Evidence for the growth effect of the EITC, especially in the 1990s, when the program was expanded, comes from Center on Budget and Policy Priorities 1998; Iceland and Kim 2001; Iceland et al. 2001.

17. Blank 2008, 237.

18. National Research Council 1995, 1–13.

19. Note that a "family" unit under the official measure can also consist of a single individual (either a person living alone or living with people not related to him or her). That is, even though these individuals are not a "family" per se, they are counted as separate units in the family unit of analysis.

20. Trends in cohabitation are found in Kennedy and Bumpass 2008. Discussion of how using different units affects poverty measurement is in Iceland 2000.

21. See National Research Council 1995; Short 2011c.

22. These themes are discussed in detail in Sen 1992; Townsend 1993.

23. Smith 1776, 519.

24. Blank 2008, 244.

25. Examples of relative poverty lines defined in this way can be found in Burtless and Smeeding 2001, 27–68; O'Higgins and Jenkins 1990, 187–211; Johnson and Webb 1992, 135–54; Smeeding et al. 2009, 6.

26. Ehrenreich 2001, 199–200.

27. Organization for Economic Cooperation and Development 2001.

28. European Commission 2000, EN version 11.

29. "India Has More Mobile Phones Than Toilets" 2010.

30. Pritamkabe 2011.

31. Rector and Sheffield 2011.

32. Cogan 1995, 385–90.

33. National Research Council 1995, 126; Sen 1983, 156.

34. See Davidson 1985.

35. UNICEF Innocenti Research Centre 2000, 6.

36. UNICEF Innocenti Research Centre 2000, 6.

37. These criticisms are discussed in National Research Council 1995, 125; Sen 1983, 156.

38. UNICEF Innocenti Research Centre 2000, 22.

39. Meyer and Sullivan 2009.

40. Discussion of hardship measures can be found in Mayer and Jencks 1989; Heflin, Sandberg, and Rafail 2009, 746–64; Iceland and Bauman 2007.

41. Beverly 2001.

42. Daly and Silver 2008.

43. Micklewright 2002, 3.

44. Atkinson and Hills 1998. See also Micklewright 2002, 9.

45. United Nations 1995.

46. Sen 1999, 87–110.

47. See, for example, United Nations 2011.

48. See Short 2011c; Short 2010; Short 2001.

49. Short 2011c.

50. Interested readers should refer to National Research Council 1995 for a more detailed discussion of these elements. Short 2011c also contains details on the actual operationalization and implementation of the SPM poverty measure.

51. Rector and Sheffield 2011; Meyer and Sullivan 2009.

52. More specifically, the SPM threshold includes a basic bundle of goods including, food, clothing, shelter, utilities, medical (termed "FSCUM"), and a little more for additional needs.

53. This question has not been asked by Gallup or the General Social Survey (the sources of the earlier data) since 1993.

54. The official and SPM measures are from Short 2011a. The relative measure is from Short 2011b.

3. CHARACTERISTICS OF THE POVERTY POPULATION

1. These stories are quoted from Contreras 2011.

2. DeNavas-Walt, Proctor, and Smith 2012, table B-2.

3. Lindsey 2009, 64–78.

4. Short 2011a, 8.

5. U.S. Census Bureau 2012k.

6. Coleman-Jensen et al. 2011.

7. U.S. Department of Housing and Urban Development 2010, i–iii.

8. U.S. Census Bureau 2011a.

9. Lichter and Crowley 2002; Chung and Myers Jr. 1999; Kaufman 1999.

10. Townsend 1993, 10.

11. Shaefer and Edin 2012, 4.

12. Bello 2012.

13. Two authors who held this view, though they had otherwise differed on many points, include Michael Harrington (1962) and Oscar Lewis (1966a).

14. Riegg Cellini, McKernan, and Ratcliffe 2008.

15. Rank and Hirschl 2001.

16. Riegg Cellini, McKernan, and Ratcliffe 2008, 594.

17. Bane and Ellwood 1986, 12.

18. Ribar and Hamrick 2003, 11.

19. Anderson 2011.

20. Stevens 1999.

21. Stevens 1994.

22. Stevens 1999.

23. Devine, Plunkett, and Wright 1992.

24. Stevens 1999.

25. Naifeh 1998.

26. Gottschalk, McLanahan, and Sandefur 1994, 85.

27. Corak 2006, 53; Isaacs, Sawhill, and Haskins 2008.

28. Isaacs 2007, 30.

29. Corak 2006, 39; Isaacs, Sawhill, and Haskins 2008.

30. Magnuson and Votruba-Drzal 2009, 155–60.

31. Magnuson and Votruba-Drzal 2009, 158.

32. Magnuson and Votruba-Drzal 2009, 158. See also Edin and Kefalas 2005.

33. U.S. Census Bureau 2012j.

34. Weinberg 1987; Lichter and Crowley 2002.

35. Mattingly, Johnson, and Schaefer 2011, 1.

36. Gibbs 2001.

37. Lichter and Crowley 2002, 23–24.

38. Lichter and Crowley 2002, 24.

39. See Jargowsky 1997. See also Wilson 1987; Kneebone, Nadeau, and Berube 2011, 2.

40. Sugrue 1993, 92–93.

41. Massey and Denton 1993, 26–59.

42. Wilson 1987; Massey and Denton 1993; Auletta 1982.

43. Jargowsky 1997, 11.

44. Jargowsky 1997, 38–43.

45. Jargowsky 1997, 38.

46. Jargowsky 2003.

47. Kneebone, Nadeau, and Berube 2011. 1–16.

48. Kneebone, Nadeau, and Berube 2011. 17.

49. Bishaw 2011.

50. Jargowsky 1996, 598.

51. McGeary 1990.

52. Massey and Denton 1993.

53. Kain 1968.

54. See Holzer 1991; Kasarda 1990; Wilson 1987.

55. Two influential proponents of this view were Charles Murray (1984) and Lawrence Mead (1992).

56. Murray 1984; Mead 1992.
57. Wilson 1987, 14.
58. Jargowsky 1997, 183.
59. U.S. Census Bureau 2012j.
60. Frey 2011, 1.
61. Kneebone, Nadeau, and Berube 2011, 17.
62. Kneebone, Nadeau, and Berube 2011, 9.

4. GLOBAL POVERTY

1. Population Reference Bureau 2011.
2. Kates and Dasgupta 2007, 16747.
3. United Nations 2010.
4. World Bank 2012c.
5. Sachs 2005; Kates and Dasgupta 2007.
6. Dollar and Svensson 2001; Killick 1995.
7. Ravallion 2009.
8. World Bank 2012c.
9. Wallerstein 1974.
10. Firebaugh 2003, 15–30. See also Milanovic 2009.
11. Ravallion 2009.
12. Firebaugh 2003.
13. Swiss Agency for Development and Cooperation (SDC) 2000, 14–61.
14. Comeliau 2000, 74–95.
15. World Bank 2001, 45.
16. Duhigg and Bradsher 2012.
17. World Bank 2012b.
18. National Center for Health Statistics 2011, 124.
19. World Bank 2012b.
20. World Bank 2012a.
21. Kristof 2007.
22. Githongo 2011.
23. Sachs 2005, 56–66.
24. See also Collier 2007.
25. Sachs 2005, 266.
26. Collier 2007.
27. Economic Research Service 2011.
28. World Bank 2011.
29. Banjerjee et al. 2010.
30. Khandker 2005; Imai, Arun, and Annim 2010; Noreen et al. 2011; Biosca, Lenton, and Mosley 2011; Banjerjee et al. 2010.
31. De Tocqueville 1840; Wood 2011; Wikipedia 2012a.
32. Gornick and Jantti 2011, table 1.
33. Gornick and Jantti 2011, table 1.
34. Gornick and Jantti 2011, table 1.
35. Gornick and Jantti 2011, table 1.
36. See Rainwater and Smeeding 1995; Rainwater and Smeeding 2003.

37. See Mayer 1996, 109.
38. Mayer 1996, 127–40. See also Bergstrom and Gidehag 2004.
39. See Sen 1999.
40. National Center for Health Statistics 2011.
41. World Bank 2012b; World Bank 2012a.
42. Corak 2006, table 1.
43. Jantti et al. 2006, 16–17.
44. Organization for Economic Cooperation and Development 2010, 17.
45. Organization for Economic Cooperation and Development 2010, 10. See also Beller and Hout 2006, 30.
46. DeParle 2012.
47. See also Jantti et al. 2006.
48. Isaacs 2007, 30. See also DeLeire and Lopoo 2010.
49. DeParle 2012.
50. Beller and Hout 2006, 30.
51. Isaacs 2007, 5–6. See also Organization for Economic Cooperation and Development 1996; Sastre and Ayala 2002.
52. Zakaria 2011.

5. CAUSES OF POVERTY

1. Lewis 1966b, quoted in Schiller 2001, 127.
2. Lichter and Crowley 2002, 19.
3. O'Connor 2001, 143.
4. Grusky 1994, 11.
5. Marx 1994a, 69–78.
6. Marx 1994b, 80–82.
7. Weber 1994a, 121.
8. U.S. Census Bureau 1993; U.S. Census Bureau 2010a.
9. U.S. Census Bureau 2011b.
10. Although the official time series of poverty statistics begins in 1959, researchers have extended the time series backward using the constant official threshold (adjusted only for inflation) as defined by Mollie Orshansky in the mid-1960s.
11. World Bank 2001.
12. See, for example, Haveman and Schwabish 1999; Blank 1997a; Blank 1997b.
13. Blank 2009, 82.
14. Iceland 2003.
15. Schumpeter 1994 [1942].
16. Sugrue 1993, 87.
17. Sugrue 1993, 88–91.
18. Sugrue 1993, 95–97.
19. Bluestone and Harrison 2000, 183.
20. Congressional Budget Office 2011, 3.
21. Congressional Budget Office 2011, x–xii.
22. U.S. Census Bureau 2011g.

23. Blank 2009, 76.
24. Blank 2009, 64–68.
25. Bureau of Labor Statistics 2011, 7.
26. Bluestone and Harrison 2000, 190–97.
27. Harrison and Bluestone 1990.
28. Krugman 2008.
29. Duhigg and Bradsher 2012.
30. Duhigg and Bradsher 2012.
31. Duhigg and Bradsher 2012.
32. Danziger and Gottschalk 1995, 130–31.
33. Bernstein et al. 2000; Bureau of Labor Statistics 2012c.
34. See Osterman 1999; Blank 2009, 77–78.
35. Duncan and Trejo 2011.
36. Congressional Budget Office 2011, xi.
37. Congressional Budget Office 2011, x–xii.
38. Interested readers should refer to Grusky's edited volume *Social Stratification in Sociological Perspective* for an in-depth discussion of these perspectives.
39. Weber 1994b, 128.
40. Blau, Duncan, and Tyree 1994, 317–29.
41. O'Hare 1996.
42. Price 1969.
43. Schiller 2001, 159–66.
44. See Bonacich 1972; Becker 1971.
45. Hogan and Pazul 1982; Piore 1994, 359–61.
46. Lundberg and Startz 2000, 273.
47. Bureau of Labor Statistics 2012d.
48. Bureau of Labor Statistics 2011, 6.
49. Taylor et al. 2011.
50. Jones 1993, 31; Trotter Jr. 1993, 60.
51. Wilson 1978.
52. Wilson 1987.
53. Loury 2000, 60.
54. Hout 1994, 531–42; Farley 1984; Sakamoto, Wu, and Tzeng 2000, 8–9; Farkas and Vicknair 1996.
55. See Pager 2009; Cross et al. 1990; Turner, Fix, and Struyk 1991.
56. Charles and Guryan 2008.
57. Massey and Denton 1993, 2–3.
58. See, for example, Johnson and Oliver 1992, 113–47; Massey and Denton 1993, 2–3; Mouw 2000.
59. Iceland 2009; Iceland, Sharp, and Timberlake 2013.
60. Bound and Freeman 1992; Bound and Holzer 1993; McCall 2001; Iceland 1997; Bound and Dresser 1999, 61–104.
61. Kasarda 1995, 215–67.
62. Western and Wildeman 2009.
63. Lin and Harris 2008, 1–17.
64. Landry and Marsh 2011.

65. Sakamoto and Furuichi 1997.

66. Martin and Midgley 2003, 16.

67. U.S. Immigration and Naturalization Service 2002, 19–21; U.S. Census Bureau 2011e.

68. Grieco 2010, 6–8.

69. See White and Glick 2009; Kasinitz et al. 2008; Alba 2009.

70. Raphael and Smolensky 2009, 123–24.

71. U.S. Census Bureau 2012a.

72. U.S. Census Bureau 2011d.

73. Thomas 2011.

74. Camarota 2007, 23.

75. Chiswick and Sullivan 1995, 211–70.

76. Camarota 2007, 18.

77. White and Glick 2009, 111. See also Bean and Stevens 2003.

78. DeNavas-Walt, Proctor, and Smith 2010, 8.

79. Isao Takei and Arthur Sakamoto 2011.

80. White and Glick 2009, 148.

81. U.S. Census Bureau 2012h.

82. Sakamoto, Wu, and Tzeng 2000; Sandefur and Scott 1983.

83. Huyser, Sakamoto, and Takei 2010.

84. Schuman et al. 2001.

85. Reardon 2011.

86. Pearce 1978.

87. U.S. Census Bureau 2012d.

88. See also Lichter and Crowley 2002, 7.

89. Bureau of Labor Statistics 2011, 62; Cancian and Reed 2009, 109.

90. Bianchi 1999.

91. England 1994, 590–603; Hartmann 1994, 570–76.

92. Polachek and Siebert 1994, 583–89; Daymont and Andrisani 1984.

93. U.S. Census Bureau 2012n.

94. Kreider and Elliott 2010.

95. CONSAD Research Corp. 2009.

96. Bureau of Labor Statistics 2011, 62–76.

97. See Bianchi 1995, 107–54.

98. Looney and Greenstone 2011.

99. Buchmann, DiPrete, and McDaniel 2008.

100. Ventura and Bachrach 2000; Martin et al. 2011. See also Wildsmith, Steward-Streng, and Manlove 2011; DeParle and Tavernise 2012.

101. DeParle and Tavernise 2012.

102. Smock and Greenland 2010.

103. U.S. Census Bureau 2011f.

104. Manning, Smock, and Majumdar 2004.

105. Frazier 1939; Frazier 1932; Myrdal 1944; Moynihan 1965; Bianchi 1990; Hogan and Lichter 1995, 93–139; Lichter 1997.

106. Murray 2012.

107. Note that poverty rates by family type reported in chapter 3, table 1, refer to the poverty rates of people in different kinds of families regardless of

whether children were present or not, while the poverty rates reported in figure 20 are for families with children. Families with children generally have higher poverty rates than families without them.

108. U.S. Census Bureau 2012e.

109. O'Hare 1996, 18, 21.

110. CONSAD Research Corp. 2009.

111. Bianchi 1999.

112. Sorenson 1994, 21–23.

113. Manning 2006.

114. Edin and Lein 1997, 126.

115. Shipler 2004, 68.

116. See Cancian and Reed 2000; Eggebeen and Lichter 1991; Lerman 1996; Hernandez 1993; Bianchi 1990; Lichter 1997.

117. Cancian and Reed 2009, 105; Haskins 2001.

118. Legal Momentum 2012.

119. Gornick and Jantti 2011, table 3.

120. UNICEF Innocenti Research Centre 2000.

121. Gornick and Jantti 2011, table 3.

122. For an extended discussion, see O'Connor 2001, 74–123.

123. Washington 1902; Myrdal 1944; Frazier 1939; Frazier 1932.

124. O'Connor 2001, 81.

125. Cherry 1995.

126. Schiller 2001, 127.

127. Banfield 1958, quoted in Katz 1989, 31–32.

128. See Murray 1984; Rector 1993.

129. See Murray 1984.

130. For a thoughtful review of Murray's book, see Edsall 2012.

131. Cancian and Reed 2009, 106. See also Becker 1991.

132. For one example of this argument, see Krugman 2012.

133. Kristof 2012.

134. Smock and Greenland 2010.

135. Gibson-Davis, Edin, and McLanahan 2005.

136. See Edin and Kefalas 2005.

137. See Lareau 2003.

138. Cherlin 2004.

139. DeParle and Tavernise 2012.

6. THE GREAT RECESSION

1. National Bureau of Economic Research 2010.

2. Bureau of Labor Statistics 2010. The October 2009 unemployment rate was slightly adjusted downward (to 10.0 rather than 10.1), as indicated in Bureau of Labor Statistics 2012a.

3. Rajan 2010.

4. Financial Crisis Inquiry Commission 2011, 5.

5. Rajan 2010, 8–9.

6. Green and Wachter 2005.

7. Rajan 2010, 8–9.
8. Financial Crisis Inquiry Commission 2011.
9. Rajan 2010, 39.
10. Financial Crisis Inquiry Commission 2011, 6.
11. Fligstein and Goldstein 2011, 23.
12. Fligstein and Goldstein 2011, 21.
13. Financial Crisis Inquiry Commission 2011, xix.
14. Financial Crisis Inquiry Commission 2011, 5–6.
15. Fligstein and Goldstein 2011, 24.
16. Financial Crisis Inquiry Commission 2011, xxv.
17. Fligstein and Goldstein 2011, 25–26.
18. Financial Crisis Inquiry Commission 2011, xx.
19. Financial Crisis Inquiry Commission 2011, xvi.
20. Burtless and Gordon 2011, 250–52.
21. Burtless and Gordon 2011, 286–88.
22. Blinder and Zandi 2010.
23. Burtless and Gordon 2011, 288–89.
24. Burtless and Gordon 2011, 289.
25. Hout, Levanon, and Cumberworth 2011, 60.
26. Bosworth 2012.
27. Bosworth 2012.
28. Bureau of Labor Statistics 2012a.
29. Hout, Levanon, and Cumberworth 2011, 60–64; Smeeding et al. 2011, 86; Hartmann, Fischer, and Logan 2012, 3.
30. Cohen 2012.
31. Cohen 2012.
32. Bureau of Labor Statistics 2012b.
33. Sherman 2011.
34. Food Research and Action Center 2012, 3.
35. Isaacs 2011.
36. Wolff, Owens, and Burak 2011, 134, 150–51.
37. Wolff, Owens, and Burak 2011, 152.
38. Hacker et al. 2011.
39. Morgan, Cumberworth, and Wimer 2011, 222–25; Guttmacher Institute 2009.
40. Morgan, Cumberworth, and Wimer 2011, 233–36.
41. Morgan, Cumberworth, and Wimer 2011, 237.
42. Jacobsen and Mather 2011, 6. See also Mykyta and Macartney 2011.
43. Kenworthy and Owens 2011, 203, 216–17.
44. Cohen 2012.
45. Williamson, Skocpol, and Coggin 2011.
46. Williamson, Skocpol, and Coggin 2011, 26. See also www.youtube.com/watch?v=zp-Jw-5Kx8k.
47. Williamson, Skocpol, and Coggin 2011, 36.
48. Stucke forthcoming.
49. Stucke forthcoming, 3–12. See also Kohut 2012.

7. POVERTY AND POLICY

1. Munsterberg 1904, 343.
2. Trattner 1994, 10–12.
3. Trattner 1994, 10–11; Katz 1996, 13–15.
4. Katz 1996, 14.
5. Trattner 1994, 23–24.
6. DuBois 1899, 269.
7. Trattner 1994, 24–26.
8. Trattner 1994, 47–56.
9. Katz 1996, 22–36.
10. Trattner 1994, 60–61.
11. Monkkonen 1993, 331–33.
12. Katz 1996, 26–36.
13. Katz 1996, 38.
14. Trotter Jr. 1993, 64–65.
15. Trattner 1994, 83–84.
16. Jones 1993, 33–34; Katz 1993b, 458.
17. Trattner 1994, 84–85.
18. Skocpol 2000, 25–26.
19. See Trattner 1994, 77–103; Katz 1996, 60–87.
20. Trattner 1994, 95.
21. Trattner 1994, 99–102.
22. Katz 1996, 197.
23. See, for example, Skocpol et al. 1993
24. Katz 1996, 148.
25. Trattner 1994, 225, 250.
26. Trattner 1994, 273–74.
27. Katz 1996, 224–54.
28. Jackson 1993, 437; Skocpol 2000, 22–58; Katz 1996, 242–55.
29. Trattner 1994, 294.
30. Katz 1996, 254.
31. Skocpol 2000, 26.
32. Trattner 1994, 313–19.
33. See Jackson 1993, 403–39; Trattner 1994, 322–31; O'Connor 2001, 166–95.
34. Trattner 1994, 304–31.
35. Katz 1993b, 476.
36. Trattner 1994, 337–51.
37. Katz 1996, 283–99; Trattner 1994, 352–65.
38. Trattner 1994, 393–97.
39. Thompson 2001, 3.
40. Greenberg 2001.
41. Scholz, Moffitt, and Cowan 2009.
42. Moffitt 2002. See also Ziliak 2009, 8.
43. Bollinger, Gonzalez, and Ziliak 2009, 66.
44. Moffitt 2002, 1, 5; Frogner, Moffitt, and Ribar 2009, 167–70.
45. A summary of the health care reform law can be found at Kaiser Family Foundation 2011.

46. DeNavas-Walt, Proctor, and Smith 2012.

47. The data for 1970 to 2005–7 in figure 22 come from Scholz, Moffitt, and Cowan 2009, table 8A.1. Data from 2009 come from Ziliak 2011, table 1.

48. Center on Budget and Policy Priorities 2011.

49. Skocpol 2000, 22–58.

50. Roemer 2000, table 2b, p. 45, reports that the problem may be most serious for estimates of family assistance, which includes TANF, where CPS aggregate income (income totaled over all respondents) in 1996 was 67.7 percent of a benchmark total estimated from administrative records. The undercount of recipients (rather than income) is likely less severe, as aggregates tend to be underestimated due to both fewer people reporting income and lower amounts reported among those who do report receipt. SSI and Social Security aggregate income from the March CPS in 1996 was 84.2 and 91.7 percent of the estimated benchmark for those two items, respectively.

51. Urban Institute 2011.

52. U.S. Census Bureau 2010d.

53. Scholz, Moffitt, and Cowan 2009, 223.

54. Scholz, Moffitt, and Cowan 2009, 219–20.

55. Scholz, Moffitt, and Cowan 2009, table 8.2.

56. Short 2011a, table 3a.

57. Ziliak 2011, 23.

58. Plotnick 2011–12, 45–46.

59. Haskins 2001; Thompson 2001. See also Currie 2006.

60. Lindsey 2009. See also Plotnick 2011–12.

61. Scholz, Moffitt, and Cowan 2009, 225.

62. For discussion of the first two, see Heclo 1994, 396–437. See also Jencks 1992, 87–91.

63. Bowles and Gintis 1998.

64. Kenworthy 2011, 106–8; Bane 2009, 373.

65. O'Hare 1996, 33.

66. Harrington 1981, xxviii–xxix.

67. Murray 1984; Rector 1993.

68. See, for example, Lindbeck et al. 1994.

69. Scholz, Moffitt, and Cowan 2009, 217. See also Knab et al. 2009, 304–5.

70. Chen and van der Klaauw 2008.

71. See, for example, Bargain and Doorley 2011.

72. Lichter, McLaughlin, and Ribar 1997.

73. Gornick and Jantti 2011, table 1.

74. See Gornick and Jantti 2011; Rainwater and. Smeeding 1995; Rainwater and Smeeding 2003.

75. McLanahan and Garfinkel 1996, 367–83; UNICEF Innocenti Research Centre 2000.

76. Adema 2010, 40; Kenworthy 2011, 104.

77. Kenworthy 2004, 148.

78. Kenworthy 2011, 105–6.

79. Atkinson 1999.

80. Lewis 2011.

81. Organization for Economic Cooperation and Development 2011.

82. Organization for Economic Cooperation and Development 2011.
83. National Public Radio 2012.
84. Katz 2001, 341.
85. Katz 2001, 62.
86. Murray 2012, 278–85.
87. Plato and Rawls cited in Adema 2010, 96; Rawls 1971, 246.
88. Katz 2001, 26–31.
89. Kenworthy 2001, 107–8.
90. Eger 2010.
91. Munsterberg 1904, 336.
92. Real Clear Politics 2012.
93. Wikipedia 2012b.
94. Smeeding and Waldfogel 2010.
95. Waldfogel 2010.
96. Smeeding and Waldfogel 2010, 403.
97. Lindsey 2009, 108.
98. Center on Budget and Policy Priorities 2009.
99. White and Morse 2011.
100. Lindsey 2009, 137–50.

References

Adema, Willem. 2010. "The Welfare State across Selected OECD Countries: How Much Does It Really Cost and How Good Is It in Reducing Poverty?" In *The Future of the Welfare State,* edited by Brigid Reynolds, Sean Healy, and Micheal Collins. Dublin: Social Justice Ireland.

Alba, Richard. 2009. *Blurring the Color Line: The Chance for a More Integrated America.* Cambridge, MA: Harvard University Press.

Anderson, Robin J. 2011. "Dynamics of Economic Well-Being: Poverty, 2004–2006." U.S. Census Bureau, Current Population Reports, P70–123, March.

Annie E. Casey Foundation. 2011. *2011 Kids Count Data Book.* Baltimore, MD: Annie E. Casey Foundation.

Atkinson, A.B. 1999. *The Economic Consequences of Rolling Back the Welfare State.* Cambridge, MA: MIT Press.

Atkinson, A.B., and John Hills. 1998. "Social Exclusion, Poverty and Unemployment." Centre for Analysis of Social Exclusion Paper no. 4.

Auletta, Ken. 1982. *The Underclass.* New York: Random House.

Bane, Mary Jo. 2009. "Poverty Politics and Policy." In *Changing Poverty, Changing Policies,* edited by Maria Cancian and Sheldon Danziger. New York: Russell Sage Foundation.

Bane, Mary Jo, and David Ellwood. 1986. "Slipping into and out of Poverty: The Dynamics of Spells." *Journal of Human Resources* 21 (Winter): 1–23.

Banfield, Edward C. 1958. *The Unheavenly City.* Boston: Little, Brown.

Banjerjee, Abhijit, Esther Duflo, Rachel Gelnnerster, and Cynthia Kinnan. 2010. "The Miracle of Microfinance? Evidence from a Randomized Evaluation." BREAD Working Paper, Bureau for Research and Economic Analysis of Development, June 30.

Bargain, Olivier, and Karina Doorley. 2011. "Caught in the Trap? Welfare's Disincentive and the Labor Supply of Single Men." *Journal of Public Economics* 95: 1096–110.

Bean, Frank D., and Gillian Stevens. 2003. *America's Newcomers and the Dynamics of Diversity.* New York: Russell Sage Foundation.

Becker, Gary S. 1971. *The Economics of Discrimination.* Chicago: University of Chicago Press.

———. 1991. *A Treatise on the Family.* Cambridge, MA: Harvard University Press.

Beller, Emily, and Michael Hout. 2006. "Intergenerational Social Mobility: The United States in Comparative Perspective." *The Future of Children* 16, no. 2: 19–36.

Bello, Marisol. 2012. "Families in Extreme Poverty Double," *USA Today,* February 24.

Bergstrom, Fredrik, and Robert Gidehag. 2004. *EU versus USA.* Stockholm: Timbro.

Bernstein, Jared, Elizabeth C. McNichol, Lawrence Mishel, and Robert Zahradnik. 2000. "Pulling Apart: A State-by-State Analysis of Income Trends." Center on Budget and Policy Priorities and Economic Policy Institute Report, January.

Beverly, Sondra G. 2001. "Measures of Material Hardship: Rationale and Recommendations." *Journal of Poverty* 5, no. 1: 23–41.

Bianchi, Suzanne. 1990. "America's Children: Mixed Prospects." *Population Bulletin* 45: 1–43.

———. 1995. "Changing Economic Roles of Women and Men." In *State of the Union: America in the 1990s,* vol. 1, edited by Reynolds Farley. New York: Russell Sage Foundation.

———. 1999. "Feminization and Juvenilization of Poverty: Trends, Relative Risks, Causes, and Consequences." *Annual Review of Sociology* 25: 307–33.

Biosca, Olga, Pamela Lenton, and Paul Mosley. 2011. "Microfinance Non-Financial Services: A Key for Poverty Alleviation? Lessons from Mexico." Sheffield Economic Research Paper Series, SERP no. 2011021, October.

Bishaw, Alemayehu . 2011. "Areas with Concentrated Poverty: 2006–2010." U.S. Census Bureau, American Community Survey Briefs, ACSBR/10–17, December.

Blank, Rebecca. 1997a. "Why Has Economic Growth Been Such an Ineffective Tool against Poverty in Recent Years?" In *Poverty and Inequality: The Political Economy of Redistribution,* edited by Jon Neil. Kalamazoo, MI: W.E. Upjohn Institute for Employment Research.

———. 1997b. *It Takes a Nation: A New Agenda for Fighting Poverty.* Princeton, NJ: Princeton University Press.

———. 2008. "Presidential Address: How to Improve Poverty Measurement in the United States." *Journal of Policy Analysis and Management* 27, no. 2: 233–54.

———. 2009. "Economic Change and the Structure of Opportunity for Less-Skilled Workers." In *Changing Poverty, Changing Policies,* edited by Maria Cancian and Sheldon Danziger. New York: Russell Sage Foundation.

Blau, Peter M., Otis Dudley Duncan, and Andrea Tyree. 1994. "The Process of Stratification." In *Social Stratification in Sociological Perspective,* edited by David B. Grusky. Boulder, CO: Westview Press.

Blinder, Alan, and Mark Zandi. 2010. "How the Great Recession Was Brought to an End." July 27. Available at www.economy.com/mark-zandi/documents/End-of-Great-Recession.pdf (accessed February 29, 2012).

Bluestone, Barry, and Bennett Harrison. 2000. *Growing Prosperity: The Battle for Growth with Equity in the Twenty-First Century.* Boston: Houghton Mifflin.

Bollinger, Christopher, Luis Gonzalez, and James P. Ziliak. 2009. "Welfare Reform and the Level of Consumption and Income." In *Welfare Reform and Its Long-Term Consequences for America's Poor,* edited by James P. Ziliak. Cambridge: Cambridge University Press.

Bonacich, E. 1972. "A Theory of Ethnic Antagonism: The Split Labor Market." *American Sociological Review* 37 (October): 547–59.

Booth, Charles. 1889. *Labour and Life of the People,* vol. 1: *East London.* London: Williams and Norgate.

———. 1892–97. *Life and Labour of the People of London,* First Series: *Poverty.* London: Macmillan; reprint, New York: AMS Press, 1970.

Bosworth, Barry. 2012. "Economic Consequences of the Great Recession: Evidence from the Panel Study of Income Dynamics." Center for Retirement Research at Boston College Working Paper, CRR WP 2012–4.

Bound, John, and Harry J. Holzer. 1993. "Industrial Shifts, Skills Levels, and the Labor Market for White and Black Males." *Review of Economics and Statistics* 75, no. 3 (August): 387–96.

Bound, John, and Laura Dresser. 1999. "Losing Ground: The Erosion of the Relative Earnings of African American Women during the 1980s." In *Latinas and African American Women at Work,* edited by Irene Browne. New York: Russell Sage Foundation.

Bound, John, and Richard Freeman. 1992. "What Went Wrong? The Erosion of Relative Earnings and Employment among Young Black Men in the 1980s." *Quarterly Journal of Economics* 107: 201–32.

Bowles, Samuel, and Herbert Gintis. 1998. *Recasting Egalitarianism: New Rules for Communities, States and Markets.* The Real Utopias Project, vol. 3, edited by Erik Olin Wright. London: Verso.

Buchmann, Claudia, Thomas A. DiPrete, and Anne McDaniel. 2008. "Gender Inequalities in Education." *Annual Review of Sociology* 34: 319–37.

Bureau of Economic Analysis. 2012. "Current-Dollar and 'Real' Gross Domestic Product." *National Accounts Data,* Times Series Estimates of Gross Domestic Product. Available at www.bea.gov/national/xls/gdplev.xls (accessed September 12, 2012).

Bureau of Labor Statistics. 2010. "Sizing up the 2007–09 Recession: Comparing Two Key Labor Market Indicators with Earlier Downturns." *Issues in Labor Statistics,* Summary 10–11 (December): 1–6.

———. 2011. "Highlights of Women's Earnings." U.S. BLS Report no. 1031 (July).

———. 2012a. "Labor Force Statistics from the Current Population Survey." Series Id LNS 14000000. Available at http://data.bls.gov (accessed February 28, 2012).

———. 2012b. "Regional and State Employment and Unemployment—December 2011." Economic News Release, Regional and State Employment and Unemployment Summary, USDL-12–0091, January 24.

———. 2012c. "Table 1. Union Affiliation of Employed Wage and Salary Workers by Selected Characteristics." BLS Economic News Release. Available at www.bls.gov/news.release/union2.to1.htm (accessed February 7, 2012).

———. 2012d. "Table A2. Employment Status of the Civilian Population by Race, Sex, and Age." BLS Economic News Release. Available at www.bls .gov/news.release/empsit.to2.htm (accessed February 13, 2012).

Burroughs, Charles. 1835. *A Discourse Delivered in the Chapel of the New Alms-House, in Portsmouth, N.H.* Portsmouth, NH: J. W. Foster.

Burtless, Gary, and Timothy M. Smeeding. 2001. "The Level, Trend, and Composition of Poverty." In *Understanding Poverty*, edited by Sheldon Danziger and Robert Haveman. Cambridge, MA: Harvard University Press, 2001.

Burtless, Gary, and Tracy Gordon. 2011. "The Federal Stimulus Programs and Their Effects." In *The Great Recession*, edited by David B. Grusky, Bruce Western, and Christopher Wimer New York: Russell Sage Foundation.

Camarota, Steven A. 2007. "Immigrants in the United States, 2007." Center for Immigration Studies Backgrounder, November.

Cancian, Maria, and Deborah Reed. 2000. "Changes in Family Structure: Implications for Poverty and Related Policy." *Focus* 21, no. 2 (Fall): 21–26.

———. 2009. "Family Structure, Childbearing, and Parental Employment: Implications for the Level and Trend in Poverty." In *Changing Poverty, Changing Policies*, edited by Maria Cancian and Sheldon Danziger. New York: Russell Sage Foundation.

Center on Budget and Policy Priorities. 1998. "Strengths of the Safety Net: How the EITC, Social Security, and Other Government Programs Affect Poverty." Center on Budget and Policy Priorities Research Report 98–020, March.

———. 2009. "Policy Basics: The Child Tax Credit." November 10 brief. Available at www.cbpp.org/files/policybasics-ctc.pdf (accessed March 13, 2012).

———. 2011. "Where Do Our Federal Tax Dollars Go?" Center on Budget and Policy Priorities Policy Basics Report, April 15.

Charles, Kerwin Kofi, and Jonathan Guryan. 2008. "Prejudice and Wages: An Empirical Assessment of Becker's *The Economics of Discrimination*." *Journal of Political Economy* 116, no. 5: 773–809.

Chen, Susan, and Wilbert van der Klaauw. 2008. "The Work Disincentive Effects of the Disability Insurance Program in the 1990s." *Journal of Econometrics* 142, no. 2: 757–84.

Cherlin, A. J. 2004. "The Deinstitutionalization of American Marriage." *Journal of Marriage and Family* 66: 848–61.

Cherry, Robert. 1995. "The Culture-of-Poverty Thesis and African Americans: The Work of Gunnar Myrdal and Other Institutionalists." *Journal of Economic Issues* 29, no. 4 (December): 1119–32.

Chiswick, Barry R., and Teresa A. Sullivan. 1995. "The New Immigrants." In *State of the Union America in the 1990s*, vol. 2, edited by Reynolds Farley. New York: Russell Sage Foundation.

Chung, Chanjin, and Samuel L. Myers Jr. 1999. "Do the Poor Pay More for Food? An Analysis of Grocery Store Availability and Food Price Disparities." *Journal of Consumer Affairs* 33, no. 2: 276–91.

Cogan, John F. 1995. "Dissent." In *Measuring Poverty: A New Approach*, edited by Constance F. Citro and Robert T. Michael. Washington, DC: National Academy Press.

Cohen, Sharon. 2012. "Frustration, Fear—and Hope: The Faces Beyond the Numbers of Long-Term Unemployed." Associated Press, February 11. Available at *http://timesdaily.com/stories/Faces-beyond-numbers-of-long-term-unemployed-Frustration-fear-and-hope,187276* (accessed December 20, 2012).

Coleman-Jensen, Alisha, Mark Nord, Margaret Andrews, and Steven Carlson. 2011. *Household Food Security in the United States in 2010*. ERR-125, U.S. Department of Agriculture, Economic Research Service, September.

Collier, Paul. 2007. *The Bottom Billion: Why the Poorest Countries Are Failing and What Can Be Done about It*. New York: Oxford University Press.

Comeliau, Christian. 2000. "Poverty—A Hopeless Battle?" In *The Challenge of Eliminating World Poverty*, edited by Swiss Agency Development and Cooperation (SDC) Publications on Development. Berne: SDC.

Congressional Budget Office. 2011. "Trends in the Distribution of Household Income between 1979 and 2007." Report, October 2011.

CONSAD Research Corp. 2009. "An Analysis of Reasons for the Disparity in Wages between Men and Women." Report prepared for the U.S. Department of Labor, January 12.

Contreras, Russell. 2011. "Behind the Poverty Statistics: Real Lives, Real Pain." Huffington Post, September 18, 2011. Available at www.huffingtonpost.com/2011/09/18/living-in-poverty-people-behind-the-statistics_n_968494.html (accessed January 5, 2012).

Corak, Miles. 2006. "Do Poor Children Become Poor Adults? Lessons from a Cross Country Comparison of Generational Earnings Mobility." Institute for the Study of Labor (IZA), Bonn, Germany, Discussion Paper no. 1993, March.

Cross, Harry, Genevieve Kenney, Jane Mell, and Wendy Zimmermann. 1990. *Employer Hiring Practices*. Washington, DC: Urban Institute Press.

Currie, Janet M. 2006. *The Invisible Safety Net: Protecting the Nation's Poor Children and Families*. Princeton, NJ: Princeton University Press.

D'Addio, Anna Cristina. 2007. "Intergenerational Transmission of Disadvantage: Mobility or Immobility Across Generations? A Review of the Evidence for OECD Countries." OECD Social, Employment and Migration Working Papers no. 52.

Dalaker, Joseph, and Mary Naifeh. 1998. "Poverty in the United States: 1997." U.S. Census Bureau, Current Population Reports, series P60–201. Washington, DC: U.S. Government Printing Office.

Daly, Mary, and Hilary Silver. 2008. "Social Exclusion and Social Capital: A Comparison and Critique." *Theory and Society* 37: 537–66.

Danziger, Sheldon H., and Peter Gottschalk. 1995. *America Unequal*. Cambridge, MA: Harvard University Press.

Davidson, James D. 1985. "Theories and Measures of Poverty: Toward a Holistic Approach." *Sociological Focus* 18, no. 3 (August): 187–88.

Daymont, T., and P. Andrisani. 1984. "Job Preferences, College Major, and the Gender Gap in Earnings." *Journal of Human Resources* 19: 408–28.

DeLeire, Thomas, and Leonard M. Lopoo. 2010. *Family Structure and the Economic Mobility of Children.* Pew Charitable Trusts, Economic Mobility Project Report, April.

DeNavas-Walt, Carmen, Bernadette D. Proctor, and Jessica C. Smith. 2010. "Income, Poverty, and Health Insurance Coverage in the United States: 2009." U.S. Census Bureau, Current Population Reports, P60–238. Washington, DC: U.S. Government Printing Office.

———. 2012. "Income, Poverty, and Health Insurance Coverage in the United States: 2011." U.S. Census Bureau Current Population Reports, P60–243. Washington, DC: U.S. Government Printing Office.

DeParle, Jason. 2012. "Harder for Americans to Rise from Lower Rungs," *New York Times,* January 4.

DeParle, Jason, and Sabrina Tavernise. 2012. "For Women under 30, Most Births Occur Outside of Marriage." *New York Times,* February 17.

De Tocqueville, Alexis. 1840. *Democracy in America.* New York: Langley.

Devine, Joel A., Mark Plunkett, and James D. Wright. 1992. "The Chronicity of Poverty: Evidence from the PSID, 1968–1987." *Social Forces* 70, no. 3 (March): 787–812.

Dollar, David, and Jakob Svensson. 2001. "What Explains the Success or Failure of Structural Adjustment Programmes?" *Economic Journal* 110, no. 446: 894–917.

DuBois, W.E.B. 1899. *The Philadelphia Negro: A Social Study.* Reprint, Philadelphia: University of Pennsylvania Press, 1996.

Duhigg, Charles, and Keith Bradsher. 2012. "How U.S. Lost Out on iPhone Work." *New York Times,* Business Day, January 22.

Duncan, Brian, and Stephen J. Trejo. 2011. "Low-Skilled Immigrants and the U.S. Labor Market." IZA Discussion Paper no. 5964, September.

Economic Research Service. 2011. "Real GDP (2005 dollars) Historical." USDA, ERS International Macroeconomic Data Set. Available at www.ers.usda.gov/Data/Macroeconomics/ (accessed January 20, 2012).

Edin, Kathryn, and Laura Lein. 1997. *Making Ends Meet: How Single Mothers Survive Welfare and Low-Wage Work.* New York: Russell Sage Foundation.

Edin, Kathryn, and Maria Kefalas. 2005. *Promises I Can Keep: Why Poor Women Put Motherhood Before Marriage* Berkeley: University of California Press.

Edsall, Thomas B. 2012. "What to Do about 'Coming Apart'," *New York Times,* Campaign Stops blog, February 12. Available at http://campaignstops.blogs.nytimes.com/2012/02/12/what-to-do-about-coming-apart/?ref=opinion (accessed February 19, 2012).

Eger, Maureen A. 2010. "Even in Sweden: The Effect of Immigration on Support for Welfare State Spending." *European Sociological Review* 26, 2: 203–217.

Eggebeen, David J., and Daniel T. Lichter. 1991. "Race, Family Structure, and Changing Poverty among American Children." *American Sociological Review* 56: 801–17.

Ehrenreich, Barbara. 2001. *Nickel and Dimed: On (Not) Getting By in America.* New York: Metropolitan Books.

England, Paula. 1994. "Wage Appreciation and Depreciation: A Test of Neoclassical Economic Explanations of Occupational Sex Segregation." In *Social Stratification in Sociological Perspective*, edited by David B. Grusky. Boulder, CO: Westview Press.

European Commission. 2000. "Presidency Conclusions." Lisbon European Council 23 and 24 March 2000, Document SN 100/00.

Farkas, G., and K. Vicknair. 1996. "Appropriate Tests of Racial Wage Discrimination Require Controls for Cognitive Skill: Comment on Cancio, Evans, and Maume." *American Sociological Review* 1: 557–60.

Farley, Reynolds. 1984. *Blacks and Whites: Narrowing the Gap?* Cambridge, MA: Harvard University Press.

Financial Crisis Inquiry Commission. 2011. *The Financial Crisis Inquiry Report: Final Report of the National Commission on the Causes of the Financial and Economic Crisis in the United States,* Official Government Edition. Washington, D.C.: U.S. Government Printing Office.

Firebaugh, Glenn. 2003. *The New Geography of Global Income Inequality.* Cambridge, MA: Harvard University Press.

Fisher, Gordon M. 1986. "Estimates of the Poverty Population under the Current Official Definition for Years before 1959." Mimeo, Office of the Assistant Secretary for Planning and Evaluation, U.S. Department of Health and Human Services.

———. 1995. "Is There Such a Thing as an Absolute Poverty Line over Time? Evidence from the United States, Britain, Canada, and Australia on the Income Elasticity of the Poverty Line." U.S. Census Bureau, Poverty Measurement Working Paper. Available at www.census.gov/hhes/povmeas /publications/povthres/fisher3.html (accessed December 20, 2012).

———. 1997a. "From Hunter to Orshansky: An Overview of (Unofficial) Poverty Lines in the United States from 1904 to 1965." U.S. Census Bureau, Poverty Measurement Working Paper. Available at www.census.gov/hhes /povmeas/publications/povthres/fisher4.html (accessed December 20, 2012).

———. 1997b. "The Development of the Orshansky Poverty Thresholds and Their Subsequent History as the Official U.S. Poverty Measure." U.S. Census Bureau, Poverty Measurement Working Paper. Available at www.census .gov/hhes/povmeas/publications/orshansky.html (accessed December 20, 2012).

Fligstein, Neil, and Adam Goldstein. 2011. "The Roots of the Great Recession." In *The Great Recession,* edited by David B. Grusky, Bruce Western, and Christopher Wimer. New York: Russell Sage Foundation.

Food Research and Action Center. 2012. "Food Hardship in America 2011." FRAC Research Report, February.

Foster, James E. 1998. "Absolute versus Relative Poverty." *American Economic Review* 88, no. 2, Papers and Proceedings of the 110th Annual Meeting of the American Economic Association (May): 335–41.

Frazier, E. Franklin. 1932. *The Negro Family in Chicago.* Chicago: University of Chicago Press.

———. 1939. *The Negro Family in the United States.* Chicago: University of Chicago Press.

Frey, William H. 2011. "Melting Pot Cities and Suburbs: Racial and Ethnic Change in Metro America in the 2000s." The Brookings Institution Metropolitan Policy Program Report, May 1.

Frogner, Bianca, Robert Moffitt, and David C. Ribar. 2009. "How Families Are Doing Nine Years after Welfare Reform: 2005 Evidence from the Three-City Study." In *Welfare Reform and Its Long-Term Consequences for America's Poor,* edited by James P. Ziliak. Cambridge: Cambridge University Press.

Galbraith, John Kenneth. 1958. *The Affluent Society.* New York: New American Library, 1964.

Gans, Herbert J. 1995. *The War against the Poor.* New York: Basic Books.

Gibbs, Robert. 2001. "Nonmetro Labor Markets in the Era of Welfare Reform." *Rural America* 16, no. 3: 11–21.

Gibson-Davis, C.M., K. Edin, and S. McLanahan. 2005. "High Hopes but Even Higher Expectations: The Retreat from Marriage among Low-Income Couples." *Journal of Marriage and Family* 67: 1301–12.

Githongo, John. 2011. "When Wealth Breeds Rage." *New York Times Sunday Review,* July 23.

Gornick, Janet C., and Markus Jantti. 2011. "Child Poverty in Cross-National Perspective: Lessons from the Luxembourg Income Study." *Children and Youth Services Review.* Available at http://dx.doi.org/10.1016/j.childyouth.2011.10.016 (accessed January 16, 2012).

Gottschalk, Peter, Sara McLanahan, and Gary Sandefur. 1994. "The Dynamics and Intergenerational Transmission of Poverty and Welfare Participation." In *Confronting Poverty,* edited by Sheldon Danziger, Gary Sandefur, and Daniel Weinberg. Cambridge, MA: Harvard University Press.

Green, Richard K., and Susan M. Wachter. 2005. "The American Mortgage in Historical and International Context." *Journal of Economic Perspectives* 19, no. 4: 93–114.

Greenberg, Mark. 2001. "Welfare Reform and Devolution." *Brookings Review* 19, no. 3 (Summer): 20–24.

Grieco, Elizabeth M. 2010. "Race and Hispanic Origin of the Foreign-Born Population in the United States: 2007." U.S. Census Bureau, American Community Survey Report ACS-11, January.

Grusky, David. 1994. "The Contours of Social Stratification." In *Social Stratification in Sociological Perspective,* edited by David B. Grusky. Boulder, CO: Westview Press.

Gurteen, S. Humphreys. 1882. *Handbook of Charity Organization.* Buffalo, NY: published by the author.

Guttmacher Institute. 2009. "A Real-Time Look at the Impact of the Recession on Publicly Funded Family Planning and Pregnancy Decisions." New York: Guttmacher Institute.

Hacker, Jacob S., Gregory A. Huber, Austin Nichols, Philipp Rehm, and Stuart Craig. 2011. "Economic Insecurity and the Great Recession: Findings from the Economic Security Index." The Rockefeller Foundation, Economic Security Index Report, November.

Harrington, Michael. 1962. *The Other America: Poverty in the United States.* New York: Macmillan.

————. 1981. *The Other America: Poverty in the United States*. Reprint with a new introduction, New York: Penguin Books.

Harrison, Bennett, and Barry Bluestone. 1990. *The Great U-Turn: Corporate Restructuring and the Polarizing of America*. New York: Basic Books.

Hartmann, Heidi. 1994. "The Unhappy Marriage of Marxism and Feminism: Towards a More Progressive Union." In *Social Stratification in Sociological Perspective*, edited by David B. Grusky. Boulder, CO: Westview Press.

Hartmann, Heidi, Jocelyn Fischer, and Jacqui Logan. 2012. "Women and Men in the Recovery: Where the Jobs Are." Institute for Women's Policy Research, Briefing Paper no. C400, August.

Haskins, Ron. 2001. "Giving Is Not Enough." *Brookings Review* 19, no. 3 (Summer): 13–15.

Haveman, Robert, and Jonathan Schwabish. 1999. "Economic Growth and Poverty: A Return to Normalcy?" *Focus* 20, no. 2 (Spring): 1–7.

Heclo, Hugh. 1994. "Poverty Politics." In *Confronting Poverty*, edited by Sheldon Danziger, Gary Sandefur, and Daniel Weinberg. Cambridge, MA: Harvard University Press.

Heflin, Colleen, John Sandberg, and Patrick Rafail. 2009. "The Structure of Material Hardship in U.S. Households: An Examination of the Coherence behind Common Measures of Well-Being." *Social Problems* 56, no. 4: 746–64.

Hernandez, Donald J. 1993. *America's Children: Resources from Family, Government, and the Economy*. New York: Russell Sage Foundation.

Hogan, Dennis, and Daniel Lichter. 1995. "Children and Youth: Living Arrangements and Welfare." In *State of the Union: America in the 1990s*, vol. 2, edited by Reynolds Farley. New York: Russell Sage Foundation.

Hogan, Dennis P., and M. Pazul. 1982. "The Occupational and Earnings Returns to Education among Black Men in the North." *American Journal of Sociology* 90: 584–607.

Holzer, Harry J. 1991. "The Spatial Mismatch Hypothesis: What Has the Evidence Shown?" *Urban Studies* 28, no. 1: 105–22.

Holzer, Harry J., Diane Whitmore, Greg J. Duncan, and Jens Ludwig. 2007. "The Economic Costs of Poverty in the United States: Subsequent Effects of Children Growing Up Poor." National Poverty Center, University of Michigan, Working Paper Series no. 07–04 (January).

Hout, Michael. 1994. "Occupational Mobility of Black Men: 1962 to 1973." In *Social Stratification in Sociological Perspective*, edited by David B. Grusky. Boulder, CO: Westview Press.

Hout, Michael, Asaf Levanon, and Erin Cumberworth. 2011. "Job Loss and Unemployment." In *The Great Recession*, edited by David B. Grusky, Bruce Western, and Christopher Wimer. New York: Russell Sage Foundation.

Hunter, Robert. 1904. *Poverty*. New York: Macmillan; reprint, New York: Harper Torchbooks, 1964.

Huyser, Kimberly R., Arthur Sakamoto, and Isao Takei. 2010. "The Persistence of Racial Disadvantage: The Socioeconomic Attainments of Single-Race and Multi-Race Native Americans." *Population Research and Policy Review* 29: 541–68.

Iceland, John. 1997. "Urban Labor Markets and Individual Transitions out of Poverty." *Demography* 34, no. 3 (August): 429–41.

———. 2000. "The 'Family/Couple/Household' Unit of Analysis in Poverty Measurement." *Journal of Economic and Social Measurement* 26: 253–65.

———. 2003. "Why Poverty Remains High: The Role of Income Growth, Economic Inequality, and Changes in Family Structure, 1949–1999." *Demography* 40, no. 3: 499–519.

———. 2009. *Where We Live Now: Immigration and Race in the United States*. Berkeley: University of California Press.

Iceland, John, Gregory Sharp, and Jeffrey M. Timberlake. 2012. "Sun Belt Rising: Regional Population Change and the Decline in Black Residential Segregation, 1970–2009." *Demography*. DOI: 10.1007/s13524-012-0136-6, published online September 11.

Iceland, John, Gregory Sharp, and Jeffrey M. Timberlake. 2013. "Sun Belt Rising: Regional Population Change and the Decline in Black Residential Segregation, 1970-2009." *Demography* 50, 1: 97–123.

Iceland, John, and Josh Kim. 2001. "Poverty among Working Families: Insights from an Improved Measure." *Social Science Quarterly* 82, no. 2 (June): 253–67.

Iceland, John, Kathleen Short, Thesia I. Garner, and David Johnson. 2001. "Are Children Worse Off? Evaluating Child Well-Being Using a New (and Improved) Measure of Poverty." *Journal of Human Resources* 36, no. 2: 398–412.

Iceland, John, and Kurt J. Bauman. 2007. "Income Poverty and Material Hardship." *Journal of Socio-Economics* 36, no. 3: 376–96.

Imai, Katsushi S., Thankrom Arun, and Samuel Kobina Annim. 2010. "Microfinance and Household Poverty Reduction: New Evidence from India." *World Development* 38, no. 2: 1760–74.

"India Has More Mobile Phones Than Toilets: UN Report." 2010. *Telegraph*, April 15. Available at www.telegraph.co.uk/news/worldnews/asia/india/7593567/India-has-more-mobile-phones-than-toilets-UN-report.html (accessed August 5, 2011).

Isaacs, Julia B. 2007. "Economic Mobility of Families across Generations." The Brookings Institution Economic Mobility Project Report, November.

———. 2011. "The Recession's Ongoing Impact on America's Children: Indicators of Children's Economic Well-Being Through 2011." The Brookings Institution First Focus Research Report, December.

Isaacs, Julia B., Isabel V. Sawhill, and Ron Haskins. 2008. "Getting Ahead or Losing Ground: Economic Mobility in America." The Brookings Institution Economic Mobility Project Report, February.

Jackson, Thomas F. 1993. "The State, the Movement, and the Urban Poor: The War on Poverty and Political Mobilization in the 1960s." In *The "Underclass" Debate: Views from History*, edited by Michael B. Katz. Princeton, NJ: Princeton University Press.

Jacobsen, Linda A. and Mark Mather. 2011. "A Post-Recession Update on U.S. Social and Economic Trends." Population Reference Bureau Bulletin Update, December.

Jantti, Markus, Bernt Bratsberg, Knut Roed, Oddbjorn Raaum, Robin Naylor, Eva Osterbacka, Anders Bjorklund, and Tor Eriksson. 2006. "American Exceptionalism in a New Light: A Comparison of Intergenerational Earnings Mobility in the Nordic Countries, the United Kingdom and the United States." IZA Discussion Paper no. 1938, January.

Jargowsky, Paul A. 1996. "Beyond the Street Corner: The Hidden Diversity of High-Poverty Neighborhoods." *Urban Geography* 17, no. 7: 579–603.

———. 1997. *Poverty and Place: Ghettos, Barrios, and the American City.* New York: Russell Sage Foundation.

———. 2003. "Stunning Progress, Hidden Problems: The Dramatic Decline of Concentrated Poverty in the 1990s." The Brookings Institution Center on Urban and Metropolitan Policy Report, Living Cities Census Series. Available at www.brook.edu/es/urban/publications/jargowskypoverty.pdf (accessed January 13, 2012).

Jencks, Christopher. 1992. *Rethinking Social Policy: Race, Poverty, and the Underclass.* New York: Harper Perennial.

Johnson, James H., and Melvin L. Oliver. 1992. "Structural Changes in the U.S. Economy and Black Male Joblessness: A Reassessment." In *Urban Labor Markets and Job Opportunity,* edited by George Peterson and Wayne Vroman. Washington, DC: Urban Institute Press.

Johnson, Paul, and Steven Webb. 1992. "Official Statistics on Poverty in the United Kingdom." In *Poverty Measurement for Economies in Transition in Eastern European Countries.* Warsaw: Polish Statistical Association and Polish Central Statistical Office.

Jones, Jacqueline. 1993. "Southern Diaspora: Origins of the Northern 'Underclass.'" In *The "Underclass" Debate: Views from History,* edited by Michael B. Katz. Princeton, NJ: Princeton University Press.

Kain, John F. 1968. "Housing Segregation, Negro Employment, and Metropolitan Decentralization." *Quarterly Journal of Economics* 82: 175–97.

Kaiser Family Foundation. 2011. "Summary of New Health Reform Law." The Henry J. Kaiser Family Foundation Focus on Health Reform Report, April 15. Available at www.kff.org/healthreform/upload/8061.pdf (accessed March 8, 2012).

Kasarda, John. 1990. "Structural Factors Affecting the Location and Timing of Underclass Growth." *Urban Geography* 11: 234–64.

———. 1995. "Industrial Restructuring and the Changing Location of Jobs." In *State of the Union: America in the 1990s,* vol. 1, edited by Reynolds Farley. New York: Russell Sage Foundation.

Kasinitz, Philip, John H. Mollenkopf, Mary C. Waters, and Jennifer Holdaway. 2008. *Inheriting the City: The Children of Immigrants Come of Age.* Cambridge, MA: Harvard University Press.

Kates, Robert W., and Partha Dasgupta. 2007. "African Poverty: A Grand Challenge for Sustainability Science." *Proceedings of the National Academy of Sciences of the United States of America* 104, no. 43: 16747–50.

Katz, Michael B. 1989. *The Undeserving Poor: From the War on Poverty to the War on Welfare.* New York: Pantheon.

———. 1993a. "The Urban 'Underclass' as a Metaphor of Social Transformation." In *The "Underclass" Debate: Views from History*, edited by Michael
B. Katz. Princeton, NJ: Princeton University Press.

———. 1993b. "Reframing the 'Underclass' Debate." In *The "Underclass"
Debate: Views from History*, edited by Michael B. Katz. Princeton, NJ:
Princeton University Press.

———. 1996. *In the Shadow of the Poorhouse: A Social History of Welfare in
America.* New York: Basic Books.

———. 2001. *The Price of Citizenship: Redefining the American Welfare State.*
New York: Metropolitan Books, Henry Holt.

Kauffman, Kyle D., and L. Lynne Kiesling. 1997. "Was There a Nineteenth
Century Welfare Magnet in the United States? Preliminary Results from
New York City and Brooklyn." *Quarterly Review of Economics and Finance*
37, no. 2 (Summer): 439–48.

Kaufman, Phil R. 1999. "Rural Poor Have Less Access to Supermarkets, Large
Grocery Stores." *Rural Development* 13, no. 3: 19–25.

Kennedy, Sheela, and Larry Bumpass. 2008. "Cohabitation and Children's Living Arrangements: New Estimates from the United States." *Demographic
Research* 19: 1663–92.

Kenworthy, Lane. 2004. *Egalitarian Capitalism: Jobs, Incomes, and Growth in
Affluent Countries.* New York: Russell Sage Foundation.

———. 2011. *Progress for the Poor.* Oxford: Oxford University Press.

Kenworthy, Lane, and Lindsay A. Owens. 2011. "The Surprisingly Weak Effect
of Recessions on Public Opinion." In *The Great Recession,* edited by David
B. Grusky, Bruce Western, and Christopher Wimer. New York: Russell Sage
Foundation.

Khandker, Shahidur R. 2005. "Microfinance and Poverty: Evidence Using Panel
Data from Bangladesh." *World Bank Economic Review* 19, no. 2: 263–86.

Kiesling, L. Lynne, and Robert A. Margo. 1997. "Explaining the Rise in Antebellum Pauperism, 1850–1860: New Evidence." *Quarterly Review of Economics and Finance* 37, no. 2 (Summer): 405–17.

Killick, Tony. 1995. "Structural Adjustment and Poverty Alleviation: An Inter-
pretive Survey." *Development and Change* 26, no. 2: 305–30.

Knab, Jean, Irv Garfinkel, Sara McLanahan, Emily Moiduddin, and Cynthia
Osborne. 2009. "The Effects of Welfare and Child Support Policies on the
Incidence of Marriage Following a Nonmarital Birth." In *Welfare Reform
and Its Long-Term Consequences for America's Poor,* edited by James P.
Ziliak. Cambridge: Cambridge University Press.

Kneebone, Elizabeth, Carey Nadeau, and Alan Berube. 2011. "The Re-
Emergence of Concentrated Poverty: Metropolitan Trends in the 2000s." The
Brookings Institution, Metropolitan Opportunity Series no. 26, November.

Kohut, Andrew . 2012. "Don't Mind the Gap." *New York Times,* January 26.

Kreider, Rose M., and Diana B. Elliott. 2010. "Historical Changes in Stay-at-
Home Mothers: 1969 to 2009." Paper presented at the annual American
Sociological Association meetings, Atlanta, GA.

Kristof, Nicholas. 2007. "Wretched of the Earth."*New York Review of Books,*
May 31, 34–36.

———. 2012. "The White Underclass," *New York Times,* February 8.

Krugman, Paul R. 2008. "Trade and Wages, Reconsidered." *Brookings Papers on Economic Activity* 1: 103–43.

———. 2012. "Money and Morals." *New York Times,* February 10.

Landry, Bart, and Kris Marsh. 2011. "The Evolution of the New Black Middle Class." *Annual Review of Sociology* 37: 373–94.

Lareau, Annette. 2003. *Unequal Childhoods: Race, Class, and Family Life.* Berkeley: University of California Press.

Legal Momentum. 2012. "Single Mothers Since 2000: Falling Farther Down." Report for the Women's Legal Defense and Education Fund. Available at www.legalmomentum.org/our-work/women-and-poverty/resources—publications/single-mothers-since-2000.pdf (accessed February 18, 2012).

Lerman, Robert I. 1996. "The Impact of the Changing U.S. Family Structure on Poverty and Income Inequality." *Economica* 63: S119–S139.

Lewis, Michael. 2011. *Boomerang: Travels in the New Third World.* New York: Penguin.

Lewis, Oscar. 1966a. "The Culture of Poverty." *Scientific American* 215: 19–25.

———. 1966b. *La Vida.* New York: Random House.

Lichter, Daniel T. 1997. "Poverty and Inequality among Children." *Annual Review of Sociology* 23: 121–45.

Lichter, Daniel T., Diane K. McLaughlin, and David Ribar. 1997. "Welfare and the Rise in Female-Headed Families." *American Journal of Sociology* 103, no. 1 (July): 112–43.

Lichter, Daniel T., and Martha L. Crowley. 2002. "Poverty in America: Beyond Welfare Reform." *Population Bulletin* 57, no. 2 (June): 1–36.

Lindbeck, A., P. Molander, T. Persson, O. Petersson, A. Sandmo, B. Swedenborg, and N. Thygesen. 1994. *Turning Sweden Around.* Cambridge, MA: MIT Press.

Lindsey, Duncan. 2009. *Child Poverty and Inequality: Securing a Better Future for America's Children.* New York: Oxford University Press.

Lin, Ann Chih, and David R. Harris. 2008. "Why Is American Poverty Still Colored in the Twenty-First Century?" In *The Colors of Poverty: Why Racial and Ethnic Disparities Persist,* edited by Ann Chih Lin and David R. Harris. New York: Russell Sage Foundation.

Looney, Adam, and Michael Greenstone. 2011. "Trends: Reduced Earnings for Men in America." The Hamilton Project Research Report, July.

Loury, Glenn C. 2000. "What's Next? Some Reflections on the Poverty Conference." *Focus* 21, no. 2 (Fall): 58–60.

Lundberg, Shelly J., and Richard Startz. 2000. "Inequality and Race: Models and Policy." In *Meritocracy and Economic Inequality,* edited by Kenneth Arrow, Samuel Bowles, and Steven Durlauf. Princeton, NJ: Princeton University Press.

Manning, Wendy D. 2006. "Children's Economic Well-Being in Married and Cohabiting Parent Families." *Journal of Marriage and Family* 68, no. 2: 345–62.

Manning, W. D., P. J. Smock, and D. Majumdar. 2004. "The Relative Stability of Cohabiting and Marital Unions for Children." *Population Research and Policy Review* 23: 135–59.

Martin J.A., B.E. Hamilton, S.J. Ventura, M.J.K. Osterman, S. Kirmeyer, T.J. Mathews, and E.C. Wilson. 2011. "Births: Final Data for 2009." National Vital Statistics Reports 60, 1. Hyattsville, MD: National Center for Health Statistics.

Martin, Philip, and Elizabeth Midgley. 2003. *Immigration: Shaping and Reshaping America*. Population Reference Bureau, Population Bulletin 58, no. 2 (June): 1–44.

Marx, Karl. 1994a. "Classes in Capitalism and Pre-Capitalism." Reprinted from *The Communist Manifesto* in *Social Stratification in Sociological Perspective*, edited by David B. Grusky. Boulder, CO: Westview Press.

———. 1994b. "Value and Surplus Value." Reprinted in *Social Stratification in Sociological Perspective*, edited by David B. Grusky. Boulder, CO: Westview Press.

Massey, Douglas S., and Nancy A. Denton. 1993. *American Apartheid*. Cambridge, MA: Harvard University Press.

Mattingly, Marybeth J., Kenneth M. Johnson, and Andrew Schaefer. 2011. "More Poor Kids in More Poor Places: Children Increasingly Live Where Poverty Persists." Carsey Institute Issue Brief no. 38, Fall.

Mayer, Susan E. 1996. "A Comparison of Poverty and Living Conditions in the United States, Canada, Sweden, and Germany." In *Poverty, Inequality, and the Future of Social Policy*, edited by Katherine McFate, Roger Lawson, and William Julius Wilson. New York: Russell Sage Foundation.

Mayer, Susan E., and Christopher Jencks. 1989. "Poverty and the Distribution of Material Hardship." *Journal of Human Resources* 24, no. 1 (Winter): 88–114.

McCall, Leslie. 2001 "Sources of Racial Inequality in Metropolitan Labor Markets: Racial, Ethnic, and Gender Differences." *American Sociological Review* 66, no. 4 (August): 520–41.

McGeary, Michael G.H. 1990. "Ghetto Poverty and Federal Policies and Programs." In *Inner-City Poverty in the United States*, edited by Laurence Lynn Jr. and Michael G.H. McGeary. Washington, DC: National Academy Press.

Magnuson, Katherine, and Elizabeth Votruba-Drzal. 2009. "Enduring Influences of Childhood Poverty." In *Changing Poverty, Changing Policies*, edited by Maria Cancian and Sheldon Danziger. New York: Russell Sage Foundation.

McLanahan, Sara, and Irwin Garfinkel. 1996. "Single-Mother Families and Social Policy: Lessons for the United States from Canada, France, and Sweden." In *Poverty, Inequality, and the Future of Social Policy*, edited by Katherine McFate, Roger Lawson, and William Julius Wilson. New York: Russell Sage Foundation.

Mead, Lawrence. 1992. *The New Politics of Poverty: The Nonworking Poor in America*. New York: Basic Books.

Meyer, Bruce D., and James X. Sullivan. 2009. "Five Decades of Consumption and Income Poverty." National Bureau of Economic Research Working Paper no. 14827 (March).

Micklewright, John. 2002. "Social Exclusion and Children: A European View for a US Debate." Center for Analysis and Social Exclusion Paper no. 51, London School of Economics, February.

Milanovic, Branko. 2009. "Global Inequality and the Global Inequality Extraction Ratio: The Story of the Past Two Centuries." World Bank Policy Research Working Paper no. 5044, September.

Moffitt, Robert. 2002. "From Welfare to Work: What the Evidence Shows." Brookings Institution Policy Brief no. 13, January.

Monkkonen, Eric H. 1993. "Nineteenth-Century Institutions: Dealing with the Urban 'Underclass.'" In The "Underclass" Debate: Views from History, edited by Michael B. Katz. Princeton, NJ: Princeton University Press.

Moore, Kristin Anderson, Zakia Redd, Mary Burkhauser, Kassim Mbwana, and Ashleigh Collins. 2009. "Children in Poverty: Trends, Consequences, and Policy Options." Child Trends Research Brief no. 2009–11, April.

Morgan, S. Philip, Erin Cumberworth, and Christopher Wimer. 2011. "The Great Recession's Influence on Fertility, Marriage, Divorce, and Cohabitation." In The Great Recession, edited by David B. Grusky, Bruce Western, and Christopher Wimer. New York: Russell Sage Foundation.

Mouw, Ted. 2000. "Job Relocation and the Racial Gap in Unemployment in Detroit and Chicago, 1980 to 1990." American Sociological Review 65, no. 5 (October): 730–53.

Moynihan, Daniel Patrick. 1965. The Negro Family: The Case for National Action. Washington, DC: U.S. Department of Labor.

Munsterberg, Emil. 1904. "The Problem of Poverty." American Journal of Sociology 10, no. 3 (November): 335–53.

Murray, Charles. 1984. Losing Ground: American Social Policy, 1950–1980. New York: Basic Books.

———. 2012. Coming Apart: The State of White America, 1960–2010. New York: Crown Forum.

Mykyta, Laryssa, and Suzanne Macartney. 2011. "The Effects of Recession on Household Composition: 'Doubling Up' and Economic Well-Being." U.S. Census Bureau, SEHSD Working Paper no. 2011–4.

Myrdal, Gunnar. 1944. An American Dilemma. 2 vols. New York: Harper and Row.

Naifeh, Mary. 1998. "Dynamics of Economic Well-Being, Poverty, 1993–94: Trap Door? Revolving Door? Or Both?" U.S. Census Bureau, Current Population Reports, series P70–63, Washington, DC: U.S. Government Printing Office.

National Bureau of Economic Research. 2010. Business Cycle Dating Committee Report, September 20, 2010. Cambridge, MA: NBER. Available at www.nber.org/cycles/sept2010.pdf (accessed July 8, 2011).

National Center for Health Statistics. 2011. Health, United States, 2010: With a Special Feature on Death and Dying. Hyattsville, MD.

National Public Radio. 2012. "What Kind of Country." This American Life, Episode 459, March 2.

National Research Council. 1995. Measuring Poverty: A New Approach, edited by Constance F. Citro and Robert T. Michael. Washington, DC: National Academy Press.

Noreen, Umara, Rabia Imran, Arshad Zaheer, and M. Iqbal Saif. 2011. "Impact of Microfinance on Poverty: A Case of Pakistan." World Applied Sciences Journal 12, no. 6: 877–83.

O'Connor, Alice. 2001. *Poverty Knowledge: Social Science, Social Policy, and the Poor in Twentieth-Century U.S. History*. Princeton, NJ: Princeton University Press.

Office of Management and Budget. 2012. *Fiscal Year 2012 Historical Tables: Budget of the U.S. Government*. Available at *www.whitehouse.gov/sites /default/files/omb/budget/fy2012/assets/hist.pdf* (accessed December 21, 2012).

O'Hare, William P. 1996. "A New Look at Poverty in America." *Population Bulletin* 51, no. 2: 1–48.

O'Higgins, Michael, and Stephen Jenkins. 1990. "Poverty in the EC: Estimates for 1975, 1980, and 1985." In *Analysing Poverty in the European Community: Policy Issues, Research Options, and Data Sources*, edited by Rudolph Teekens and Bernard M. S. van Praag. Luxembourg: Office of Official Publications of the European Communities.

Organization for Economic Cooperation and Development. 1996. "OECD Employment Outlook 1996—Countering the Risks of Labour Market Exclusion." Paris.

———. 2001. *OECD Employment Outlook*. Paris: OECD, June.

———. 2010. "A Family Affair: Intergenerational Social Mobility across OECD Countries." Economic Policy Reforms, Going for Growth Report.

———. 2011. "Labour Force Statistics, Unemployment." Available at http:// stats.oecd.org/Index.aspx?DatasetCode=MEILABOUR (accessed March 9, 2012).

Orshansky, Mollie. 1963. "Children of the Poor." *Social Security Bulletin* 26, no. 7 (July): 3–13.

———. 1965. "Counting the Poor: Another Look at the Poverty Profile." *Social Security Bulletin* 28, no. 1 (January): 3–29.

Osterman, Paul. 1999. *Securing Prosperity*. Princeton, NJ: Princeton University Press.

Pager, Devah. 2009. "Discrimination in a Low-Wage Labor Market: A Field Experiment." *American Sociological Review* 74, no. 5: 777–99

Patterson, James T. 2000. *America's Struggle against Poverty in the Twentieth Century*. Cambridge, MA: Harvard University Press.

Pearce, Diana. 1978. "The Feminization of Poverty: Women, Work, and Welfare." *Urban Sociological Change* 11: 128–36.

Piore, Michael J. 1994. "The Dual Labor Market: Theory and Implications." In *Social Stratification in Sociological Perspective*, edited by David B. Grusky. Boulder, CO: Westview Press.

Plotnick, Robert D. 2011–12. "The Alleviation of Poverty: How Far Have We Come?" University of Washington, Daniel J. Evans School of Public Affairs Working Paper, 2011–02. Available at http://evans.washington.edu/files /EvansWorkingPaper-2011-02.pdf (accessed March 6, 2012).

Plotnick, Robert D., Eugene Smolensky, Eirik Evenhouse, and Siobhan Reilly. 1998. "The Twentieth Century Record of Inequality and Poverty in the United States." Paper presented at the General Conference of the International Association for Research on Income and Wealth. Cambridge, England, August 23–29.

Polachek, Solomon W., and W. Stanley Siebert. 1994. "Gender in the Labour Market." In *Social Stratification in Sociological Perspective*, edited by David B. Grusky. Boulder, CO: Westview Press.

Population Reference Bureau. 2011. "2011 World Population Data Sheet." Available at www.prb.org/pdf11/2011population-data-sheet_eng.pdf (accessed January 23, 2012).

Price, C. 1969. "The Study of Assimilation." In *Sociological Studies: Migration*, edited by J. A. Jackson. Cambridge: Cambridge University Press.

Pritamkabe. 2011. "The Mobile Phone Revolution in the Developing World." February 12. Available at http://pritamkabe.wordpress.com/2011/02/12/the-mobile-phone-revolution-in-the-developing-world/ (accessed August 5, 2011).

Rainwater, Lee, and Timothy M. Smeeding. 1995. "Doing Poorly: The Real Income of American Children in a Comparative Perspective." In *Crisis in American Institutions*, edited by J. H. Skolnick and E. Currie. Boston: Allyn and Bacon, 1995.

———. 2003. *Poor Kids in a Rich Country: America's Children in Comparative Perspective*. New York: Russell Sage Foundation.

Rajan, Raghuram G. 2010. *Fault Lines: How Hidden Fractures Still Threaten the World Economy*. Princeton, NJ: Princeton University Press.

Rank, Mark R., and Thomas A. Hirschl. 2001. "Rags or Riches? Estimating the Probabilities of Poverty and Affluence across the Adult American Life Span." *Social Science Quarterly* 82, no. 4: 651–69.

Raphael, Steven, and Eugene Smolensky. 2009. "Immigration and Poverty in the United States." In *Changing Poverty, Changing Policies*, edited by Maria Cancian and Sheldon Danziger. New York: Russell Sage Foundation.

Ravallion, Martin, Shaohua Chen, and Prem Sangraula. 2008. "Dollar a Day Revisited." The World Bank Policy Research Working Paper no. 4620. Washington, DC: World Bank.

———. 2009. "A Comparative Perspective on Poverty Reduction in Brazil, China, and India." World Bank Policy Research Working Paper no. 5080, October.

Rawls, John. 1971. *A Theory of Justice*. Cambridge, MA: Harvard University Press.

Real Clear Politics. 2012. "Congressional Job Approval." Available at www.realclearpolitics.com/epolls/other/congressional_job_approval-903.html (accessed March 12, 2012).

Reardon, Sean R. 2011. "The Widening Achievement Gap Between the Rich and the Poor: New Evidence and Possible Explanations." In *Whither Opportunity? Rising Inequality, Schools, and Children's Life Chances*, edited by Greg J. Duncan and Richard Murnane. New York: Russell Sage Foundation.

Rector, Robert. 1993. "Welfare Reform, Dependency Reduction, and Labor Market Entry." *Journal of Labor Research* 14, no. 3 (Summer): 283–97.

Rector, Robert, and Rachel Sheffield. 2011. "Air Conditioning, Cable TV, and an Xbox: What Is Poverty in the United States Today?" Heritage Foundation Backgrounder no. 2575, July 18.

Ribar, David C., and Karen S. Hamrick. 2003. "Dynamics of Poverty and Food Sufficiency." United States Department of Agriculture, Food Assistance and Nutrition Research Report no. 36, September.

Riegg Cellini, Stephanie, Signe-Mary McKernan, and Caroline Ratcliffe. 2008. "The Dynamics of Poverty in the United States: A Review of Data, Methods, and Findings." *Journal of Policy Analysis and Management* 27, no. 3: 577–605.

Roemer, Marc. 2000. "Assessing the Quality of the March Current Population Survey and the Survey of Income and Program Participation Income Estimates, 1990–1996." U.S. Census Bureau Staff Paper on Income, Internet Release Data, June 16. Available at www.census.gov/hhes/income/papers.html.

Ryan, John. 1906. *A Living Wage: Its Ethical and Economic Aspects.* New York: Macmillan Co.

Sachs, Jeffrey D. 2005. *The End of Poverty: Economic Possibilities of Our Time.* New York: Penguin Books.

Sakamoto, Arthur, and Satomi Furuichi. 1997. "Wages among White and Japanese-American Male Workers." *Research in Stratification and Mobility* 15: 177–206.

Sakamoto, Arthur, Huei-Hsia Wu, and Jessie M. Tzeng. 2000. "The Declining Significance of Race among American Men during the Latter Half of the Twentieth Century." *Demography* 37, no. 1: 41–51.

Sandefur, Gary, and W. J. Scott. 1983. "Minority Group Status and the Wages of Indian and Black Males." *Social Science Research* 12: 44–68.

Sastre, Mercedes, and Luis Ayala. 2002. "Europe vs. the United States: Is There a Tradeoff Between Mobility and Inequality?" Working Paper no. 2002–26. Colchester, UK: University of Essex, Institute for Social and Economic Research.

Schiller, Bradley R. 2001. *The Economics of Poverty and Discrimination,* 8th ed. Upper Saddle River, NJ: Prentice Hall.

Scholz, John Karl, Robert Moffitt, and Benjamin Cowan. 2009. "Trends in Income Support." In *Changing Poverty, Changing Policies,* edited by Maria Cancian and Sheldon Danziger. New York: Russell Sage Foundation.

Schuman, Howard, Charlotte Steeh, Lawrence Bobo, and Maria Krysan. 2001. *Racial Attitudes in America: Trends and Interpretations,* rev. ed. Cambridge, MA: Harvard University Press.

Schumpeter, Joseph A. 1994. [1942] *Capitalism, Socialism and Democracy.* London: Routledge.

Second Annual Report of the Children's Aid Society of New York. 1855. New York.

Sen, Amartya. 1983. "Poor, Relatively Speaking." *Oxford Economic Papers* 35, no. 2: 153–69.

———. 1992. *Inequality Reexamined.* Cambridge, MA: Harvard University Press.

———. 1999. *Development as Freedom.* New York: Anchor Books.

Shaefer, H. Luke, and Kathryn Edin. 2012. "Extreme Poverty in the United States, 1996 to 2011." National Poverty Center Policy Brief no. 28, University of Michigan, February.

Sherman, Arloc. 2011. "Poverty and Financial Distress Would Have Been Substantially Worse in 2010 without Government Action, New Census Data Show." Center on Budget and Policy Priorities Research Report, November 7.

Shipler, David K. 2004. *The Working Poor: Invisible in America*. New York: Vintage Books.

Short, Kathleen S. 2001. "Experimental Poverty Measures: 1999." U.S. Census Bureau, Current Population Reports, Consumer Income, series P60–216. Washington, DC: U.S. Government Printing Office.

———. 2010. "Experimental Modern Poverty Measures 2007." Census Bureau Working Paper, January 3. Available at www.census.gov/hhes/povmeas /publications/overview/shortsge2010.pdf (accessed August 10, 2011).

———. 2011a. "The Research Supplemental Poverty Measure: 2010." U.S. Census Bureau, Current Population Reports, P60–241, Washington, DC: U.S. Government Printing Office.

———. 2011b. "The Supplemental Poverty Measure: Examining the Incidence and Depth of Poverty in the U.S. Taking Account of Taxes and Transfers." U.S. Census Bureau, SEHSD Working Paper no. 2011–20. Available at www.census.gov/hhes/povmeas/methodology/supplemental/research /WEA2011.kshort.071911_2.rev.pdf (accessed January 3, 2012).

———. 2011c. "Who Is Poor? A New Look with the Supplemental Poverty Measure." Paper presented at the 2011 Allied Social Science Association, Society of Government Economists meetings. Available at www.census.gov /hhes/povmeas/methodology/supplemental/research/SGE_Short.pdf (accessed August 5, 2011).

Skocpol, Theda. 2000. *The Missing Middle: Working Families and the Future of American Social Policy*. New York: W. W. Norton.

Skocpol, Theda, Marjorie Abend-Wein, Christopher Howard, and Susan Goodrich Lehmann. 1993. "Women's Associations and the Enactment of Mothers' Pensions in the United States." *American Political Science Review* 87, no. 3 (September): 686–701.

Smeeding, Timothy M., and Jane Waldfogel. 2010. "Fighting Poverty: Attentive Policy Can Make a Huge Difference." *Journal of Policy Analysis and Management* 29, no. 2: 401–7.

Smeeding, Timothy M., Jeffrey P. Thompson, Asaf Levanon, and Esra Burak. 2011. "Poverty and Income Inequality in the Early Stages of the Great Recession." In *The Great Recession*, edited by David B. Grusky, Bruce Western, and Christopher Wimer. New York: Russell Sage Foundation.

Smeeding, Timothy M., Karen Robson, Coady Wing, and Jonathan Gershuny. 2009. "Income Poverty and Income Support for Minority and Immigrant Children in Rich Countries." Luxembourg Income Study Working Paper Series no. 527, December.

Smith, Adam. 1776. *An Inquiry into the Nature and Causes of the Wealth of Nations*. 1776; reprint, Oxford: Clarendon Press, 1976.

Smock, Pamela, and Fiona Rose Greenland. 2010. "Diversity in Pathways to Parenthood: Patterns, Implications, and Emerging Research Directions." *Journal of Marriage and Family* 72, no. 3: 576–93.

Sorenson, Elaine. 1994. "Noncustodial Fathers: Can They Afford to Pay More Child Support?" Urban Institute Working Paper, December.

Stevens, Ann Huff. 1994. "The Dynamics of Poverty Spells: Updating Bane and Ellwood." *AEA Papers and Proceedings* 84, no. 2 (May): 34–37.

————. 1999. "Climbing out of Poverty, Falling Back In: Measuring the Persistence of Poverty over Multiple Spells." *Journal of Human Resources* 34, no. 3 (Summer): 557–88.

Stucke, Maurice E. Forthcoming. "Occupy Wall Street and Antitrust." *Southern California Law Review Postscript,* SSRN id2014312, posted February 10, 2012.

Sugrue, Thomas J. 1993. "The Structure of Urban Poverty: The Reorganization of Space and Work in Three Periods of American History." In *The "Underclass" Debate: Views from History,* edited by Michael B. Katz. Princeton, NJ: Princeton University Press.

Swarns, Rachel L. 2008. "Bipartisan Calls for New Federal Poverty Measure." *New York Times,* September 2.

Swiss Agency for Development and Cooperation (SDC). 2000. "The SDC Policy for Social Development." In *The Challenge of Eliminating World Poverty,* edited by SDC Publications on Development. Berne: SDC.

Takei, Isao, and Arthur Sakamoto. 2011. "Poverty among Asian Americans in the 21st Century." *Sociological Perspectives* 54, no. 2: 251–76.

Taylor, Paul , Rakesh Kochhar, Richard Fry, Gabriel Velasco, and Seth Motel. 2011. "Wealth Gaps Rise to Record Highs Between Whites, Blacks, and Hispanics." Pew Research Center Social & Demographic Trends Research Report, July 26.

Thomas, Kevin J. A. 2011. "Familial Influences on Child Poverty in Black Immigrant, US-Born Black, and Non-Black Immigrant Families." *Demography* 48, no. 2: 437–60.

Thompson, Tommy G. 2001. "Welfare Reform's Next Step." *Brookings Review* 19, no. 3 (Summer): 2–3.

Townsend, Peter. 1993. *The International Analysis of Poverty.* Hemel Hempstead, UK: Harvester-Wheatsheaf.

Trattner, Walter I. 1994. *From Poor Law to Welfare State: A History of Social Welfare in America.* New York: Free Press.

Trotter, Joe William, Jr. 1993. "Blacks in the Urban North: The 'Underclass Question' in Historical Perspective." In *The "Underclass" Debate: Views from History,* edited by Michael B. Katz. Princeton, NJ: Princeton University Press.

Turner, Jonathan H., Leonard Beeghley, and Charles H. Powers. 1989. *The Emergence of Sociological Theory.* Belmont, CA: Wadsworth.

Turner, Margery, Michael Fix, and Raymond Struyk. 1991. *Opportunities Denied, Opportunities Diminished: Discrimination in Hiring.* Washington, DC: Urban Institute Press.

UNICEF Innocenti Research Centre. 2000. "Child Poverty in Rich Nations." *Innocenti Report Card* no. 1 (June): 1–28.

United Nations. 1995. "World Summit on Social Development." Copenhagen. Available at http://social.un.org/index/Home/WSSD1995.aspx (accessed August 10, 2011).

————. 2010. "The Millennium Development Goals Report: 2010." New York. Available at www.un.org/millenniumgoals/poverty.shtml (accessed March 26, 2012).

———. 2011. "The Millennium Development Goals Report 2011." Available at www.un.org/millenniumgoals/reports.shtml (accessed August 10, 2011).

Urban Institute. 2011. "Earned Income Tax Credit by State, Tax Year 2009." Tax Policy Center Tax Facts Table. Available at www.taxpolicycenter.org /taxfacts/Content/PDF/eitc_state.pdf (accessed March 6, 2012).

U.S. Census Bureau. 1993. "Population and Housing Unit Counts," 1990 Census of Population and Housing Report 1990 CPH-2-1.

———. 2000. "DP-1. Profile of General Demographic Characteristics: 2000." Summary file I (SF 1), 100-Percent Data Quick Table, American Fact Finder Tabulation. Available at http://factfinder.census.gov (accessed January 12, 2012).

———. 2009. "*Table 10*. Percent of Households with Selected Measures of Material Well-Being: 1992, 1998, 2003, 2005." Detailed Tables on Extended Measures of Well-Being: Living Conditions in the United States, 2005, from the Survey of Income and Program Participation. Available at www.census.gov /hhes/well-being/publications/extended-05.html (accessed January 9, 2012).

———. 2010a. "2010 Census of Population." Public Law 94–171 Redistricting Data File.

———. 2010b. "POV06: Families by Number of Working Family Members and Family Structure." Detailed Poverty Tables, Table POV06. Available at www.census.gov/hhes/www/cpstables/032010/pov/new06_100_01.htm (accessed September 16, 2010).

———. 2010c. "Poverty Thresholds for Two-Adult-Two-Child Family Following NAS Recommendations: 1999–2009." Tables of NAS-Based Poverty Estimates, Internet Rerelease Data. Available at www.census.gov/hhes /povmeas/data/nas/tables/index.html (accessed August 16, 2011).

———. 2010d. "Table 7. Income of Households from Specified Sources, by Poverty Status: 2009." Current Population Survey, Annual Social and Economic Survey, Effects of Benefits and Taxes on Income and Poverty (R&D), Internet Release Data. Available at www.census.gov/hhes/www/cpstables/032010/rdcall/7_001.htm (accessed March 6, 2012).

———. 2011a. *American Housing Survey for the United States: 2009.* Current Housing Reports, Series H150/09. Washington, DC: U.S. Government Printing Office.

———. 2011b. "Percent of People 25 Years Old and Over Who Have Completed High School or College, by Race, Hispanic Origin and Sex: Selected Years 1940 to 2010." Educational Attainment Historical Tables, Table A-2. Available at www.census.gov/hhes/socdemo/education/data/cps/historical /(accessed September 13, 2012)

———. 2011c. "Poverty Status of People by Family Relationship, Race, and Hispanic Origin: 1959 to 2010." Historical Poverty People Tables, Table 2. Available at www.census.gov/hhes/www/poverty/data/historical/hstpov2.xls (accessed February 1, 2012).

———. 2011d. "Table 1.5. Educational Attainment of the Population 25 Years and Over by Sex, Nativity, and U.S. Citizenship Status: 2010." Current Population Survey, Annual Social and Economic Supplement, 2010. Available at www .census.gov/population/foreign/data/cps2010.html (accessed February 15, 2012).

———. 2011e. "Table DP02: Selected Social Characteristics in the United States, 2010 American Community Survey 1-Year Estimates." Available at http://FactFinder2.census.gov (accessed February 14, 2012).

———. 2011f. "Table FM-2. All Parent/Child Situations, by Type, Race, and Hispanic Origin of Householder or Reference Person: 1970 to Present." Current Population Survey data, 2011. Available at www.census.gov /population/socdemo/hh-fam/fm2.xls, (accessed February 17, 2012).

———. 2011g. "Table H-4. Gini Ratios for Households, by Race and Hispanic Origin of Householder: 1967 to 2010." Current Population Survey, Annual Social and Economic Supplements, Historical Income Inequality Tables. Available at www.census.gov/hhes/www/income/data/historical/inequality /(accessed February 6, 2012).

———. 2012a. Current Population Survey Table Creator, Annual Social and Economic Supplement, 2012. Available at www.census.gov/hhes/www /cpstc/cps_table_creator.html (accessed September 12, 2012).

———. 2012b. Detailed Poverty Tables, Current Population Survey, Annual Social and Economic Supplement, 2012. Available at www.census.gov/hhes /www/cpstables/032012/pov/toc.htm (accessed September 13, 2012).

———. 2012c. Historical Poverty Tables for People and Families, Current Population Survey, Annual Social and Economic Supplement, 2012. Available at www.census.gov/hhes/www/poverty/data/historical/index.html (accessed September 13, 2012).

———. 2012d. "Poverty of People, by Sex: 1966 to 2011." Historical Poverty Tables, Table 7. Available at www.census.gov/hhes/www/poverty/data /historical/people.html (accessed September 12, 2012).

———. 2012e. "Poverty Status of Families, by Type of Family, Presence of Related Children, Race and Hispanic Origin: 1959 to 2011." Family Historical Poverty Tables, Table 4. Available at www.census.gov/hhes/www /poverty/data/historical/families/html (accessed September 12, 2012).

———. 2012f. "Poverty Status of People, by Age, Race, and Hispanic Origin: 1959 to 2011." Historical Poverty People Tables, Table 3. Available at www.census.gov/hhes/www/poverty/data/historical/people.html (accessed September 12, 2012).

———. 2012g. "S1701. Poverty Status in the Past 12 Months." 2011 American Community Survey 1-Year Estimates, Internet Release Data. Available at http://factfinder2.census.gov (accessed September 20, 2012).

———. 2012h. "Table B17001C. Poverty Status in the Past 12 Months by Sex by Age (American Indian and Alaska Native Alone)." 2011 American Community Survey data. Available at http://FactFinder2.census.gov (accessed September 20, 2012).

———. 2012i. "Table B17001C. Poverty Status in the Past 12 Months by Sex by Age (American Indian and Alaska Native Alone Population for Whom Poverty Status Is Determined." 2011 American Community Survey 1-Year Estimates downloaded from American FactFinder. Available at http:// factfinder2.census.gov/ (accessed September 20, 2012).

———. 2012j. "Table 9. Poverty of People, by Region: 1959 to 2011." 2011 Annual Social and Economic Supplement of the Current Population Survey

Historical Tables. Available at www.census.gov/hhes/www/poverty/data/historical/people.html (accessed September 12, 2012).

———. 2012k. "Table POV01. Age and Sex of All People, Family Members and Unrelated Individuals Iterated by Income-to-Poverty Ratio and Race." 2011 Annual Social and Economic Supplement of the Current Population Survey Detailed Poverty Tables. Available at www.census.gov/hhes/www/cpstables/032012/pov/toc.htm (accessed September 12, 2012).

———. 2012l. "Table POV02: People in Families by Family Structure, Age, and Sex, Iterated by Income-to-Poverty Ratio and Race: 2011." Current Population Survey, 2012 Annual Social and Economic Supplement Detailed Tables on Poverty. Available at www.census.gov/hhes/www/cpstables/032012/pov/toc.htm (accessed September 12, 2012).

———. 2012m. "Table POV29: Years of School Completed by Poverty Status, Sex, Age, Nativity, and Citizenship: 2011." Current Population Survey, 2012 Annual Social and Economic Supplement Detailed Tables on Poverty. Available at www.census.gov/hhes/www/cpstables/032012/pov/toc.htm (accessed September 12, 2012).

———. 2012n. "Women's Earning as a Percentage of Men's Earning by Race and Hispanic Origin: 1960–2011." Historical Income People Tables, Table P-40. Internet Release Data, Available at www.census.gov/hhes/www/income/data/historical/people/ (accessed September 12, 2012).

U.S. Department of Housing and Urban Development. 2010. *The 2009 Annual Homeless Assessment Report to Congress.* Office of Community Planning and Development Report, June 18.

U.S. Energy Information Administration. 2009. 2009 Residential Energy Consumption Survey Data Tables. Available at www.eia.gov/consumption/residential/data/2009/ (accessed January 9, 2012).

U.S. Immigration and Naturalization Service. 2002. *Statistical Yearbook of the Immigration and Naturalization Service, 2000.* Washington, D.C: U.S. Government Printing Office.

Vanden Heuvel, Katrina. 2011. "Colbert Challenges the Poverty Deniers." *The Nation* blog, July 28. Available at www.thenation.com/blog/162421/colbert-challenges-poverty-deniers (accessed August 3, 2011).

Vaughan, Denton R. 1993. "Exploring the Use of the Public's Views to Set Income Poverty Thresholds and Adjust Them over Time." *Social Security Bulletin* 56, no. 2 (Summer): 22–46.

Ventura, S. J. and C. A. Bachrach. 2000. Nonmarital Childbearing in the United States, 1940–99. National Vital Statistics Reports 48, 16. Hyattsville, MD: National Center for Health Statistics.

Waldfogel, Jane. 2010. *Britain's War on Poverty.* New York: Russell Sage Foundation.

Wallerstein, Immanuel. 1974. *The Modern World System: Capitalist Agriculture and the Origins of the European World-Economy in the 16th Century.* New York: Academic Press.

Washington, Booker T. 1902. *The Future of the American Negro.* New York: Metro Books, 1969.

Weber, Max. 1994a. "Class, Status, Party." In *Social Stratification in Sociological Perspective*, edited by David B. Grusky. Boulder, CO: Westview Press.

———. 1994b. "Open and Closed Relationships." In *Social Stratification in Sociological Perspective*, edited by David B. Grusky. Boulder, CO: Westview Press.

Weinberg, Daniel H. 1987. "Rural Pockets of Poverty." *Rural Sociology* 52: 398–408.

Western, Bruce, and Christopher Wildeman. 2009. "The Black Family and Mass Incarceration." *Annals of the American Academy of Political and Social Science* 621, no. 1: 221–42.

White, Michael J., and Jennifer E. Glick. 2009. *Achieving Anew: How New Immigrants Do in American Schools, Jobs, and Neighborhoods*. New York: Russell Sage Foundation.

White, Vernica, and Kristin Morse. 2011. "Innovate, Research, Repeat: New York City's Center for Economic Opportunity." *Pathways: A Magazine on Poverty, Inequality, and Social Policy*, Summer, 14–17.

Wikipedia. 2012a. "American Exceptionalism." Available at http://en .wikipedia.org/wiki/American_exceptionalism (accessed January 30, 2012).

———. 2012b. "Parental Leave." Available at http://en.wikipedia.org/wiki /Parental_leave (accessed March 13, 2012).

Wildsmith, Elizabeth, Nicole R. Steward-Streng, and Jennifer Manlove. 2011. "Childbearing Outside of Marriage: Estimates and Trends in the United States." Child Trends Research Brief, 2011–29, November.

Williamson, Vanessa, Theda Skocpol, and John Coggin. 2011. "The Tea Party and the Remaking of Republican Conservatism." *Perspectives on Politics* 9, no. 1: 25–43.

Wilson, William Julius. 1978. *The Declining Significance of Race: Blacks and Changing American Institutions*. Chicago: University of Chicago Press.

———. 1987. *The Truly Disadvantaged: The Inner City, the Underclass, and Public Policy*. Chicago: University of Chicago Press.

Wood, Gordon. 2011. *The Idea of America: Reflections on the Birth of the United States*. New York: Penguin Press.

Wolff, Edward N., Lindsay A. Owens, and Esra Burak. 2011. "How Much Wealth Was Destroyed in the Great Recession?" In *The Great Recession*, edited by David B. Grusky, Bruce Western, and Christopher Wimer. New York: Russell Sage Foundation.

World Bank. 2001. *World Development Report, 2000/2001: Attacking Poverty*. Oxford: Oxford University Press.

———. 2011. "Microfinance." International Finance Issue Brief, September, 13. Available at www1.ifc.org/wps/wcm/connect/ef58a800486a807b-be89fff995bd23db/AM211IFCIssue+Brief_Microfinance.pdf?MOD=AJPERES (accessed March 28, 2012).

———. 2012a. "Health." World Development Indicators data. Available at http://data.worldbank.org/topic/health (accessed January 19, 2012).

———. 2012b. "Mortality Rate, Infant (per 1,000 Live Births)." World Development Indicators data. Available at http://data.worldbank.org/indicator /SP.DYN.IMRT.IN (accessed January 19, 2012).

————. 2012c. "Replicate the World Bank's Regional Aggregation." PovcalNet poverty calculations. Available athttp://iresearch.worldbank.org/PovcalNet /povDuplic.html (accessed January 17, 2012).

Zakaria, Fareed. 2011. "Zakaria: Fix Education, Restore Social Mobility." CNN, November 6. Available at http://globalpublicsquare.blogs.cnn .com/2011/11/06/zakaria-fix-education-restore-social-mobility/?hpt=hp_c1 (accessed February 2, 2012).

Ziliak, James P. 2009. "Introduction." In *Welfare Reform and Its Long-Term Consequences for America's Poor,* edited by James P. Ziliak. Cambridge: Cambridge University Press.

————. 2011. "Recent Developments in Antipoverty Policies in the United States." University of Kentucky Center for Poverty Research Discussion Paper, DP 2011–05.

Index

absolute poverty. *See also* official U.S.
 poverty measure; poverty thresholds:
 compared wealthier countries and,
 71–72, 72*fig.*; comparison of poverty
 measures and, 34–36, 35*fig.*, 36*fig.*; in
 developing world, 62–63; economic
 growth and, 30, 162; measures of, 23,
 24–27, 30, 37; in U.S., 47, 81–82, 82*fig.*
ACA. *See* Patient Protection and Affordable
 Care Act (ACA)
ADC. *See* Aid to Dependent Children
 (ADC)
AFDC. *See* Aid to Families with Dependent
 Children (AFDC)
Affluent Society, The (Galbraith), 19–20
African Americans: "culture of poverty"
 and, 107; Great Recession and,
 123*table*, 125; immigrant *vs.* native-
 born poverty rates and, 97; myths about
 poverty and, 4; New Deal programs
 and, 135; poverty rates among, 42*table*,
 43, 90–93, 96*table*, 97, 160; spells of
 poverty among, 48, 49; before the
 twentieth century, 15–16, 131, 132–33;
 urban poverty and, 55, 56, 59
age. *See also* child poverty; elderly, the;
 Social Security program: gender wage
 gap and, 101; impacts of Great

Recession and, 125; trends in U.S.
 poverty rates and, 40–43, 41*fig.*, 42*table*
Aid to Dependent Children (ADC), 135
Aid to Families with Dependent Children
 (AFDC), 135, 136, 138
AIG. *See* American International Group
 (AIG)
American Dream, 77
"American exceptionalism," 70, 76, 149
American Health Benefit Exchanges,
 138–39
American ideology, 70, 132, 133, 149
American International Group (AIG), 119
American Recovery and Reinvestment Act
 (2009), 119–20
Anglophone countries, 70*fig.*, 72*fig.*
Appalachia, 53
Apple Computer, 87–88
Asian Americans, 42*table*, 43, 94–98,
 96*table*, 160
"assimilation," 95
Associated Press, 2012 story, 121–22
Atkinson, A. B., 31–32
Australia, 71, 72*fig.*

Banfield, Edward, 107–8
bank lending practices, 115–19
Bargy, Ken, 39

barrio poverty, as term, 54
basic goods, and U.S. poor, 46–47, 46*fig.*, 59–60
Bear Stearns, 119
Blinder, Alan, 120
Booth, Charles, 18
Brace, Charles Loring, 14
Brazil, 71
Burroughs, Charles, 13
Burtless, Gary, 120
Bush, George W., 117, 119

California, 122
Cambodia, 65–66
CAP. *See* Community Action Program (CAP)
"capability failure," poverty as, 73
car ownership, 28, 46
causes of poverty. *See also* segregation: culture and, 107–11; discrimination and, 89–90; economic processes and, 81–88; ethnic minorities and, 94–99; family structure and, 102–6; gender and, 99–106; race and, 90–93; social stratification and, 80–88
CEA. *See* Council of Economic Advisors (CEA)
CETA. *See* Comprehensive Employment and Training Act (CETA)
charitable organizations, 132, 133, 134
Cherlin, Andrew, 110
child care: public programs and, 152–53; single parents and, 105
child mortality, 69, 73–74. *See also* infant mortality
child poverty, 40–43, 53; programs for reduction of, 144, 152–54
Children's Bureau (U.S.), 134
Children's Health Insurance Program (CHIP), 141, 152
Childress, J. R., 121–22
Child Tax Credit (CTC), 122
Child Trust Fund program, 153–54
China, 61, 63
Chinese Exclusion Act (1882), 94
CHIP. *See* Children's Health Insurance Program (CHIP)
cities. *See* concentration of poverty; urban poverty
citizenship, and poverty rate, 42*table,* 43
civil rights movement, 9, 135–36
class, concept of, 80. *See also* social stratification
Clinton, Bill, 137–38

Clinton Administration, 117
cohabiting relationships, 27, 103, 105, 110, 113, 125. *See also* family structure
Colbert, Stephen, 23
Colombia, 71
Colorado Springs, Colorado, 148–49
Coming Apart: The State of White America, 1960–2010 (Murray), 103–4, 108–9
common good, 149–50
Community Action Program (CAP), 136
Comprehensive Employment and Training Act (CETA), 137
Comte, Auguste, 17
concentration of poverty. *See also* high-poverty neighborhoods; urban poverty: factors affecting changes in, 57–59; growth trends in, 54–56; in nineteenth-century cities, 14–16; significance of, 54
consumer debt, 31, 115–16, 117–19
consumer goods. *See also* hardship: percent of households with various, 46*fig.*; poor in other countries and, 72–73; poor in U.S. and, 7, 28, 46–47, 72–73
Consumer Price Index (CPI), 167n10
consumption measures, 30–31
Continental Europe, 70*fig.*, 72*fig.*
contract *vs.* contact discrimination, 92
corporations, and economic inequalities, 83–84
Council of Economic Advisors (CEA), 1, 20
"creative destruction," 83
credit rating agencies, 118
cross-national comparisons. *See also* developed countries; developing countries; Europe: response to recession of 2008 and, 148; single parenting and, 106
CTC. *See* Child Tax Credit (CTC)
"cultural breakdown," concept of, 107
"culture of poverty," 50, 58, 107–11, 138, 146. *See also* intergenerational transfer of poverty
"cumulative disadvantages," 93
Current Population Survey (CPS), 141, 142*table*
cycle of poverty, 4–5, 20, 108

Dasgupta, Partha, 61–62
deindustrialization in U.S., 51, 87, 92, 93, 109
Denmark, 71, 76*table,* 147
Denton, Nancy, 57, 92
dependency. *See* welfare dependency

deregulation of banks, 115, 116–19
deserving vs. undeserving poor, 5, 12–13, 107, 134
developed countries: child mortality in, 69, 73–74; father-son earning elasticity in, 49–50, 74–75, 75fig.; measures of well-being in, 73–74; median income in, 70–71; poverty rates in, 69–73, 147; responses to recession of 2008 in, 148; single-parent families in, 106; social spending in, 72, 147–48
developing countries, 61–69; decline in absolute poverty in, 62–63; external causes of poverty in, 68–69; impacts of globalization on, 63–67, 68–69; internal causes of poverty in, 67–68; relative poverty measures and, 28–29; welfare policies in, 67–69
disabled Americans, 131, 136
discrimination, 89–92, 94. See also African Americans; job opportunity; segregation; women
District of Columbia, 124
divorce rates, 110, 125. See also family structure
DuBois, W. E. B., 15–16, 18

Earned Income Tax Credit (EITC), 10, 122, 137, 138, 140, 142, 143, 144, 153
East Asia, 62–63
Eastern Europe, 70fig., 71, 72fig.
economic crises. See Great Depression (1930s); Great Recession (2007–9); recessions, in late twentieth century
economic growth, 81; in developing world, 68; as goal of social policies, 144–49; poverty measures and, 30, 162; poverty rates and, 112, 162; stimulus package in 2009 U.S. and, 119–20; trade-off between federal spending and, 146–49
economic mobility, 74–77, 128, 157; education and, 158; father-son earning elasticity and, 74–75, 75fig.; of individuals, 76–77, 76table; relative vs. absolute mobility and, 76–77
Economic Opportunity Act, 136
economic processes: non-marital births and, 109–11; poverty trends and, 81–88
economic system, and income inequality, 82–88
Edelman, Peter, 23
Edin, Kathryn, 105
education: child poverty and, 152–53, 154; economic mobility and, 75–76, 128,

158; as goal of early relief programs, 132; income inequality and, 85–86, 89, 92–93, 96–97, 98; single parenting and, 102–3, 104, 105; U.S. poverty rates and, 8, 42table, 43; women and, 102, 161
Ehrenreich, Barbara, 28
EITC. See Earned Income Tax Credit (EITC)
elderly, the. See also Medicare; Social Security program: poverty among, 40–43, 100, 122, 144; programs for, 133, 136, 143–44
eligibility requirements, 138; means-tested programs and, 139, 140fig.; residency rules and, 131–32
Elizabethan Poor Law (1601), 131
employment. See job opportunity; unemployment; unemployment insurance (UI)
End of Poverty, The (Sachs), 67–68
Estonia, 71
Europe. See also Continental Europe; developed countries; Eastern Europe; entries for specific European countries: economic mobility in, 49, 77; government social spending in, 72, 146; immigration to U.S. from, 94; infant mortality in, 65; poverty measures in, 17, 23, 28, 70fig.; poverty rates in, 70fig., 71fig., 72fig., 78, 106

Fair Housing Authority (FHA), 117
Fallon, Kris, 39
Family and Medical Leave Act (1993), 152
family background, and poverty, 49, 98, 158. See also intergenerational transfer of poverty
family structure, 8, 112–13, 161, 173n107; Great Recession and, 125–26; official poverty measure and, 27; single parenting and, 102–6; U.S. poverty rates and, 42table, 43, 71–72
Family Support Act (1988), 137
Fannie Mae. See Federal National Mortgage Association (Fannie Mae)
Farm Security Administration, 134
father-son earning comparisons, 49–50, 74–75, 75fig.
Fault Lines (Rajan), 115, 117
Federal Emergency Relief Act (1933), 135
Federal Housing Administration (FHA), 115–16
Federal National Mortgage Association (Fannie Mae), 115–16

Federal Reserve, 117–18
federal spending: on compared social
    programs, 140*fig.*; percentage of
    households receiving social benefits
    from, 142*table;* on social programs, 72,
    139–41, 140*fig.*, 147; social programs
    as percentage of total budget, 141*fig.*;
    trade-off between economic growth and,
    146–49
feminization of poverty, as term, 99
FHA. *See* Federal Housing Administration
    (FHA)
financial aid, effectiveness of, 10, 68.
    See also government transfers
Fisher, Gordon M., 18, 19, 25–26
"floating proletariat," 13
food assistance, 43, 47, 136, 140. *See also*
    Supplemental Nutrition Assistance
    Program (SNAP)
food insecurity, 11, 44, 45*table,* 124. *See*
    also absolute poverty; hardship
Food Stamp Act (1964), 136. *See also*
    Supplemental Nutrition Assistance
    Program (SNAP)
Ford, Henry, 74
Foxconn City, in China, 64
France, 147
Frazier, E. Franklin, 103, 107
Freddie Mac, 116–17
Freedmen's Bureau, 132–33
"friendly visitors," 133

Galbraith, John Kenneth, 19–20
Garn-St. Germain Depository Institutions
    Act (1982), 116
GDP. *See* Gross Domestic Product (GDP)
gender. *See* women
General Motors, 87
General Social Survey (1993), 11–12, 34
geography of poverty, 51–59. *See also*
    regional differences in poverty
Georgia, 51
Germany, 71, 74, 147, 148
ghetto, as term, 54
Githongo, John, 66
global inequality, 7, 61–62; declines in, and
    globalization, 7, 63–64; political unrest
    and, 66–67
globalization: declines in global poverty
    and, 7, 63–64; inequality within
    countries and, 64, 86–88
Gordon, Tracy, 120
Gornick, Janet C., 71, 72*fig.*
government programs. *See also* Earned

Income Tax Credit (EITC); government
    transfers; Medicare; public policy in
    U.S.; Social Security program: Great
    Depression and, 134–36; Great
    Recession and, 119–20, 122–24, 127,
    128; measurement of success of, 34,
    158–59; 1960s policies and, 136–37;
    perceptions of size of, 10; post-1970s
    policies and, 137–39; public attitudes
    toward, 127, 128, 141, 149–51;
    spending on, 1970–2009, 140*fig.*; types
    of current programs, 139–44
government transfers. *See also* federal
    spending; public assistance policies;
    public policy in U.S.; social insurance
    policies: equalizing effect of, 88; goal of,
    150; in other countries, 106, 147; U.S.
    poverty rate and, 10, 71–72, 78, 88,
    124, 142–44, 143*fig.*
Gramm-Leach-Bliley Act (1999), 116
Great Depression (1930s), 11, 16, 99; policy
    and, 115, 134–35, 154, 155, 159
Great Plains, 53
Great Recession (2007–9), 1, 8–9, 59,
    114–29, 161; causes of, 114–20,
    128–29; consequences of, 9, 120–28,
    129, 161; federal actions and, 119–20,
    122–24, 127, 128; local governments
    and, 148–49; measures of well-being
    and, 124–26; politics of, 9, 127–28,
    129; poverty before and after,
    123*table*
Greece, 148–49
Greene, Jerome, 127
Greenland, Fiona Rose, 110
Greenspan, Alan, 117–18
Gross Domestic Product (GDP), 81–82,
    120, 121, 147
Gross National Product (GNP), 7–8
Grusky, David, 80
Guatamala, 71
Gurteen, S. Humphreys, 14

hardship. *See also* Great Recession
    (2007–9): effects of, 3–4; meaning of
    poverty and, 31, 160; in U.S., 44–47,
    45*table,* 59–60
hardship measures of poverty, 31
Harrington, Michael, 20, 145
Hart-Cellar Act. *See* Immigration and
    Nationality Act (Hart-Cellar Act,
    1965)
health care in U.S., 44, 45*table,* 138–39,
    151, 162–63. *See also* Medicare

health indicators. *See* child mortality; infant mortality; life expectancy; mental health; well-being, measures of
Heller, Walter, 20
high-poverty neighborhoods, 54–59. *See also* concentration of poverty; definition of, 55; social problems and, 7; total and poor population in, 56*fig.*
Hispanic Americans: Great Recession and, 123*table*, 125; poverty rates among, 42*table*, 43, 94–98, 96*table*, 160; spells of poverty among, 48, 49; urban poverty and, 55
HOLC. *See* Home Owners' Loan Corporation (HOLC)
homelessness, 45. *See also* "tramps"; vagrants
Home Owners' Loan Corporation (HOLC), 115
Hoover, Herbert, 134
housing conditions in U.S., 28, 44–45, 45*table*, 116*fig.*–118*fig. See also* mortgage-backed securities; housing policy and, 115–17; impact of Great Recession and, 117–18, 125; residential segregation and, 8, 57, 59, 92–93
Hout, Michael, 120–21
human capital, 79–80, 81, 93
human capital skills differentials, 93
humanitarian views on policy, 145
Hungary, 74
Hunter, Robert, 15, 18

IMF. *See* International Monetary Fund (IMF)
immigrants, 76, 94–98, 160. *See also* Asian Americans; Hispanic Americans; minority groups
Immigration and Nationality Act (Hart-Cellar Act, 1965), 94
income, definition of, 25, 33
income inequality. *See also* individual wealth in U.S.: within countries, 74–77, 75*fig.*, 76*table*, 158; gender wage gap and, 99–102, 101*fig.*; globalization and, 64, 86–88; Great Recession and, 115; market system and, 82–83; mobility and, 74–77, 75*fig.*, 76*table;* Occupy Wall Street movement and, 128; policy and, 159, 162; post-1970s growth in, 84–89
India, 61
Indiana, 51
individualism, 70, 132, 133, 149

individual responsibility, and poverty, 79, 133. *See also* "culture of poverty"
individual wealth in U.S. *See also* economic inequality; income inequality; wealthy Americans: differentials in, 85*fig.*, 90–91, 112, 160; growth in, by income group, 84*fig.;* impacts of Great Recession on, 9, 120, 121, 125, 129
"indoor relief" (poorhouses), 13–14, 132
industrialization, 15–16, 64, 78, 83, 131, 134. *See also* concentration of poverty
inequality. *See* discrimination; global inequality; income inequality
infant mortality, 7, 64–65, 65*fig.*, 78
intergenerational transfer of poverty, 47–51, 152. *See also* "culture of poverty"
International Monetary Fund (IMF), 62, 63
Iowa Bureau of Labor Statistics, 18

Jantti, Markus, 71, 72*fig.*
Japan, 64, 65*fig.*, 73*fig.*, 74, 147; immigration from, 94, 98
Jargowsky, Paul, 58–59
Jim Crow system, 15, 89, 91
Job Corps, 136
Job Opportunities and Basic Skills (JOBS) program, 137
job opportunity: decline in, and inequality, 108–11; discrimination and, 89–90, 91–92, 93, 98; Freedmen's Bureau and, 132–33; Native Americans and, 98–99; nineteenth-century poverty and, 13, 15, 17; urban poverty and, 58–59
Jobs, Steve, 74, 77
Johnson, Lyndon, 1, 20, 49, 136

Kates, Robert, 61–62
Katz, Michael, 14–15, 149
Kennedy administration, 20, 136
Kenworthy, Lane, 150
Kristof, Nicholas, 65–66, 109–10

labor unions, 83–84, 88, 93
Lampman, Robert, 20, 25
Latin America, 70*fig.*, 71, 72*fig. See also* Hispanic Americans
Latinos. *See* Hispanic Americans
Legal Services Corporation, 136
Lehman Brothers bankruptcy, 119
Lein, Laura, 105
Lewis, Oscar, 79, 107
life expectancy: in developed countries, 7, 74; in developing countries, 7, 65, 78; gender and, 100; U.S. trends in, 16, 83

Lindsey, Duncan, 153
line of poverty (term), 18. *See also* poverty thresholds
local relief programs, 131–32, 136, 138, 141, 154–55. *See also* states
Longhua, Shenzhen, China, 64
Loury, Glenn, 92
Lowell, Josephine Shaw, 133
low-income working families, 83, 144, 153. *See also* working poor
Lundberg, Shelly, 90
Luxembourg, 70*fig.*, 71, 72*fig.*, 74

Making Work Pay tax credit, 122
March, Madalyn, 47
marginalization. *See* social exclusion
marriage, decline in, 109–11, 113, 125, 146. *See also* cohabiting relationships; family structure; single-parent families
Marx, Karl, 17, 80, 82
Massachusetts, 16
Massey, Douglas S., 57, 92
material hardship. *See* hardship
MDGs. *See* Millennium Development Goals (MDGs)
means-tested programs, 139. *See also* public assistance policies
measurement of poverty. *See* poverty measures
median income: ethnic and racial differences in, 90, 98; mobility and, 76; post-1960s period and, 2; relative poverty and, 28, 29, 33, 70–71, 70*fig.*; single-mother households and, 106
Medicaid, 136, 139, 140*fig.*, 142*fig.*, 143
Medicare, 10, 136, 140*fig.*, 143; public support for, 127; use of, 141, 142*fig.*
mental health, 126, 138
Michigan, 51, 124
microfinance, 69
Midwestern U.S. poverty rates, 51–53, 52*table*, 59
Millennium Development Goals (MDGs), 62
minority groups. *See also* African Americans; Asian Americans; Hispanic Americans; Native Americans; social stratification; women: concentrations of poverty among, 6, 107, 160; depth of poverty among, 43–47; Great Recession poverty levels and, 122–24, 123table; poverty over time in, 8, 39–43; single parenting and, 102–4, 103*fig.*; social stratification and, 89–102

Mississippi (state), 124
Mississippi Delta (region), 53
Moffitt, Robert, 146
mortgage-backed securities, 115, 116–19
Moynihan, Daniel Patrick, 103
Mozilo, Angelo, 118
Munsterberg, Emil, 130, 151
Murray, Charles, 103–4, 108–9, 149
mutual aid societies, 132
Myrdal, Gunnar, 103, 107

NAS. *See* U.S. National Academy of Sciences (NAS)
National Labor Relations Act (Wagner Act), 134
Native Americans, 42*table*, 43, 98–99, 131
naturalized citizens, 95–97, 96*table*
Nevada, 122
New Deal programs, 134–35
New Mexico, 124
New York Charity Organization Society, 133
New York City, 153
New York Times, 65–66, 87
Nickel and Dimed: On (Not) Getting By in America (Ehrenreich), 28
Nordic countries, 70*fig.*, 71, 72*fig. See also* Denmark; Sweden
Northeastern U.S. poverty rates, 51–53, 52*table*, 122

Obama, Barack, 127, 138–39
"Obamacare." *See* Patient Protection and Affordable Care Act (ACA)
Occupy Wall Street movement (OWS), 9, 77, 127, 128, 129
OEDC. *See* Organization for Economic Cooperation and Development (OEDC)
OEO. *See* Office of Economic Opportunity (OEO)
Office of Economic Opportunity (OEO), 20–21
Office of Management and Budget (OMB), 21
official poverty rates. *See also* absolute poverty: by age group, 41*fig.*; effects of government assistance and, 122–24; trends in, across U.S. groups, 40–43, 41*fig.*, 42*table*; War on Poverty and, 2
official U.S. poverty measure: compared poverty measures and, 34–36, 35*fig.*, 36*fig.*; components of, 24–25; need for change in, 22–23; pros and cons of, 26–27

Ogburn, William, 19
OMB. *See* Office of Management and
    Budget (OMB)
Operation Head Start, 136
Oregon, 124
Organization for Economic Cooperation
    and Development (OEDC): compared
    social spending in, 147–48; poverty in
    member countries and, 64–65; poverty
    measures and, 28
Orshansky, Mollie, 20, 24–25, 171n10
Other America, The (Harrington), 20, 145
"outdoor relief," 13–14, 132
OWS. *See* Occupy Wall Street movement
    (OWS)

Pacific, the, poverty in, 62–63
parental leave policies, 152
parties, concept of, 80. *See also* social
    stratification
Patient Protection and Affordable Care Act
    (ACA), 138–39
Patterson, James T., 11
pauperism, 13–15, 18, 131, 132
Pearce, Diana, 99
Pennsylvania, 53*fig.*, 126, 131. *See also*
    Philadelphia, Pennsylvania
personal narratives of poverty, 39, 47,
    65–66, 87–88, 105, 111, 121–22, 127
Personal Responsibility and Work
    Opportunity Reconciliation Act
    (PRWORA), 138
Philadelphia, Pennsylvania, 15–16, 132
Plato, 149
political unrest, and global inequality,
    66–67
poorhouses ("indoor relief"), 13–14,
    132, 154
population growth, 81
Portugal, 73
Poverty (Hunter), 15, 18
poverty, definitions of, 11–12, 23–24, 37,
    158–60
poverty, depth of, in U.S., 43–47, 44*fig.*
poverty line. *See* poverty measures; poverty
    thresholds
poverty measures. *See also* absolute poverty;
    official U.S. poverty measure; poverty
    thresholds; relative poverty; Supplemen-
    tary Poverty Measure (SPM): compari-
    son of, 34–36; development of official
    measure and, 19–21; origins of, 17–19;
    theoretical issues in, 36–37; types of, 6,
    23–34, 37–38

poverty myths, 4–5
poverty rates. *See also* absolute poverty;
    official poverty rates; relative poverty:
    depth of poverty in U.S. and, 43–47,
    44*fig.*; in developing world, 61–63,
    63*fig.*; economic processes and, 81–88,
    82*fig.*, 84*fig.*, 85*fig.*; family structure
    and, 104*fig.*; Great Recession and,
    122–24, 123*table*; by measure, 6*fig.*,
    36*fig.*; racial/ethnic groups in U.S. and,
    96*table*, 104*fig.*; 1970's shift in, 81–82,
    82*fig.*; trends in, by age group, 40–43,
    41*fig.*, 42*table*; in U.S., 72, 96*table*,
    139–41, 140*fig.*, 143*fig.*, 147; in
    wealthier countries, 69–73, 70*fig.*,
    72*fig.*, 147
poverty thresholds. *See also* absolute
    poverty; official U.S. poverty measure;
    poverty measures; relative poverty:
    absolute measures and, 5, 6, 24–27;
    comparison of, 34–36, 35*fig.*, 36*fig.*;
    early measures and, 18–19; as flawed,
    27; for four-person families, 35*fig.*;
    income elasticity of, 25–26; ratio of
    family income to, 44*fig.*; relative
    measures and, 23–24, 28; SPM measure
    and, 33; subjective threshold and,
    11–12, 34, 35*fig.*
PPP. *See* purchasing power parity (PPP)
    exchange rates
private charities, 132, 134
PRWORA. *See* Personal Responsibility and
    Work Opportunity Reconciliation Act
    (PRWORA)
public assistance policies (means-tested
    programs), 139. *See also* Earned Income
    Tax Credit (EITC); Medicaid;
    Supplemental Nutrition Assistance
    Program (SNAP); Temporary Assistance
    for Needy Families (TANF); impacts on
    poverty, 142–44, 143*fig.*; spending on,
    139–41, 140*fig.*
public attitudes. *See also* Occupy Wall
    Street movement; Tea Party movement:
    causes of poverty and, 79; confidence in
    government and, 126, 151; as divided
    on social policy, 137–38, 144–46,
    149–51, 162–63; pre-*1900* views of
    poverty and, 12–17
public policy in U.S. *See also* federal
    spending; government programs: basic
    goals of, 145; current debates on,
    144–51; current welfare programs,
    139–44; effects on inequality, 9,

public policy in U.S. *(continued)*
142–44, 143*fig.*, 159; future options for, 151–54; historical origins of, in U.S., 131–39; impact on poverty and, 142–44, 143*fig.*; limits of, 149–51, 162–63; origins of debates on, 130–39; program implementation and, 148–49; public dissatisfaction with, 137–38; reduction of child poverty and, 144, 152–54; reform in 1990s and, 10, 137–38, 146; role of government and, 149–51; urban poverty and, 58; work disincentives and, 9, 106, 108, 146, 147
purchasing power parity (PPP) exchange rates, 71

quasi-relative poverty measure. *See* Supplementary Poverty Measure (SPM)

racial poverty gap, 160. *See also* African Americans; Hispanic Americans
Rajan, Raghuram, 115, 117
Rawls, John, 149
Reagan, Ronald, 1, 137
real estate industry, 57, 117. *See also* Great Recession (2007–9)
recessions. *See also* Great Depression (1930s); Great Recession (2007–9): global recession of 2008 and, 148; in late twentieth century, 137–38
regional differences in poverty, 7, 64. *See also* concentration of poverty; developed countries; developing countries; in U.S., 51–54, 52–53*table*
relative poverty. *See also* Supplementary Poverty Measure (SPM): in compared wealthier countries, 70–71, 70*fig.*; comparison of poverty measures and, 34–36, 35*fig.*, 36*fig.*; Great Recession and, 115; measures of, 23–24, 27–30, 37; single parenting and, 106; trends in, across U.S. groups, 40–43, 41*fig.*, 42*table*; trends in, and economic growth, 82
residency rules, 131–32
Ricker, Bill, 39
Rio Grande Valley, 53
Roosevelt, Franklin D., 17, 134–35
Roosevelt, Theodore, 83–84, 159
rural poverty in U.S., 7, 53–54
Ryan, John, 15

Sachs, Jeffrey, 67–68
Santelli, Rick, 127

Sargoza, Eric, 87–88
SBTC. *See* "skill-based technological change" (SBTC)
Schlumpeter, Josepn, 83
Scholz, John Karl, 142, 146
scientific charity societies, 133–34, 154
segregation: class and, 54, 59, 92; gender and, 100; Jim Crow system and, 15, 89, 91; racial, 57, 59, 89, 92–93, 94; residential, 8, 57, 59, 92–93
Sen, Amartya, 32, 73
Sheppard-Towner Act (1921), 134
Sherman, Arloc, 123
Shipler, David, 105
single-parent families. *See also* family structure; women: culture and, 108–9, 111; employment and, 106, 138, 146; poverty rate and, 104–6, 104*fig.*, 112–13
"skill-based technological change" (SBTC), 85–86
"skills mismatch" hypothesis, 58
Slovak Republic, 74
Smith, Adam, 12, 27
Smock, Pamela, 110
SNAP. *See* Supplemental Nutrition Assistance Program (SNAP)
social conditions, and views of poverty, 12–17
social exclusion, 28–29, 31–32, 37. *See also* relative poverty
social insurance policies, 139. *See also* Medicare; Social Security program; impacts on poverty, 142–44, 143*fig.*; number receiving benefits from, 141–42, 142fig.; popularity of, 127, 141; spending on, 139–41, 140*fig.*
social safety net: in Europe, 150–51; global poverty and, 66, 75; U.S. welfare programs and, 10, 17, 40, 124, 141, 143–45; weakness of local programs and, 154–55
social science research: longitudinal studies of individual poverty and, 47–48; nonmarital births and, 110–11; poverty measures and, 17–19
Social Security Act (1935), 135; Public Amendments to (1962), 136
Social Security Bulletin (journal), 20
Social Security program: impact on poverty, 10, 143–44; public support for, 127; receipts from, 142; spending on, 140*fig.*; use of, 141
social stratification, 80–81, 112; culture and, 107–11; discrimination and,

89–90; economic system and, 81–88; ethnic groups and, 93–99; family structure and, 102–6; gender and, 99–102; process of, 89; race and, 90–93
social work, professionalization of, 133, 134
South Asian poverty, 62
Southern U.S., 15, 51–53, 52table, 122
"spatial mismatch" hypothesis, 58
spells of poverty, 7, 47–49, 60; duration of, 48–49; vs. permanent underclass, 47–48
Spencer, Herbert, 17
SPM. See Supplementary Poverty Measure (SPM)
"standard budgets," 17, 18
standard of living, and poverty measures, 23–25. See also relative poverty
Startz, Richard, 90
states. See also local relief programs: differences in poverty rate, 51–53, 52–53table, 60; welfare programs in, 134, 138
statistical discrimination, 90
status groups, concept of, 80. See also social stratification
stereotyping, 90
Strader, Amber, 111
structural adjustment programs, 63
subjective threshold, 11–12, 34, 35fig.
sub-Saharan Africa, 62, 65
suburban poverty, 7, 59
Sugrue, Thomas J., 16
Supplemental Nutrition Assistance Program (SNAP), 122, 124, 136, 139, 140, 144
Supplemental Security Income Program (1974), 136, 142fig.
Supplementary Poverty Measure (SPM), 33–34, 35–36, 38; basic goods and, 168n52; comparison of poverty measures and, 34–36, 35fig., 36fig.; poverty trends across U.S. groups, 40–43, 41fig., 42table
Sweden, 106, 147, 148, 150–51, 152
Switzerland, 71, 72

TANF. See Temporary Assistance for Needy Families (TANF)
TARP. See Troubled Asset Relief Program (TARP)
tax policy, 75, 122, 124, 159. See also Child Tax Credit (CTC); Earned Income Tax Credit (EITC)
Tea Party movement, 127
technological change: deindustrialization

and, 51, 87, 92, 93, 109; economic growth and, 81; income inequality and, 85–88; "skill-based technological change" (SBTC) and, 85–86; social unrest and, 66–67
Temporary Assistance for Needy Families (TANF), 138, 139, 141, 142fig., 144, 177n50
Tennessee, 124
Tocqueville, Alexis de, 70
Townsend, Peter, 12, 47
"tramps," 13, 15
Trenton, New Jersey, 148
Troubled Asset Relief Program (TARP), 119
Truly Disadvantaged, The (Wilson), 58

UI. See unemployment insurance (UI)
underclass, as term, 31, 54–55. See also social exclusion
unemployment. See also job opportunity; unemployment insurance (UI); work disincentives: global recession of 2008 and, 148; Great Depression and, 16–17, 134; poverty rate and, 82; racial disparities and, 90; support for non-working families and, 144; U.S. rates of, 114, 121–22, 148, 151; work disincentives and, 9, 106, 108, 146, 147
unemployment insurance (UI), 122, 124, 140fig., 144
UNICEF Innocente Research Centre, 29–30
United Kingdom: child poverty and, 152–53; early poor laws in, 131; relative poverty in, 71; social exclusion and, 31
United Nations, 32, 62
U.S. Bureau of the Budget, 21
U.S. Census Bureau, definition of income, 25, 33
U.S. Congress, 134–35, 151. See also government programs; government transfers; public policy in U.S.
U.S. National Academy of Sciences (NAS): National Research Council, 33; Panel on Poverty and Family Assistance, 38; poverty measures and, 6, 24, 32–34, 123 (See also Supplementary Poverty Measure (SPM))
universal child allowance, 153
urban poverty, 52table, 53, 58–59. See also concentration of poverty

vagrants, 131. See also homelessness; "tramps"

values. *See also* individualism: culture of poverty debate and, 107–10; social policy and, 149–51
veterans, aid to, 132–33, 135

Wagner Act. *See* National Labor Relations Act (Wagner Act)
Wagner-Steagall Act , 135
War on Poverty, 1, 2, 9, 136, 155–56
Washington, Booker T., 107
wealthier countries. *See* developed countries
Wealth of Nations, The (Smith), 12, 27
wealthy Americans. *See also* individual wealth in U.S.: measures of poverty and, 31; standards of living and, 161; structural benefits to, 63, 88, 128, 157; top 1 percent incomes and, 88
Weber, Max, 80, 89
welfare dependency: high-poverty areas and, 54, 58; poor laws and, 132; prevention of, 10, 153, 154–55; reduction of, 138, 150; social programs as fostering, 58, 108, 146
well-being, measures of, 73–74, 124–26. *See also* child mortality; hardship; infant mortality; life expectancy
Wells, Brandi, 39
Western U.S. poverty rates, 51–54, 52*table,* 122
white Americans: disparities in wealth and, 90–91; education and, 98, 160; low-skill

workers and, 48, 98, 108–10; median income and, 98; poverty rates of, 42*table,* 43, 44*fig.,* 91*fig.,* 96*table,* 97*fig.,* 104*fig.,* 123*table;* race-based assistance imbalances and, 133, 135; racial attitudes of, 16; rural poverty and, 54, 135; time in poverty and, 48–49; urban poverty and, 55, 56
Wilson, William Julius, 58, 91–92
women, 99–102, 160–61. *See also* single-parent families; earnings gap and, 8, 86, 100–102; education and, 8, 86; Great Recession and, 121, 122; program effectiveness and, 138; views on marriage among, 109, 110–11
work disincentives, 9, 106, 108, 146, 147
working poor, 4, 105, 137. *See also* low-income working families
Works Progress Administration (WPA), 134
World Bank, 12, 62, 63, 69
World War II, 84, 135

Yen, Nhem, 65–66
young adults, 125–26, 128. *See also* family structure

Zakaria, Fareed, 77
Zandi, Mark, 120